THE MISTAKE LAB

THE MISTAKE LAB

How to Build a Classroom Where Failure Fuels Learning

By Jeffrey O. Porter

COPYRIGHT PAGE

THE MISTAKE LAB
How to Build a Classroom Where Failure Fuels Learning

Published by The JP Moment Educational Consultants, LLC
First Edition, 2026

ISBN: 979-8-9956712-0-6

Printed in the United States of America

For bulk orders, workshops, or speaking engagements, contact:
info@thejpmoment.com
www.thejpmoment.com

DEDICATION

For every teacher who has ever thought:
"I should know this by now."
"I can't ask for help."
"If I admit I don't know, they won't respect me."

You are not alone.
You are not failing.
You are learning.

And that's exactly what you're teaching your students to do.

For Derek and Edward—
You've had a front-row seat to my journey,
watching me grow through every challenge and every mistake.
I hope it teaches you to embrace every lesson,
own every mistake, and never stop becoming who you're meant to be.

INTRODUCTION

Why I Wrote This Book

I've spent over twenty-five years in education—as a classroom teacher, assistant principal, principal, and assistant superintendent.

And for most of those years, I believed that leadership meant having all the answers.

I thought admitting uncertainty would undermine my authority.
I thought asking for help was a sign of weakness.
I thought struggling meant I wasn't cut out for the role.

I was wrong.

And that belief nearly destroyed me—and the teachers and students I was supposed to serve.

The Turning Point

The turning point came during my third year as a principal.

A veteran teacher came to my office, frustrated. She'd tried a new teaching strategy I'd championed in a faculty meeting. It had flopped. Students were confused. She felt like she'd failed.

My instinct was to defend the strategy—to explain what she'd done wrong, to suggest she hadn't implemented it with fidelity, to maintain my image as the instructional leader who knows best.

But something stopped me.

I looked at her and said, "I don't know why it didn't work. Let's figure it out together."

The relief on her face was immediate.

We spent the next hour analyzing what happened.

I didn't have the answers. I asked questions. We thought out loud together.

She showed me student work. We identified where the breakdown occurred. We brainstormed adjustments.

At the end, she said: "This is the most helpful conversation I've had all year."

I asked why.

She said, "Because you didn't just tell me what to do. You listened. You admitted you didn't know. We figured it out together."

What I Learned

That moment changed how I lead.

I realized three things:

First, teachers don't need leaders who pretend to be perfect. They need leaders who model learning.

Second, teachers need to see that not knowing is the beginning of inquiry, not a failure of leadership.

Third, teachers need leaders who run experiments, analyze what works, and adjust when things don't.

But I couldn't ask teachers to build mistake-literate classrooms if I wasn't willing to lead a mistake-literate school.

Over the next several years—as principal and then assistant superintendent—I worked to build systems where:

Teachers could experiment without fear of failure
Mistakes were analyzed as data, not punished as incompetence.
Professional learning was iterative—try, reflect, revise—not one-shot workshops.
Administrators modeled vulnerability alongside teachers.

It wasn't easy.

The system educators exist to resist this approach. Accountability measures demand certainty. Parents expect answers. Boards want guarantees.

Nevertheless, throughout my journey in the field, one thing became clear to me: Despite the expectation that school leaders have all of the answers, the reality is different.

The most innovative schools aren't led by people who have all the answers.

They're led by people who are brave enough to ask the best questions.

Why This Book Exists

This book emerged from those years of learning.

I wrote it because:

As a teacher, I struggled with perfectionism and saw my students absorb that fear.

As an assistant principal, I watched teachers burn out trying to maintain an impossible standard of expertise.

As a principal, I saw what happened when we created space for professional risk-taking—teachers thrived, innovation flourished, student learning deepened.

As an assistant superintendent, I learned to navigate the tension between systemic constraints and transformative practice.

This book is written primarily for teachers—because classrooms are where the transformation begins.

But it's also for administrators who want to support this work.

Throughout the book, I will speak from the teacher's perspective because that's where the day-to-day practice happens.

But I've also included guidance for navigating policies, working within systems, and building administrator support—because I've lived on both sides of that dynamic.

The Challenges You Face

I know the challenges you face:

If you're a teacher:
You're being evaluated on test scores.
You're working within rigid pacing guides.
You're navigating district grading policies.
You're managing parent expectations.
You're exhausted
If you're an administrator:
You're balancing accountability with innovation.
You're supporting teachers while managing board expectations.
You're trying to change culture within systemic constraints.
You're protecting your teachers while pushing for growth

I've been in both roles. I know the tension. The pressure to always be right is real.

This book addresses it head-on.

What I Believe

Here's what I believe:

You can build mistake-literate classrooms even within traditional systems.
You can advocate for policy change while working within current constraints.
You can model vulnerability as a teacher or administrator without sacrificing credibility.
You can sustain this work without burning out.

But it requires strategy. It requires community. It requires understanding how systems work and how to navigate them.

That's what this book provides.

Why I Had to Write This

I wrote this book because:

I've seen what happens when classrooms are treated as performance stages rather than labs—students stop trying, internalize failure, and believe they're not capable.

I've seen what happens when teachers believe they must be perfect: isolation, burnout, and leaving the profession.

I've seen what happens when administrators demand certainty instead of supporting inquiry—a compliance culture, innovation dies, and teachers stop taking risks.

I've seen what's possible when schools embrace the scientist mindset—teachers experiment, students own their learning, growth becomes the norm.

What This Book Will Ask of You

This book will challenge you.

It will ask you to confront your own beliefs about mistakes and perfection.

It will ask you to run experiments that might fail.

It will ask you to say "I don't know" when you don't—whether you're a teacher in front of students or an administrator in front of staff.

It will ask you to navigate systems strategically while advocating for change.

That's uncomfortable.

But it's transformative.

A Personal Note

I want you to know: I'm not writing from ivory-tower theory.

I've been in your classroom, grading papers at midnight.
I've been in your office, navigating angry emails from parents.
I've been in board meetings defending innovative practices.

I've made every mistake in this book—and learned from them.

This book is the distillation of more than twenty-five years of learning, failing, adjusting, and trying again.

Welcome to The Mistake Lab.

Whether you're a teacher building your classroom culture or an administrator supporting that work, this book is for you.

Let's begin the experiment.

Jeffrey O. Porter
Former Teacher, Assistant Principal, Principal, and Assistant Superintendent

HOW TO USE THIS BOOK

For Different Teaching Contexts

This book is designed for K-12 teachers across all subjects and grade levels.

But not every strategy works the same way for kindergarteners and high schoolers.

Here's how to adapt this book to your context:

If You Teach K-2- Think of your classroom as a **"Discovery Lab."**

Focus on:

- Modeling experiments that don't work: "I tried this. It didn't work. Let me try something else."
- Using language they understand: "Scientists make lots of mistakes. That's how they learn!"
- Building safety through predictable routines
- Celebrating "oops moments."

Lab language for this age:

- "We're scientists! Scientists try things!"
- "What happened in your experiment?"
- "Let's try it a different way!"

Key chapters for you:

- Chapter 2: Modeling fallibility
- Chapter 4: Psychological safety
- Chapter 7: First week routines—setting up your lab
- Chapter 12: Simplified mistake analysis: What happened? What will you try?

If You Teach 3-5- Think of your classroom as an **"Experiment Station."**

Focus on:

- Teaching the scientific method explicitly and applying it to ALL learning, not just science
- Introducing hypothesis → test → revise cycle
- Building peer culture—scientists collaborate
- Documenting experiments through written reflection

Lab language for this age:

- "What's your hypothesis?"
- "Let's test it and see what happens."
- "What did the data tell you?"
- "Time to revise your hypothesis."

Key chapters for you:

- All of Part 1: Foundation
- Chapter 8: Teacher as co-researcher
- Chapters 12-14: Mistake analysis, error analysis, revision as iteration
- Chapter 11: Equity—especially learning disabilities and EL students

If You Teach 6-8- Think of your classroom as a **"Research Lab."**

Focus on:

- Addressing perfectionism head-on—middle schoolers are intensely self-conscious
- Building psychological safety—peer judgment is brutal at this age
- Teaching sophisticated data analysis
- Lab notebooks for documenting learning, mistakes, and revisions

Lab language for this age:

- "What did the data show?"
- "How can we replicate this experiment?"
- "What variables do we need to control?"
- "Let's peer-review each other's work."

Key chapters for you:

- The entire book is relevant
- Especially Chapter 4: Psychological safety—critical for middle school
- Chapter 9: Peer culture—peer review
- Chapter 10: Grading as feedback, not judgment
- Chapter 17: When students are obsessed with grades

If You Teach 9-12- Think of your classroom as an **"Advanced Research Lab."**

Focus on:

- Deconstructing years of perfectionism—many have internalized it deeply
- Publication and presentation of findings, not just grades
- Sophisticated metacognition and self-assessment
- Student ownership of research questions

Lab language for this age:

- "What's your research question?"
- "What does the literature say?"—What have others discovered?
- "What are your findings?"
- "How will you present your research?"

Key chapters for you:

- Chapter 3: Your perfectionism—high schoolers will see through performance
- Chapter 10: Grading revolution—move toward portfolio and research model
- Chapter 16: Student ownership—students design their own experiments
- Chapters 17-19: Working within system constraints

The Lab Metaphor Across All Grades

What makes a good lab?

- **Safety first:** Psychological safety equals protective equipment
- **Clear protocols:** Mistake analysis equals scientific method
- **Documentation:** Lab notebooks, reflection journals
- **Iteration:** Experiments get revised and re-run
- **Peer review:** Scientists share findings and get feedback
- **Curiosity-driven:** Questions matter more than answers
- **Failure is expected:** Not every experiment works—that's data

This is what your classroom can become.

If You Teach Special Education- Your classroom is an "**Adaptive Lab.**"

Pay special attention to:

- Chapter 11: Equity—students with disabilities
- Visual supports for lab protocols
- Scaffolded experiments—break into smaller steps
- Celebrating small discoveries

Lab adaptations:

- Concrete manipulatives for experiments
- Visual lab notebooks—pictures plus words
- More frequent check-ins
- Partner scientists for peer support

If You Teach English Learners- Your classroom is a "**Language Lab.**"

Pay special attention to:

- Chapter 11: Equity—language mistakes are part of language acquisition
- Sentence frames for scientific discussion
- Multilingual lab notebooks
- Experiments that don't require advanced language

Lab strategies:

- Model the language of science: "I hypothesize that..."
- Sentence stems for peer feedback.
- Visual representations of experiments
- Celebrate language experiments—trying new words and phrases

If You Teach Advanced or Gifted Students- Your classroom is an "**Innovation Lab.**" These students often have the most perfectionism due to fear of losing "gifted" status.

Pay special attention to:

- Experiments designed to induce productive struggle
- Questions without known answers
- Self-designed research projects
- Failure is essential to innovation

Lab challenges:

- "Design an experiment where you don't know the outcome."
- "Research a question no one has answered yet."
- "Replicate a famous failed experiment—what can you learn?"

General Lab Setup Guidance

Start with Part 1: Lab Safety Training

Before you start running experiments, you need to have safety protocols in place. Part 1 equals psychological safety, language, and beliefs. Don't skip Chapter 3: Your Perfectionism Problem—your own lab notebook.

Set up your lab gradually:

- Week 1: Establish lab norms
- Week 2: Practice basic protocols
- Month 1: Run simple experiments
- Semester 1: Students design their own experiments

Use the appendices as lab manuals:

- Student Mistake Analysis Protocol equals Lab Protocol
- Teacher Tools equals Lab Equipment
- Age-appropriate adaptations equal different lab levels
- Subject-specific applications equal different types of experiments

Find a lab partner:

This work is easier with a colleague. Find one other teacher. Build your labs together.

Document your experiments:

Keep your own lab notebook—a teacher journal:

- What did you try?
- What worked?
- What didn't?
- What will you revise?

Model what you're asking students to do.

Be patient with the setup:

Building a lab takes time. You're not just rearranging furniture—you're changing culture. Give it a semester. Give it a year. The results will be worth it.

Welcome to The Mistake Lab. Let's set up your experiment.

TABLE OF CONTENTS

INTRODUCTION

THE CLASSROOM THAT CHANGED EVERYTHING

Two classrooms. Same school. Same students. Different outcomes.

Let me tell you about both.

Classroom A: Where Mistakes Were Shameful

September. Mr. Harrison's 8th-grade math class.

A student—I'll call her Maya—is working on a problem at the board.

She writes: $3x + 5 = 20$

She solves: $3x = 15$

Then: $x = 3$

Wrong.

Mr. Harrison sighs. "No, Maya. You forgot to subtract 5 from both sides. Who can show her the right way?"

Three hands shoot up. Maya's face turns red. She sits down, silent.

She doesn't volunteer again for the rest of the semester.

By December:

Students stop raising hands. Too risky.

Students stop asking questions. Don't want to look stupid.

Students copy answers without understanding. Just want to get it right.

Test scores are mediocre.

Engagement is low.

Maya believes she's "not a math person."

Mr. Harrison thinks: "These students aren't trying. They don't care about learning."

But that's not true.

They care deeply.

They're just terrified of being wrong.

Classroom B: Where Mistakes Were Data

Same school. Same semester. Ms. Rodriguez's 8th-grade math class.

A student—I'll call him James—is working on the same problem at the board.

He writes: $3x + 5 = 20$

He solves: $3x = 25$

Then: $x = 8.33$

Wrong.

Ms. Rodriguez pauses. "Interesting. Walk me through your thinking, James."

James explains: "I added 5 to both sides."

Ms. Rodriguez nods. "So you did the opposite of what you needed. What operation would undo the +5?"

James thinks. "Subtraction?"

"Exactly. Try again."

James erases. Solves correctly. Smiles.

"That's it. You found your error and corrected it. That's how scientists work. That's how mathematicians work. You just ran an experiment, got data, and revised your approach."

By December:

Students volunteer frequently. Mistakes are normalized.

Students ask clarifying questions. Curiosity is encouraged.

Students show their work and explain their thinking.

Test scores improve significantly.

Engagement is high.

James believes he can figure things out, even when stuck.

Ms. Rodriguez thinks: "These students are becoming problem-solvers."

And they are.

Because her classroom isn't a performance stage, it's a lab.

What Made the Difference?

Same students. Same content. Same standards.

Different beliefs about mistakes.

In Classroom A:

Mistakes equal failure.

Mistakes equal evidence you're not smart.

Mistakes equal something to hide.

The classroom operates like a theater:

- Performance matters
- You get one shot
- Mistakes are embarrassing
- The audience—your peers—judges you

Result: Students stop trying. Fear of failure paralyzes learning.

In Classroom B:

Mistakes equal data.

Mistakes equal information about what you need to learn next.

Mistakes are an equal part of the process.

The classroom operates like a lab:

- Experimentation is expected
- You run trials and revise
- Mistakes are documented and analyzed
- Peers are collaborators, not judges

Result: Students take risks. Learning accelerates.

The difference wasn't the curriculum. The difference wasn't resources.

The difference was the teacher's belief about mistakes—and how that belief shaped the culture.

The Lab Metaphor

Think about a science lab. What happens in a lab?

Scientists run experiments. Some work, some don't.

They document results, including failures.

They analyze what went wrong—not who failed, but what the data shows.

They revise their hypotheses. Iteration is the process.

They collaborate. Peer review. Sharing findings.

Failure is expected. Edison didn't fail 1,000 times—he found 1,000 ways that didn't work.

Now think about a typical classroom. What happens when a student makes a mistake?

The mistake is marked wrong. Red X. Points deducted.

The student feels ashamed, especially in public.

The mistake is discarded. Move on. Don't dwell on it.

No analysis happens. What went wrong? Why? What's next?

Peers judge. Whispers. Eye rolls. "I can't believe they didn't know that."

Failure is unacceptable. You should get it right the first time.

See the problem?

We tell students: "Learn from your mistakes!"

But we've designed classrooms that punish mistakes.

We say: "It's okay to fail!"

But we grade in ways that make failure permanent.

We want students to be scientists—curious, experimental, resilient.

But we've built theaters, not labs.

What Is a Mistake Lab?

A Mistake Lab is a classroom where:

Mistakes are expected, not avoided.

Mistakes are documented. Students keep records of what they tried and what happened.

Mistakes are analyzed using a protocol, like the scientific method.

Mistakes are revised. Iteration is the process.

Mistakes are shared. Collaboration, not competition.

Mistakes fuel learning. They're data, not disasters.

In a Mistake Lab:

The teacher is a lead scientist, not a performer or expert who knows everything.

Students are junior scientists, running experiments, collecting data, and drawing conclusions.

Assignments are experiments—hypotheses to test.

Grades are feedback on current mastery, not punishment for past failures.

Revision is expected. Scientists revise hypotheses. Students revise their work.

Peers are lab partners—collaborators who help each other analyze results.

But Here's the Question

How did Ms. Rodriguez create that culture?

Did she just tell students "mistakes are okay"?

No.

Because students don't believe what you say, they believe what you model.

Here's what Ms. Rodriguez did differently:

First, she modeled being a scientist herself.

When she made a mistake—solved a problem wrong on the board, forgot a step, explained something unclearly—she treated it like data:

"Wait, I made an error. Let's analyze it. Where did I go wrong?"

Students saw: My teacher runs experiments too. She makes mistakes and learns from them.

Second, she responded to student mistakes with curiosity, not judgment.

When a student got something wrong, she didn't say: "No, that's wrong."

She said: "Interesting result. Walk me through your experiment. What were you testing? What did you observe?"

Students learned: My mistakes are interesting data points, not shameful failures.

Third, she separated experiments from demonstrations of mastery.

Lab work—practice, drafts, formative assignments—was feedback only. No grade.

Demonstrations of mastery—tests and final projects—were graded but could be revised after reteaching. Grades reflected current understanding, not the average of all attempts.

Students learned: I'm not being punished for experimenting. Failures during practice are expected.

Fourth, she taught students to run their own experiments and analyze results.

When students made errors, she didn't just correct them.

She taught them the Mistake Analysis Protocol, a simplified scientific method:

1. What was your hypothesis? What were you trying to do?
2. What was your result? What actually happened?
3. Analyze the data: Why didn't it work?
4. Revise your hypothesis: What will you try differently?
5. Run the experiment again.

Students learned: I can figure this out. I'm a scientist. I analyze data and adjust.

Fifth, she built a culture in which peer scientists collaborated rather than competed.

When students mocked each other's mistakes—it happened at first—she stopped class:

"In a lab, we don't laugh when an experiment fails. We ask: What did we learn? How can we help? What should we try next?"

"Let's practice responding like scientists."

Students practiced:

- "I had a similar result. Here's what I tried next."
- "What were you testing? I'm curious about your hypothesis."
- "Want to collaborate? Maybe we can figure it out together."

Students learned: We're all scientists. We help each other run better experiments.

By December, Ms. Rodriguez's classroom looked like a lab.

Students were experimenting. Hypothesizing. Analyzing. Revising. Collaborating. Not because they were smarter than Mr. Harrison's students. Because the culture allowed them to learn like scientists.

The Problem With Most Classrooms

Most classrooms—like Mr. Harrison's—are designed around perfectionism:

Get it right the first time.

Don't ask questions. You should already know.

Don't make mistakes. Or hide them if you do.

Grades punish errors.

One shot to succeed.

This is how theaters work, not labs.

In a theater:

- You rehearse in private, hiding the messy process
- You perform in public, showing only the polished result
- Mistakes are disasters—the show must go on
- You get one shot: opening night
- The audience judges: applause or silence

This system:

Kills curiosity. Too risky to try new things.

Increases anxiety. Fear of public failure.

Widens achievement gaps. Students who struggle early never catch up.

Drives students away from "hard" subjects—STEM, writing, anything that requires struggle.

And here's the tragedy:

This isn't how learning works.

This isn't how science works.

This isn't how the real world works.

In the real world:

Scientists run experiments that fail repeatedly.

Engineers build prototypes that don't work and learn from them.

Writers produce terrible first drafts, then revise.

Athletes practice skills badly before mastering them.

Entrepreneurs launch products that flop, then pivot.

Failure is data. Revision is the process. Iteration leads to mastery.

But we don't teach students this.

We teach them to hide failure. To get it right the first time. To never let anyone see you struggle.

No wonder they're anxious. No wonder they give up.

The Science Says: Mistakes Are How We Learn

Neuroscience is clear:

When you make a mistake and correct it, your brain releases dopamine—a learning signal.

Your brain literally grows stronger in that moment.

But here's the catch:

This only happens if the environment is psychologically safe.

If mistakes equal shame, your brain releases cortisol instead—a stress response.

Cortisol blocks learning.

Translation:

In Mr. Harrison's classroom—high shame, low safety:

Student makes mistake → cortisol released → learning blocked → student shuts down

In Ms. Rodriguez's Mistake Lab—low shame, high safety:

Student makes mistake → dopamine released → brain strengthens → student learns

Same mistake. Different brain chemistry. Different outcome.

The research is extensive:

Carol Dweck on growth mindset: Students who see mistakes as learning opportunities outperform students who see them as evidence of fixed ability.

John Hattie on feedback research: Feedback is one of the highest-impact teaching strategies—but only if it's separated from grades and focused on learning.

Claude Steele on stereotype threat: When students fear confirming negative stereotypes, their performance drops. Creating safe environments eliminates this effect.

Dylan Wiliam on formative assessment: The most effective teaching happens when students receive feedback, revise, and try again.

The science is unambiguous:

Mistakes → Analysis → Revision = Learning

Mistakes → Shame → Hiding = Stagnation

The Promise of This Book

This book will show you how to build a Mistake Lab.

A classroom where:

Students see mistakes as data, not identity.

Students run experiments, analyze results, and revise their approach.

Students ask questions without fear. Students collaborate like scientists—peer review and shared discoveries.

Students take intellectual risks. Learning accelerates.

But here's what you need to know:

You can't build a Mistake Lab if you're still operating like Mr. Harrison.

You can't tell students "experiments fail sometimes" if you believe your mistakes are failures.

You can't ask students to document their failed attempts if you hide yours.

The work starts with you.

Your Lab Needs a Lead Scientist

In a lab, the lead scientist:

Runs experiments. Tries new teaching strategies.

Documents results. What worked, what didn't.

Analyzes failures. Why didn't that lesson land?

Revises approaches. Iteration is the process.

Models the scientific mindset: curiosity, humility, persistence.

That lead scientist is you.

Before you can teach students to be scientists, you must become one.

This Book Is Structured in Five Parts

PART 1: THE FOUNDATION (Lab Safety & Setup)

Before you start running experiments, you need safety protocols and foundational knowledge.

Chapter 1: The science of learning from mistakes—neuroscience, research, evidence

Chapter 2: Why you hide mistakes from students—the infallible teacher myth

Chapter 3: Your perfectionism problem—your own relationship with failure (Most important chapter)

Chapters 4-6: How to build psychological safety, shift language, teach the concept

This is lab safety training. Don't skip it.

PART 2: THE LAB CULTURE

How to set up your classroom as a functioning lab.

First week routines. Establishing lab protocols.

Teacher as co-researcher, not just expert.

Peer culture: lab partners, collaboration.

Grading as feedback, not judgment.

Equity. Who gets to experiment safely?

This is a lab setup. The environment matters.

PART 3: LAB PROTOCOLS

The specific procedures students use to analyze their mistakes.

The Student Mistake Analysis Protocol—four steps

Error analysis as a learning tool

Revision as iteration—the scientific method applied to all learning

Metacognition—thinking about your thinking

Student ownership—students design their own experiments

This is the lab manual. The systematic approach.

PART 4: WORKING WITHIN THE SYSTEM

How to run a lab in a high-stakes, test-driven, grade-obsessed school.

When students are obsessed with grades

When parents pressure perfection

When standardized tests loom

When your school culture is perfectionist

This is running a lab under constraints. Real-world challenges.

PART 5: SUSTAINING THE LAB
How to make this last all year and beyond.
When students resist—reluctant scientists
Mid-year check-ins—is your lab working?
End-of-year reflection—what did we discover?
This is long-term lab management.

Who This Book Is For

This book is for K-12 teachers who:

Are tired of students who won't try because they're afraid of failing

Are frustrated by grade-obsessed students who care more about points than learning

Want to build cultures where students take risks, ask questions, and grow

Are willing to become scientists of their own, teaching—run experiments, analyze results, revise

Are you ready to do your own work first—confront your perfectionism before addressing theirs

This book is not for teachers who:

Just want tips and tricks—this requires a deeper cultural transformation

Aren't willing to model vulnerability—students learn from what you model, not what you say

Want to maintain traditional grading while claiming "mistakes are okay"—those are incompatible

Expect instant results—lab setup takes time; cultural change takes a semester or more.

Before You Begin: Three Things You Need to Know

First, this will feel uncomfortable.

Running an experiment that fails feels vulnerable.

Admitting you don't know something feels risky.

Documenting your mistakes publicly feels scary.

Letting go of control—grading for compliance, performing expertise—feels disorienting.

Do it anyway.

Discomfort is where growth happens.

Scientists embrace uncertainty. So must you.

Second, this takes time.

You won't transform your classroom in a week.

Students have been trained to fear mistakes for years. Unlearning that takes time.

Your own perfectionism didn't develop overnight. Undoing it will take patience.

Give it a month. Give it a semester. Give it a year.

Cultural transformation is gradual.

But the results are exponential.

Third, the work starts with you.

The lead scientist.

Before you ask students to embrace mistakes, you must embrace yours.

Before you teach them to run experiments, you must run experiments yourself.

Before you build a Mistake Lab for them, you must become a scientist of your own practice.

Chapter 3 is the foundation. Don't skip it.

Your relationship with your own mistakes will determine whether this approach works.

The Experiment Begins

Imagine it's six months from now.

You walk into your classroom.

Students are collaborating at lab stations.

One group is analyzing why their hypothesis didn't work. They're debating, revising, trying again.

Another student approaches you: "Can you look at my experiment? It failed, but I think I know why. I want to test a new variable."

A student raises their hand: "I don't understand this part. Can you explain it differently?"

No shame. No fear. Just curiosity.

That's your Mistake Lab.

It's not a fantasy. It's possible.

But it starts with you.

Ready to begin the experiment?

Turn the page.

Let's set up your lab.

PART 1

THE FOUNDATION (Lab Safety & Setup)

Why Students Can't Learn From Mistakes (Yet)

Before you run experiments, you need lab safety training.

In a science lab, safety comes first:

Protective equipment—goggles, gloves, procedures

Understanding hazards—chemicals, heat, sharp instruments

Emergency protocols—what to do when something goes wrong

In a Mistake Lab, psychological safety comes first:

Protective norms—no mockery, no shame

Understanding threats—judgment, comparison, grades as punishment

Response protocols—how to handle mistakes when they occur

Part 1 is your lab safety training.

You'll learn:

The science of learning from mistakes (Chapter 1)

Why teachers hide mistakes (Chapter 2)

Your own relationship with failure (Chapter 3)—very important

How to build psychological safety for students (Chapter 4)

The language that creates safety (Chapter 5)

How to teach students the core concept (Chapter 6)

Don't rush through this.

Just like you wouldn't skip lab safety training before working with chemicals, don't skip this foundation before building your Mistake Lab.

The culture you build in Part 1 determines whether everything else works.

Let's begin.

CHAPTER 1

THE SCIENCE OF LEARNING FROM MISTAKES

This Isn't Just Feel-Good Pedagogy. It's Brain Science.

Let's start with the evidence.

Because when a parent questions you, when a colleague challenges you, when a student pushes back, you need more than good intentions.

You need science.

The Neuroscience: How the Brain Actually Learns

Here's how learning works in the brain:

The Prediction-Error Cycle

Step 1: Your brain makes a prediction

"Based on what I know, here's what should happen if I do X."

Example:

Student thinks: "If I add 3x + 5 on both sides, I'll get the answer."

The teacher thinks, "If I explain it this way, students will understand."

Step 2: You test the prediction—run the experiment

The student solves the problem. The teacher delivers the lesson.

Step 3: You get a result

The result either matches your prediction—success—or doesn't—error.

Step 4: Your brain processes the error

This is the critical moment.

When your prediction is wrong, your brain has two possible responses:

Response A: Safe Environment (Mistake Lab)

What happens in your brain:

Your brain releases dopamine, a neurotransmitter.

Dopamine says, "Pay attention! This is important! You just learned something!"

Your brain encodes the correct information more strongly.

The neural pathway associated with the error strengthens, not weakens.

Why?

Because your brain is wired to learn from prediction errors. That's literally how learning happens.

Result: You remember the mistake and the correction. You're less likely to repeat the error.

Response B: Unsafe Environment (Theater Classroom)

What happens in your brain:

Your brain releases cortisol, a stress hormone.

Cortisol says: "Danger! Protect yourself!"

Your brain goes into fight, flight, or freeze mode.

The neural pathway associated with learning is blocked. Why?

Because your brain prioritizes survival over learning, when you feel threatened—by shame, judgment, public humiliation—learning shuts down.

Result: You remember the shame, not the lesson. You're likely to avoid similar situations in the future.

Let's make this concrete:

Scenario: Student makes a math mistake in front of the class

Response A (Mistake Lab):

Teacher: "Interesting. Walk me through your thinking."

Student's brain: Dopamine release. "This is safe. I can explain my thinking. Let me analyze what happened."

Outcome: Student learns from the error. The brain encodes correction. Less likely to repeat a mistake.

Response B (Theater):

Teacher: "No, that's wrong. You should know this. Who can show them the right way?"

Student's brain: Cortisol release. "Danger! Everyone's looking at me. I feel stupid. I need to hide."

Outcome: Student remembers the shame, not the math. The brain is in survival mode. Learning is blocked. The student avoids volunteering in the future.

Same mistake. Different environment. Different brain chemistry. Different outcome.

The Research: Eduardo Briceño

Eduardo Briceño, a performance researcher, identified two zones:

1. Performance Zone

Goal: Execute what you already know

Mistakes equal failures

Emphasis: Don't mess up

2. Learning Zone

Goal: Improve, acquire new skills

Mistakes equal data

Emphasis: Experiment, fail, learn

His finding:

High achievers spend time in both zones.

They practice in the learning zone, where failure is expected.

They perform in the performance zone, where execution matters.

But most classrooms are all performance zones.

Every assignment is graded. Every mistake counts. There's no safe space to practice.

Result: Students never develop skills. They just execute, or hide.

Translation for classrooms:

You need both zones:

Learning Zone (Lab work):

- Practice assignments—feedback only, no grades
- Rough drafts—expected to be messy
- Formative assessments—diagnostic, not evaluative
- Experiments—failure is data

Performance Zone (Demonstrations of mastery):

- Tests—but retakes allowed after reteaching
- Final projects—after revision
- Presentations—after practice

Most classrooms only have a Performance Zone. Your Mistake Lab needs both.

The Feedback Research: John Hattie

John Hattie analyzed 1,400-plus meta-studies involving 300-plus million students.

Question: What teaching strategies have the biggest impact on student learning?

Finding:

Feedback is one of the highest-impact strategies, with an effect size of 0.70.

For context:

- Average effect size equals 0.40
- Homework equals 0.29
- Feedback equals 0.70—nearly double the average

Translation: Feedback is powerful.

But here's the problem:

Not all feedback is created equal.

Hattie identified what makes feedback effective:

Timely—soon after the task. Specific—not "good job," but what specifically worked?

Focused on the task, not the person—"This paragraph is unclear" versus "You're not a good writer."

Actionable—tells the student what to do next

Separated from grades—this is critical

The Problem With Grades Plus Feedback

Research from Ruth Butler, 1988:

She gave students three types of feedback on their work:

Group A: Comments only, no grade

Group B: Grade only, no comments

Group C: Comments plus grade

Then she measured:

- Motivation
- Performance on the next task
- What students paid attention to

Results:

Group A (Comments only):

- Read the comments carefully
- Used feedback to improve
- Performed better on the next task
- Increased motivation

Group B (Grade only):

- Looked at the grade
- Compared with peers
- Didn't improve much on the next task
- Motivation depended on grade—high grade equals happy, low grade equals discouraged

Group C (Comments plus grade):

- Looked at the grade, ignored the comments
- Compared with peers
- Similar to Group B—grade only

The finding:

When you give comments and a grade, students focus on the grade and ignore the feedback.

The grade erases the value of the feedback.

Translation for your Mistake Lab:

Practice work—learning zone—equals feedback only, no grade

Demonstrations of mastery—performance zone—equals feedback plus grade

But even then, allow revision. Scientists revise hypotheses. Students revise their work.

We'll cover this more in Chapter 10: Grading Revolution.

The Motivation Research: What Actually Drives Learning?

For decades, schools have operated on this assumption:

Grades motivate students. If we grade everything, students will try harder."

The research says: This is backward.

Alfie Kohn: Punished by Rewards

Alfie Kohn reviewed decades of research on motivation.

Finding: Extrinsic rewards—grades, points, prizes, stickers—undermine intrinsic motivation.

When you reward a behavior:

- People do it for the reward, not because they care
- When the reward is removed, the behavior stops
- Creativity and deep engagement decrease

Example:

Study: Kids who loved drawing were given rewards for drawing.

Result: They drew less when rewards stopped. Drawing became work, not play.

Translation for classrooms:

When grades drive learning:

- Students learn for the grade, not because they're curious
- They ask: "Is this going to be on the test?" Not: "Why does this work?"
- They avoid challenge—high grades come from doing what you already know
- They cheat or cut corners—grade matters more than learning

When learning is driven by intrinsic motivation:

- Students learn because they're curious
- They ask: "How does this work? What if I try this?"
- They embrace challenge—growth is the goal
- They're honest about what they don't know—no need to perform

Self-Determination Theory (Deci & Ryan)

Researchers Edward Deci and Richard Ryan identified what drives intrinsic motivation:

Three psychological needs:

1. Autonomy

- Feeling of control over your learning
- Choice in what and how you learn
- Self-direction

2. Competence

- Feeling that you're getting better
- Mastery over time
- Growth, not just grades

3. Relatedness

- Connection to others
- Belonging
- Collaboration

When these three needs are met, intrinsic motivation flourishes.

When these needs are thwarted—by controlling teachers, grades as punishment, competitive classrooms—intrinsic motivation dies.

Translation for your Mistake Lab:

Autonomy: Students help design experiments, choose topics, and direct their own learning

Competence: Students see growth over time—revision, retakes, mastery-based grading

Relatedness: Students collaborate—lab partners, peer review, shared discoveries

Result: Students are intrinsically motivated. They learn because they want to, not because they're being graded.

Daniel Pink: Drive

Daniel Pink synthesized motivation research into three factors:

1. Autonomy (same as Deci & Ryan)
2. Mastery—the desire to get better at something
3. Purpose—the sense that what you're doing matters

His finding:

For complex, creative tasks—like learning—extrinsic rewards, such as grades, actually decrease performance.

Intrinsic motivation—autonomy, mastery, purpose—is what drives excellence.

Translation for classrooms:

Old model, extrinsic:

"Study hard so you can get an A. If you don't, your grade will suffer."

Result: Students study for the grade. Motivation is fragile—it disappears when grades aren't at stake.

New model, intrinsic—Mistake Lab:

"We're exploring this because it's fascinating. You're going to run experiments, make discoveries, and see how much you can grow. Mistakes are part of the process."

Result: Students learn because they're curious. Motivation is sustainable—learning becomes its own reward.

The Equity Research: Why Psychological Safety Matters More for Marginalized Students

Not all students experience mistakes the same way.

For marginalized students, mistakes carry additional weight.

Claude Steele: Stereotype Threat

Claude Steele, a social psychologist, studied how stereotypes affect performance.

His classic study:

He gave Black and white students the same difficult test.

Group A: Told it was a test of intelligence

Group B: Told it was a problem-solving exercise, not evaluative

Results:

When told it was an intelligence test:

- Black students underperformed compared to their actual ability
- White students performed normally

When told it was just problem-solving:

- Black students performed just as well as white students

What happened?

Stereotype threat:

When Black students were told it was an intelligence test, they were aware of the stereotype: "Black students aren't as smart."

That awareness created anxiety.

Anxiety → cortisol → learning blocked → performance dropped.

Not because they were less capable. Because the environment triggered a threat.

This has been replicated with:

- Women in math and science—stereotype: "Women aren't good at math."
- Latino students—stereotype: "Latinos don't value education."
- Students from poverty—stereotype: "Poor kids can't achieve."

The finding is consistent:

When students from stereotyped groups are in high-stakes, evaluative situations, performance drops.

When the environment is low-threat—growth-focused rather than evaluative—the performance gap disappears.

Translation for your Mistake Lab:

Traditional classroom, high-stakes, evaluative:

- Students of color face stereotype threat
- Every mistake feels like confirmation of stereotypes
- Performance drops

Mistake Lab, low-threat, growth-focused:

- Mistakes are normalized for everyone
- No one is confirming or disconfirming stereotypes
- Performance gaps shrink

Building a Mistake Lab is an equity imperative.

We'll cover this more in Chapter 11: Equity.

Gloria Ladson-Billings: Culturally Responsive Teaching

Gloria Ladson-Billings studied teachers who were effective with students of color.

Her finding:

Effective teachers had:

- High expectations—believed students were capable of excellence
- High support—scaffolded learning, provided feedback, created safe environments
- Cultural responsiveness—valued students' backgrounds, connected to their experiences

Ineffective teachers had:

- Low expectations—deficit thinking: "These kids can't."
- Low support—sink or swim
- Cultural mismatch—ignored or devalued students' identities

Translation for your Mistake Lab:

High expectations without high support equals a perfectionist culture:

"You should know this. Figure it out. If you can't, you're not capable."

High support without high expectations equals low rigor:

"I'll make it easier for you. You probably can't handle this."

High expectations plus high support equals Mistake Lab:

"This is hard. You're capable of figuring it out. I'm going to help you. Mistakes are part of the process."

Zaretta Hammond: Culturally Responsive Teaching and the Brain

Zaretta Hammond connected neuroscience to culturally responsive teaching.

Her finding:

Trauma and chronic stress—which disproportionately affect marginalized students—impair the brain's ability to learn.

Cortisol, the stress hormone, blocks the prefrontal cortex, where higher-order thinking happens.

When students don't feel safe:

- Their brains are in survival mode
- Learning is blocked
- Mistakes feel like threats, not learning opportunities

When students do feel safe:

- Their brains can engage in complex thinking
- Learning accelerates
- Mistakes are curiosity-provoking, not threatening

Translation for your Mistake Lab:

For students who've experienced trauma, instability, or chronic stress:

Traditional classroom equals threat:

- High stakes
- Public failure
- Unpredictable consequences
- Triggers fight, flight, freeze

Mistake Lab equals safety:

- Predictable routines
- Private practice before public performance
- Clear protocols
- Mistakes are expected and analyzed, not punished

Psychological safety isn't "nice to have." It's neurologically necessary.

The Growth Mindset Research: Carol Dweck

You've probably heard of the growth mindset.

But let's be clear about what the research actually says—not the watered-down version.

Carol Dweck's Research

Dweck studied how students respond to challenge and failure.

She identified two mindsets:

Fixed Mindset:

"Intelligence is fixed. You're either smart, or you're not."

When students with a fixed mindset encounter difficulty:

- They think: "I'm not good at this. I should give up."
- They avoid challenge—failure equals proof they're not smart
- They hide mistakes
- They compare themselves to others—"Am I the smartest?"

Result: Stagnation. They don't grow.

Growth Mindset:

"Intelligence is malleable. You get smarter by working hard and learning from mistakes."

When students with a growth mindset encounter difficulty:

- They think: "This is hard. I need to try a different strategy."
- They embrace challenge—difficulty equals opportunity to grow
- They analyze mistakes
- They compare themselves to their past selves—"Am I better than I was before?"

Result: Growth. They improve over time.

Dweck's key finding:

Mindsets can be taught.

When you praise effort and strategy rather than intelligence, students develop growth mindsets.

When you praise intelligence—"You're so smart!"—students develop fixed mindsets.

But here's where most schools get it wrong:

They tell students: "Have a growth mindset! Mistakes are good!"

But they grade in ways that punish mistakes.

They say: "Effort matters!"

But they reward students who get it right the first time—no effort needed.

Translation for your Mistake Lab:

You can't just tell students to have a growth mindset.

You have to build a system that rewards growth:

- Revision and retakes allowed—improvement is what matters
- Feedback on process, not just product—"I like how you tried three different strategies."
- Mistakes analyzed, not punished
- Growth tracked over time—students see their own improvement

Growth mindset isn't a poster on the wall. It's a culture.

The Bottom Line: What the Science Says

Here's what we know from neuroscience, psychology, and education research:

The brain learns through prediction errors. Mistakes are literally how learning happens.

Mistakes only lead to learning in safe environments—dopamine, not cortisol.

Feedback is powerful, but only when separated from grades. Comments get ignored when paired with grades.

Extrinsic motivation—grades—undermines intrinsic motivation. Students learn for points, not curiosity.

Intrinsic motivation requires autonomy, mastery, and purpose—not compliance.

Stereotype threat harms marginalized students in high-stakes environments. Safety reduces gaps.

High expectations plus high support equals culturally responsive teaching—rigor plus care.

Mindsets can be taught, but only if systems align. You can't say "growth mindset" while grading punitively.

In other words:

Everything you're about to build in this book is grounded in science.

This isn't just a nice idea. It's how the brain works.

So, Why Don't More Classrooms Operate This Way?

Good question.

If the science is clear, why do most classrooms still:

Punish mistakes with grades?

Create high-threat environments?

Use extrinsic motivation—points, rewards?

Emphasize performance over learning?

Two reasons:

Reason One: The system is designed this way

Schools were built for compliance and sorting, not learning.

The factory model:

- Standardized inputs
- Standardized processes
- Standardized outputs
- Sort students into categories: A, B, C, D, F

This worked for an industrial economy—workers who follow instructions.

It doesn't work for a knowledge economy—workers who problem-solve, innovate, and adapt.

We'll address this in Part 4: Working Within the System.

Reason Two: Teachers believe they should be infallible

And here's where the work starts with you.

If you believe:

"Good teachers don't make mistakes."

"I should know everything."

"Admitting I don't know makes me look incompetent."

Then you can't authentically build a Mistake Lab.

Because students will see through it.

They'll hear: "Mistakes are okay."

But they'll see: "My teacher never makes mistakes. My teacher hides when they're confused. My teacher is an expert."

And they'll learn from what they see, not what they hear.

That's why the next two chapters are the most important in this book.

Chapter 2: Why you hide mistakes—the infallible teacher myth

Chapter 3: Your perfectionism problem—your relationship with your own failures

You can't teach students to be scientists if you're still performing perfectly.

Let's address that next.

REFLECTION QUESTIONS

Personal Reflection:

1. What surprised you most about the neuroscience of learning from mistakes?
2. Think about a time you learned something deeply. Did it involve making mistakes? Revising? Iterating?
3. How does your classroom currently operate? More like a theater, a performance, or a lab—experimentation?
4. What would need to change for your classroom to align with the science in this chapter?

Classroom Audit:

Rate your current classroom on a 1-5 scale:

1. Psychological safety:

- 1 equals students are terrified of mistakes
- 5 equals students freely share confusion and errors

Your rating: _____

2. Learning versus performance:

- 1 equals everything is high-stakes and graded
- 5 equals a clear distinction between practice—safe—and performance—evaluated

Your rating: _____

3. Feedback:

- 1 equals only grades, no comments
- 5 equals detailed feedback separated from grades

Your rating: _____

4. Motivation:

- 1 equals extrinsic—grades, rewards
- 5 equals intrinsic—curiosity, mastery, purpose

Your rating: _____

5. Mindset culture:

- 1 equals a fixed mindset dominates
- 5 equals a growth mindset embedded in systems

Your rating: _____

Scoring:

20-25: Your classroom already operates like a lab

15-19: You're partway there

5-14: Significant changes needed—that's okay, this book will help

Action Planning:

Based on this chapter, what's one thing you could try this week?

- Separate one assignment into practice—feedback only—versus performance—graded
- Give comments-only feedback on one assignment, no grade yet.
- Explicitly tell students: "This is practice. Mistakes are expected. No grade."
- Ask yourself after a lesson: "Did students get dopamine—safe to fail—or cortisol—threat—today?"
- Identify one way to increase autonomy, mastery, or purpose in your class.

Further Exploration

Read:

- *Mindset: The New Psychology of Success* by Carol Dweck
- *Drive: The Surprising Truth About What Motivates Us* by Daniel Pink
- *Punished by Rewards* by Alfie Kohn
- *Visible Learning* by John Hattie
- *Whistling Vivaldi* by Claude Steele
- *Culturally Responsive Teaching and the Brain* by Zaretta Hammond

Watch:

- Eduardo Briceño's TED Talk: "How to Get Better at the Things You Care About"
- Carol Dweck's TED Talk: "The Power of Believing That You Can Improve"

Listen:

- "Hidden Brain" podcast episode on stereotype threat
- "WorkLife with Adam Grant" episode on feedback

Ready to continue?

CHAPTER 2

THE INFALLIBLE TEACHER MYTH

Students Think Teachers Never Make Mistakes Because Teachers Hide Them

October. 7th-grade science class.

The teacher—I'll call her Ms. Patterson—is demonstrating how to balance a chemical equation.

She writes on the board:

$H_2 + O_2 \rightarrow H_2O$

Then she adds coefficients:

$2H_2 + O_2 \rightarrow H_2O$

A student raises their hand: "Ms. Patterson, shouldn't there be a 2 in front of the H_2O?"

Ms. Patterson's internal panic: *Oh no. I messed up. In front of the whole class. They're going to think I don't know chemistry. I'll lose credibility.*

What she says: "Let me check my notes."

She turns away, pretends to consult her teacher's edition, erases quickly, and rewrites:

$2H_2 + O_2 \rightarrow 2H_2O$

Then: "Yes, that's correct. Good catch."

She moves on quickly, hoping no one noticed she made a mistake.

But here's what the students noticed:

Ms. Patterson didn't want to admit she made an error.

She had to check her notes—she wasn't sure.

She moved on fast—uncomfortable with the mistake.

And here's what they learned:

"Teachers aren't supposed to make mistakes. If I make one, I should hide it too."

The Same Week, Same School, Different Teacher

Mr. Chen is demonstrating the same equation.

He writes: $H_2 + O_2 \rightarrow H_2O$

Adds coefficients:

$2H_2 + O_2 \rightarrow H_2O$

A student raises their hand: "Mr. Chen, I think you're missing a coefficient."

Mr. Chen pauses. Looks at the board.

"You're absolutely right. I didn't balance the oxygen atoms on the right side. Can someone help me figure out what coefficient I need?"

Students call out: "Two!"

"Exactly." He writes $2H_2O$.

"Thanks for catching that. This is exactly what scientists do—check each other's work. I made a prediction error, you caught it, and I corrected it. That's how we learn. Everyone, make a note of this common mistake in their notebooks."

Students write: "Common mistake: forgetting to balance both sides."

What students learned:

"Mr. Chen makes mistakes. He admits them. He learns from them. Scientists check each other's work. Mistakes are normal."

Same mistake. Different response. Different lesson.

The Myth: Teachers Should Be Infallible

Here's the myth that most teachers have internalized:

"Good teachers know everything."

"Good teachers don't make mistakes."

"Good teachers always have the answer."

"If I admit I don't know something, students will lose respect for me."

This is the Infallible Teacher Myth.

And it's destroying your ability to build a Mistake Lab.

Why?

Because students don't learn from what you say.

They learn from what you model.

If you say: "Mistakes are how we learn!"

But you model: "I never make mistakes, and when I do, I hide them."

Students absorb the model, not the words.

Translation:

You can hang as many growth-mindset posters as you want.

You can tell students, "It's okay to fail!"

But if you won't admit when you don't know something, if you won't acknowledge when a lesson bombs, if you perform expertise instead of modeling learning...

Students will learn: "Mistakes are shameful. I should hide mine too."

Where the Myth Comes From

The Infallible Teacher Myth didn't come from nowhere.

You were taught this.

Here's where:

Source One: Teacher Training

Think about your teacher preparation program.

What were you taught?

Master your content. "Know your subject inside out."

Plan thoroughly. "Be prepared for every scenario."

Appear confident. "Students need to trust you know what you're doing."

Manage the classroom. "Don't let them see you sweat."

What were you not taught?

How to say "I don't know."

How to admit when a lesson fails

How to ask students for help

How to model learning alongside students

Student teaching:

You were evaluated on appearing competent.

Your supervisor observed and took notes:

Did you know the content? Check.

Did you execute the lesson plan? Check.

Did you manage behavior? Check.

No one asked:

Did you model intellectual humility?

Did you admit when you didn't know something?

Did you show students what learning looks like?

The message you absorbed:

"Good teachers are experts who have it all figured out."

Source Two: First-Year Survival Mode

Your first year of teaching, you were drowning.

Lesson planning took hours. Classroom management was a nightmare. You had no idea what you were doing.

But you couldn't admit that.

Why?

You didn't want colleagues to think you were incompetent.

You didn't want your principal to regret hiring you.
You didn't want students to lose confidence in you.
You were afraid you'd get fired.
So you performed competently.
You stayed late. You researched frantically. You pretended you had it together.
The message you absorbed:
"Hide your struggles. Never let them see you don't know."

Source Three: The Culture of Teaching

Teaching is an isolated profession.
You're alone in your classroom. You close the door. No one sees what happens inside.

Staff meetings are performative:

Teachers share successes. "Here's what's working in my class!"
Teachers don't share struggles. "I'm drowning and have no idea what I'm doing."

The teacher's lounge:

Complaints about students, parents, and admin.
Not: "I need help. I don't know how to teach this concept."

Professional development:

The presenter acts like an expert.
Teachers sit and receive—passive.
No one says: "I tried this and it failed. Can we troubleshoot together?"
The message you absorbed:
"Everyone else has it figured out. I'm the only one struggling. I need to hide that."

Source Four: The Evaluation System

Your performance reviews focus on deficits.
The document says:
Strengths: Brief paragraph
Areas for improvement: Long list of what you're doing wrong
Observations feel like gotcha moments:
Did you differentiate?
Did you check for understanding?
Did you manage transitions effectively?
You're being evaluated on what you don't know, what you didn't do.
The message you absorbed:
"Mistakes equal poor evaluation equals job insecurity. I can't afford to fail."

Source Five: Societal Expectations

Society has impossible expectations for teachers.

You're supposed to be:

Selfless—work nights and weekends, buy supplies with your own money

Tireless—never complain, never burn out

Perfect—save every child, close every gap, fix every problem

Media portrayals of teachers:

Saints who sacrifice everything—*Stand and Deliver*, *Freedom Writers*

Incompetent failures—*Bad Teacher*, negative news coverage

No middle ground. No humanity.

Parents expect you to know everything:

"You're the expert. Why doesn't my child understand fractions?"

Not: "Let's figure this out together."

The message you absorbed:

"I have to be perfect, or I'm letting everyone down."

The Cost of the Myth

When you believe you should be infallible, here's what happens:

Cost One: You Hide Your Mistakes From Students

Scenario:

You're teaching a lesson. It's not landing. Students are confused.

Old response—Infallible Teacher:

You push through. You don't acknowledge the confusion. You finish the lesson and hope they figure it out from the homework.

What students learn:

"When something doesn't work, don't acknowledge it. Just move on."

New response—Mistake Lab Lead Scientist:

You pause. "This isn't working. You're confused. I can see that. Let me try explaining it a different way."

What students learn:

"When an experiment doesn't work, you acknowledge it and revise your approach."

Cost Two: You Don't Say "I Don't Know"

Scenario:

A student asks a question you don't know the answer to.

Old response—Infallible Teacher:

You deflect:

"That's a great question. Let me think about it." Never bring it up again.

"Look it up for homework."

"That's beyond the scope of this class."

Or worse: You make something up.

What students learn:

"Teachers always know. If I don't know, something's wrong with me."

New response—Mistake Lab Lead Scientist:

"I don't know. That's a great question. Let's research it together."

You and your students look it up in real time, or you say, "I'm going to research this tonight and share what I find tomorrow." Then you actually do it.

Next day:

"I researched your question. Here's what I found." Share findings. "This led me to another question:" New question. "Anyone want to explore that with me?"

What students learn:

"Not knowing is the beginning of inquiry, not a failure. Scientists say 'I don't know' all the time—it's what drives research."

Cost Three: You Perform Expertise Instead of Modeling Learning

Scenario:

You're teaching a concept you don't fully understand yourself.

Old response—Infallible Teacher:

You study it the night before. You present it as if you've always known it. You perform with confidence.

What students learn:

"Learning happens in private. You should already know things before you show up."

New response—Mistake Lab Lead Scientist:

"I'm learning this concept alongside you. I studied it last night, but I'm still working through some of the nuances. Let's explore it together."

As you teach, you think aloud:

"Wait, I'm not sure I understand why that works. Let me re-read this part."

"I thought it would work this way, but I'm seeing something different. What do you notice?"

What students learn:

"Learning is a process. Even teachers are still learning. It's okay to think out loud and revise your understanding."

Cost Four: Students Absorb Your Perfectionism

Here's the most insidious cost:

When you model perfection, students think:

"My teacher never makes mistakes."

"My teacher always knows the answer."

"My teacher never struggles."

"Therefore, I shouldn't make mistakes. I should always know the answer. I shouldn't struggle."

"If I do struggle, something's wrong with me."

This creates:

Performance anxiety—fear of being exposed as "not smart."

Hiding behaviors—pretend to understand when you don't, copy answers, avoid asking questions.

Fixed mindset—"I'm either smart, or I'm not."

Shame spirals—"I made a mistake. I'm stupid. I should give up."

Your perfectionism becomes their perfectionism.

Cost Five: You Burn Out

Performing perfection is exhausting.

You can't sustain it.

Eventually:

You're working nights and weekends, trying to stay ahead.

You're avoiding trying new strategies. Failure is too risky.

You're isolated. Can't ask for help.

You're questioning whether you're cut out for teaching.

This is burnout.

And it's not because you're not good enough.

It's because you're trying to be something no one can be: perfect.

The Fallibility Paradox

Here's the paradox:

You think: "If I admit I don't know, students will lose respect for me."

But research shows the opposite:

Students respect teachers more when they're vulnerable.

Research: Brené Brown on Vulnerability

Brené Brown has spent two decades researching vulnerability, courage, and shame.

Her core finding:

"Vulnerability is not weakness. It's the most accurate measure of courage."

In her research on teachers specifically:

Students report higher trust in teachers who:

Admit when they don't know something

Acknowledge when lessons don't work

Share their own learning process

Show humanity, not perfection

Why?

Because vulnerability equals authenticity equals trust.

When you pretend to be perfect, students know it's performance.

When you're honest about your limitations, students see you as real.

Research: Social Psychology—The Pratfall Effect

The Pratfall Effect, Aronson, 1966:

People are more likable after they make a minor mistake, as long as they're perceived as competent overall.

Why?

Because perfection is off-putting, it creates distance.

Mistakes humanize you. They make you relatable.

Translation for teachers:

When you admit a mistake, students think:

"Oh, my teacher is human. They're not some untouchable expert. They make mistakes too. Maybe it's okay if I make mistakes."

This increases your credibility, not decreases it.

What Students Actually Need

Students don't need you to be perfect.

They need you to be:

1. Honest

When you don't know something: Say it.

When a lesson fails: Acknowledge it.

When you make a mistake: Own it.

Students trust honesty more than they trust perfect performance.

2. A Learner

Show them your learning process:

"I'm reading this book to get better at teaching writing."

"I tried a new strategy last year, and it didn't work. Here's what I learned from that."

"I don't know how to solve this problem yet. Let's figure it out together."

Students need to see that learning is lifelong, not something that ends when they become adults.

3. Curious

Model curiosity, not certainty.

Instead of: "Here's the answer."

Try: "Here's what I think. What do you notice? What questions does this raise?"

Instead of: "You should know this."

Try: "I'm curious why you approached it that way. Walk me through your thinking."

4. Willing to Experiment

Tell students when you're trying something new:

"I've never taught this lesson before. I'm experimenting. It might not work perfectly, and that's okay. We'll adjust as we go."

This normalizes:

Experimentation

Iteration

Learning from what doesn't work

5. A Co-Learner, Not Just an Expert

Position yourself as a fellow learner, not an all-knowing sage.

"I'm learning alongside you."

"This is new for me, too."

"Let's figure this out together."

This shifts the dynamic from:

Teacher equals expert, Student equals recipient

To:

Teacher equals lead scientist, Student equals junior scientist, Both equals researchers.

Real Examples: Modeling Fallibility

Let me show you what this looks like in practice.

Example One: You Make a Mistake on the Board

Old response:

Erase it quickly. Hope no one noticed. Move on.

What students learn:

"Mistakes are embarrassing. Hide them."

New response:

"Wait, I made an error. Can someone help me find it?"

Students identify the error.

"Thanks for catching that. This is exactly what I want you to do in your own work—check your thinking. Let's analyze where I went wrong."

You walk through your mistake, identify the error, and correct it.

What students learn:

"Everyone makes mistakes. Finding them is part of the process. We help each other."

Example Two: A Student Asks a Question You Don't Know

Old response:

"That's a great question. Look it up for homework."

What students learn:

"Teachers know everything. If you don't, you should hide it."

New response:

"I don't know the answer to that. But I'm curious now. Let's research it."

You pull it up on the projector, or you say, "I'm going to research this tonight and share what I find tomorrow."

Next day:

"I researched your question. Here's what I found." Share findings. "This led me to another question:" New question. "Anyone want to explore that with me?"

What students learn:

"Not knowing is the start of inquiry. Questions lead to more questions. That's how learning works."

Example Three: A Lesson Bombs

Old response:

Push through. Finish the lesson. Grade the assignment. Don't acknowledge it didn't work.

What students learn: "When things don't work, pretend they did."

New response:

Mid-lesson, you pause.

"This isn't working. I can see you're confused. Let me try a different approach."

You pivot. Try a new explanation, a different activity, a visual.

"That's better. I should have started with that. Let me know if you need me to explain it a different way."

What students learn:

"When an experiment doesn't work, you adjust in real-time. You don't just push through."

Example Four: You're Learning Something New

Old response:

Learn it in private. Present it as if you've always known it.

What students learn:

"Learning happens behind the scenes. You should show up already knowing."

New response:

"I'm learning how to use this new software. I've never used it before. I might make mistakes as we go. If you notice something I'm doing inefficiently, let me know."

As you teach, you think aloud:

"Hmm, I thought that button would do X, but it did Y. Let me try this instead."

"I'm not sure how to do this part. Let's look at the help menu together."

What students learn:

"Learning is messy. Experts are learners too. It's okay to figure things out in public."

Example Five: You Try a New Teaching Strategy, and It Fails

Old response:

Never try new things again. Stick with what's safe.

What students learn:

"Don't take risks. Failure is unacceptable."

New response:

Next class:

"I tried a new activity yesterday. It didn't go as well as I hoped. Here's what I think went wrong:" Analyze. "Here's what I'm going to try differently next time:" Revise. "What did you notice about the activity? What would make it better?"

What students learn:

"Teachers experiment. Not all experiments work. We analyze, revise, and try again. Failure is data."

How to Start Modeling Fallibility

If you've been performing perfection for years, this will feel uncomfortable.

Here's how to start:

Step One: Start Small—Low-Stakes Vulnerability

You don't have to announce your biggest teaching failure on Day 1.

Start with low-stakes admissions:

Admit small errors: "I misspelled a word on the board. Let me fix that."

Say "I don't know" to factual questions: "I don't know what year that happened. Let's look it up."

Acknowledge when you forget something: "I forgot to bring the handouts. My mistake. I'll have them tomorrow."

These are small, but they signal: "I'm human. I make mistakes. It's okay."

Step Two: Build to Medium-Stakes Vulnerability

Once small admissions feel normal, increase the stakes slightly:

Share when a lesson doesn't work: "That activity was confusing. Let me re-teach this a different way."

Ask students for feedback: "What worked about today's lesson? What didn't? How can I explain this better?"

Admit when you're trying something new: "I've never taught this lesson before. I'm experimenting. Give me feedback as we go."

Step Three: Model High-Stakes Vulnerability

Eventually, share bigger struggles and learning processes:

Share your learning journey: "I'm working on getting better at giving feedback. I'm reading a book about it. Here's what I'm trying this semester."

Acknowledge when you don't know how to teach something well: "I'm still learning how to teach this concept effectively. Let's figure it out together."

Share when you made a decision you regret: "I graded that assignment too harshly. I'm going to re-grade it. I learned something about my grading approach."

The Vulnerability Ladder

Think of vulnerability as a ladder:

Rung 1—Low-stakes:

- Typos and small errors
- "I don't know" to factual questions
- Forgetting minor things

Rung 2—Medium-stakes:

- Lessons that don't work
- Trying new strategies publicly
- Asking for student feedback

Rung 3—High-stakes:

- Sharing your learning process
- Acknowledging gaps in your teaching
- Revising grading or policies based on reflection

Climb the ladder gradually.

Don't start at Rung 3. Build your courage and your students' trust by starting at Rung 1.

Common Fears—And Why They're Unfounded

You might be thinking: "But what if students lose respect for me?"

"What if the admin thinks I'm incompetent?" "What if I lose control of the classroom?"

Let's address these fears:

Fear One: "Students Will Lose Respect for Me"

What do you think will happen:

You admit you don't know something. Students think: "This teacher is clueless. I'm not learning anything."

What actually happens:

You admit you don't know something. Students think: "Wow, my teacher is honest. They're human. It's okay for me not to know things, too."

Remember the research:

Students trust vulnerable teachers more, not less.

The key:

Be vulnerable from a place of confidence, not insecurity.

Low confidence vulnerability: "I don't know. Sorry. I'm probably a bad teacher."

High confidence vulnerability: "I don't know. Great question. Let's find out together."

The first signals incompetence. The second signals curiosity.

Fear Two: "Admin Will Think I'm Incompetent"

What do you think will happen:

Your principal observes you admitting a mistake. They write in your evaluation: "Teacher lacks content knowledge."

What actually happens:

Your principal observes you admitting a mistake and learning from it. They write: "Teacher models growth mindset and intellectual humility for students."

Most administrators want teachers who reflect and grow.

They're less impressed by teachers who pretend to be perfect—they know it's performance.

If you're worried about this:

Talk to your principal:

"I'm working on modeling a growth mindset for students by being more transparent about my own learning process. You might observe me saying 'I don't know' or acknowledging when a lesson doesn't work. I want you to know this is intentional—I'm teaching students that learning is iterative." Frame it as intentional pedagogy, not incompetence.

Fear Three: "I'll Lose Control of the Classroom"

What do you think will happen:

You admit you don't know something. Students think: "The teacher doesn't know what they're doing. Chaos ensues."

What actually happens:

You admit you don't know something. Students respect your honesty. Classroom culture becomes more collaborative, less hierarchical.

You don't lose control. You shift the dynamic.

From: Teacher equals authority who must be obeyed

To: Teacher equals lead scientist who guides inquiry

This is actually more effective classroom management because students are invested in the learning, not just complying with rules.

The Bottom Line

You cannot build a Mistake Lab if you're performing perfectly.

Students learn from what you model.

If you model:

- Hiding mistakes
- Pretending to know everything
- Never saying "I don't know."

Students will:

- Hide their mistakes
- Pretend to understand when they don't
- Never ask for help

If you model:

- Acknowledging mistakes and learning from them
- Saying "I don't know" and researching together
- Sharing your learning process

Students will:

- Analyze their mistakes openly
- Ask questions without shame
- See themselves as learners, like you

The Infallible Teacher Myth is destroying your classroom culture.

It's time to let it go.

But here's the catch:

You can't just start modeling vulnerability if you haven't addressed your own beliefs about mistakes.

If you believe deep down, "I should know everything. Making mistakes means I'm failing."

Then, the modeling vulnerability will feel fake. And students will sense it.

That's why Chapter 3 is the most important in this book. Before you can model fallibility for students, you have to confront your own perfectionism. Let's do that next.

REFLECTION QUESTIONS

Personal Reflection:

1. When was the last time you publicly admitted a mistake to your students? What happened?
2. When was the last time you said "I don't know" to a student's question? What stopped you?
3. On the Vulnerability Ladder—Rung 1, 2, or 3—where are you currently operating? Where do you want to be?
4. What fears come up when you think about being more vulnerable with students?

Scenario Reflection:

Imagine this scenario:

You're teaching a lesson. Mid-lesson, you realize you explained a concept incorrectly. Students are confused.

What would you do?

Option A: Push through, finish the lesson, and hope they figure it out from the homework.

Option B: Pause, acknowledge the error, re-explain correctly, move on quickly.

Option C: Pause, acknowledge the error, ask students what they noticed, analyze the mistake together, re-explain, and invite questions.

Which option feels most natural to you? Which option would you want to choose?

Action Planning:

This week, try one act of vulnerability:

Rung 1—Low-stakes: Admit a small mistake—typo, forgot something minor, didn't know a factual answer

Rung 2—Medium-stakes: Acknowledge when a lesson doesn't work and pivot in real-time

Rung 3—High-stakes: Share your learning process with students—"I'm working on getting better at..."

After you try it, reflect:

How did it feel?

How did students respond? What did you learn?

Further Exploration

Read:

- *Daring Greatly* by Brené Brown—on vulnerability and courage
- *The Courage to Teach* by Parker Palmer—on teaching from the heart
- *Thanks for the Feedback* by Douglas Stone & Sheila Heen—on receiving feedback as a learning opportunity

Watch:

- Brené Brown's TED Talk: "The Power of Vulnerability"
- Rita Pierson's TED Talk: "Every Kid Needs a Champion"—on authentic relationships with students

Ready to continue?

CHAPTER 3

YOUR PERFECTIONISM PROBLEM

Why You Believe You Should Be Infallible—And How to Shift That Belief

Sunday night. 11:47 PM.

You're still awake, planning tomorrow's lessons.

You've rewritten the warm-up three times. You've anticipated every possible student question. You've created backup activities in case the main lesson doesn't work.

You're exhausted.

But you can't stop. Because if you're not perfectly prepared, the lesson might fail. And if the lesson fails, you're failing.

You finally go to bed at 1 AM.

You wake up at 5:30 AM, already anxious.

"What if they don't understand?"

"What if I can't answer their questions?"

"What if the principal walks in during the messy part?"

Monday, 3rd Period

A student asks a question you don't know the answer to.

Your internal reaction:

Panic. I should know this. I studied this content. Why don't I know? They're going to think I'm incompetent. I need to deflect.

What you say:

"That's a great question. Let me think about it and get back to you."

You never bring it up again.

You go home that night feeling like a fraud.

Sound familiar?

The Voice in Your Head

This chapter is about the voice in your head.

The one that says:

"You should know better."

"You shouldn't struggle with this."

"Good teachers don't make these kinds of mistakes."

"If people knew how much you don't know, they'd realize you're not cut out for this."

That voice is perfectionism. And it's not just affecting you. It's affecting your students.

The Problem: You Believe You Should Be Infallible

Chapter 2 was about what you do: You hide mistakes from students. You don't say "I don't know." You perform with expertise.

Chapter 3 is about what you believe: You genuinely believe you shouldn't make mistakes. You believe struggling means you're failing. You believe asking for help means you're incompetent.

This isn't just performance—what you show students.

This is internalized perfectionism—what you believe about yourself.

And here's the critical insight:

You can't authentically model vulnerability for students if you haven't confronted your own perfectionism.

You can't teach students that mistakes equal data if you believe your mistakes equal failure.

The work starts with you.

Part A: The Problem—You Believe You Should Be Infallible

Let's start by naming what's happening inside you.

The Internal Dialogue of Perfectionism

These are things perfectionistic teachers say to themselves:

"I should know how to do this by now."

"I've been teaching for X years—why am I still struggling with classroom management?"

"Other teachers seem to have it figured out. What's wrong with me?"

"If I ask for help, people will realize I don't know what I'm doing."

"I can't admit I'm overwhelmed—they'll think I can't handle it."

"I should be better at this."

"I made a mistake in front of students. I'm a terrible teacher."

"Good teachers don't struggle like this." Do any of these sound familiar? If yes, you've internalized perfectionism.

Here's the problem:

This isn't just "being hard on yourself."

This belief system is sabotaging your teaching.

Because:

You're treating your mistakes as evidence of failure—identity thinking.

You're isolating yourself—can't ask for help.

You're burning out—perfectionism is exhausting.

You're modeling this for students—they absorb your perfectionism.

Part B: Where the Belief Comes From

Perfectionism didn't come from nowhere.

You were taught this.

Here's where:

Source One: How You Were Trained

Think about your teacher preparation program.

What was emphasized?

Content mastery

"You need to know your subject inside and out."

The assumption: By the time you're a teacher, you should know everything in your content area.

Thorough planning

"Plan for every possible scenario. Anticipate every question. Have backup activities."

The assumption: Good teachers are perfectly prepared.

Appearing confident

"Students need to trust you know what you're doing. Project authority."

The assumption: Uncertainty equals incompetence.

What was not emphasized:

Intellectual humility

"It's okay not to know. Saying 'I don't know' is powerful."

Learning alongside students

"You're a learner too. Model your learning process."

Asking for help

"Collaboration makes you stronger, not weaker."

The message you absorbed:

"By the time you're certified, you should have it all figured out."

But here's the reality:

Teacher training can't prepare you for everything.

You can't predict every student's question.

You can't master every teaching strategy before Day 1.

You can't know how to handle every classroom situation.

You're going to encounter things you don't know.

You're going to struggle. You're going to make mistakes.

That doesn't mean you're failing. It means you're learning.

But your training didn't prepare you to believe that.

Source Two: First-Year Survival Mode

Your first year of teaching, you were drowning.

The reality of first-year teaching:

Lesson planning took 3-4 hours every night.

Classroom management was chaos.

You had no idea what you were doing half the time.

You cried in your car more than once.

But you couldn't admit that.

Why?

Because you thought:

"Everyone else has it together. If I admit I'm struggling, they'll know I'm not cut out for this."

"If my principal finds out I'm overwhelmed, they'll regret hiring me."

"If students sense I don't know what I'm doing, I'll lose control."

"If I ask a colleague for help, they'll think I'm incompetent."

So you performed competently.

Stayed until 7 PM every night, so no one knew you were behind.

Smiled and said "Fine!" when colleagues asked how you were doing.

Googled frantically in secret: "How to teach photosynthesis," "What to do when students won't stop talking." Never admitted you were struggling.

The message you absorbed:

"Struggling equals failing. I need to hide this."

But here's the truth:

Every first-year teacher is drowning. Veteran teachers remember drowning, too.

But because everyone hides it, first-year teachers think they're the only ones who do.

This isolation reinforces perfectionism.

Source Three: The Culture of Teaching

Teaching is an isolated, performative profession.

Here's what that looks like:

Isolation:

You're alone in your classroom. You close the door. No one sees what happens inside.

You don't see other teachers teach, except maybe during observations, which are performances.

You have no idea if other teachers:

Are struggling with the same things you are. Make the same mistakes you do.

Feel as overwhelmed as you feel. You assume everyone else has it figured out.

Performative Culture:

Staff meetings:

Teachers share successes:

"I tried this new strategy, and it worked great!"

"My students loved this activity!"

Teachers don't share struggles:

"I tried this strategy, and it bombed."

"I have no idea how to reach this student."

Professional development:

The presenter acts like an expert:

Polished slides

Confident delivery

"Here's what works!"

No one says:

"I tried this, and it failed. Here's what I learned."

"I'm still figuring this out."

Teacher's lounge:

Complaints about students, parents, and admin.

But not:

"I need help. I don't know how to teach this concept."

"Can someone watch me teach and give me feedback?"

The message you absorbed:

"Everyone else has it together. I'm the only one struggling. I need to hide this."

But here's the reality:

Everyone is struggling.

Veteran teachers are still figuring things out.

But because the culture is performative, no one talks about it.

Source Four: The Evaluation System

Your performance reviews focus on what you're doing wrong.

The document structure:

Strengths: Brief paragraph

Areas for improvement: Long, detailed list of deficits

Observations feel like gotcha moments:

Your principal walks in with a clipboard.

They're looking for:

Did you differentiate?

Did you check for understanding?

Were transitions smooth?

Did you call on a variety of students?

They're not noticing:

The beautiful moment when a struggling student finally got it

The relationship you've built with your most challenging student

How much you've grown since last year

They're looking for what's missing.

Post-observation conference:

"Here's what you need to work on..."

The message you absorbed:

"I'm being evaluated on my deficits. Mistakes equal poor evaluation equals job insecurity."

This creates hypervigilance:

"I can't let the principal see me struggle."

"I need to have perfect lessons every time I'm observed."

"If I make a mistake during an observation, my evaluation will suffer."

The result:

Teaching becomes a performance, not a practice.

Source Five: Societal Expectations

Society has impossible, contradictory expectations for teachers.

Expectation One: You should be selfless.

"Teachers should work nights and weekends."

"Teachers should spend their own money on supplies."

"Teachers should sacrifice their personal lives for their students."

If you set boundaries, you're "not dedicated enough."

Expectation Two: You should be tireless.

"Teachers should never complain."

"Teachers should never burn out."

"Teachers should be endlessly patient and energetic."

If you're exhausted, you're "not resilient enough."

Expectation Three: You should be perfect.

"Teachers should save every child."

"Teachers should close every achievement gap."

"Teachers should never make mistakes that harm students."

If a student struggles, you "should have done more."

Media portrayals of teachers:

Option A: Saints

Stand and Deliver

Freedom Writers

Dead Poets Society

Teachers who sacrifice everything, work miracles, never give up.

Option B: Failures

Negative news coverage

"Failing schools," "Bad teachers"

Politicians blame teachers for societal problems

No middle ground.

No portrayal of teachers as normal humans who:

Try their best

Make mistakes

Learn and grow

Have boundaries

Parents expect you to be the expert:

"You're the teacher. You should know why my child isn't learning."

Not:

"Let's figure this out together."

The message you absorbed:

"I have to be perfect, or I'm letting everyone down."

"If I admit I'm struggling, I'm confirming that I'm not good enough."

Source Six: Impostor Syndrome

Many teachers experience impostor syndrome.

Impostor syndrome equals the persistent belief that you're a fraud and will be "found out."

What it sounds like in your head:

"I don't really know what I'm doing."

"Other teachers are better than I am."

"I got lucky getting this job. They'll eventually realize I'm not qualified."

"If anyone knew how much I don't know, they'd fire me."

Impostor syndrome is especially common among:

First-year teachers: "I'm faking it until I make it." Teachers who switched careers: "I'm not a 'real' teacher."

Teachers in new contexts: "I've never taught this grade or subject before."

Teachers from marginalized backgrounds: "I don't fit the stereotype of what a teacher should be."

The result:

You overcompensate by projecting expertise. "If I admit I don't know, they'll realize I'm a fraud."

The message you absorbed:

"I need to prove I belong here. I can't let anyone see my uncertainty."

Part C: The Cost of This Belief

When you believe you should be infallible, here's what happens:

Cost One: Shame When You Make Mistakes

Scenario:

You're teaching a lesson. You explain a concept incorrectly. A student points it out.

External reaction—what students see:

You correct it and move on.

Internal reaction—what you feel:

Intense shame.

"I can't believe I got that wrong. I should know this. What kind of teacher makes that mistake? They're going to think I'm incompetent. I'm so stupid."

The spiral: Shame → Rumination → Self-criticism → Shame about feeling shame

You replay the mistake in your head for days.

This is exhausting. And it's not helping you grow.

Because you're focused on: "I'm a bad teacher"—identity

Not: "What happened and how can I improve?"—data

Cost Two: Anxiety About Being Observed

Scenario:

Your principal schedules an observation.

Your reaction:

Panic. Overplan. Stay up late perfecting the lesson. Rehearse it multiple times.

The day of the observation, you're hyper-aware of every mistake.

After the observation, you replay it in your head:

"I forgot to call on that student."

"That transition was messy."

"I should have explained that differently."

The belief driving this:

"I need to be perfect. If the principal sees me struggle, my evaluation will suffer."

The cost:

Observations become performances, not learning opportunities.

You don't try new strategies—too risky.

You teach the safest, most polished version of yourself, not your most authentic or experimental self.

Cost Three: Burnout

Perfectionism is exhausting.

You're constantly:

Working late, trying to create perfect lessons

Second-guessing yourself: "Should I have done that differently?"

Comparing yourself to others: "Other teachers seem to have it together. Why don't I?"

Hiding struggles—can't ask for help

This leads to:

Physical exhaustion—never enough sleep

Emotional exhaustion—constant anxiety

Cognitive exhaustion—decision fatigue, rumination

Eventually:

You burn out.

You start questioning:

"Am I cut out for teaching?"

"Should I leave the profession?"

But the problem isn't you.

The problem is perfectionism.

Cost Four: Isolation

When you believe you should be perfect, you can't ask for help.

Because asking for help feels like admitting:

"I don't know what I'm doing."

"I'm not as good as other teachers."

"I'm failing."

So you suffer in silence.

You don't ask colleagues for feedback.

You don't observe other teachers.

You don't share what's not working.

You struggle alone.

The result:

You don't grow as quickly as you could.

Because growth requires:

Feedback, which requires vulnerability

Collaboration, which requires admitting you don't have all the answers

Experimentation, which requires accepting failure. Perfectionism blocks all of these.

Cost Five: You Can't Authentically Model Vulnerability for Students

This is the most important cost:

If you believe your mistakes equal failure, you can't authentically teach students that mistakes equal data.

Why?

Because students sense inauthenticity.

You might say:

"Mistakes are how we learn! It's okay to fail!"

But if you:

Hide your mistakes

Beat yourself up internally when you make errors

Feel shame when you don't know something

Perform expertise instead of modeling learning

Students will learn from what you model, not what you say.

They'll think:

"My teacher says mistakes are okay. But they never make mistakes. So mistakes must not be okay."

Your perfectionism becomes their perfectionism.

Cost Six: You Stop Trying New Things

Perfectionism kills innovation.

Because trying new things equals risk of failure.

And if failure equals proof you're not good enough, you'll avoid it.

So you:

Stick with lessons you've taught before—safe, polished

Don't experiment with new strategies—might fail

Don't try new technology—it might not work perfectly

Don't take risks—failure feels too dangerous

The result:

Your teaching stagnates.

You don't grow. Your students don't benefit from innovation.

All because you're afraid of failing.

Part D: The Shift You Need to Make

Here's the shift:

From—Identity Thinking:

"Good teachers don't make mistakes."

"If I'm making mistakes, I'm failing."

"Struggling means I'm not good enough."

To—Data Thinking:

"Good teachers learn from mistakes."

"Making mistakes means I'm growing."

"Struggling means I'm working on something challenging—that's where growth happens."

The core shift:

Separate your identity from your performance.

Identity thinking:

"I made a mistake. I'm a bad teacher."

Data thinking:

"I made a mistake. That's information about what I need to learn next."

This is the same shift you need students to make, covered in Chapter 6.

But you can't teach them this if you haven't done it yourself.

Part E: How to Make the Shift—Seven Steps

Here's how to confront your perfectionism and develop a scientist mindset about your own teaching:

Step One: Acknowledge Your Perfectionism

The first step is awareness. You can't change what you don't acknowledge.

Take the Teacher Perfectionism Self-Assessment:

Rate yourself on a 1-5 scale:

1 = Strongly disagree

5 = Strongly agree

1. When I make a mistake in front of students, I feel intense shame.

Your rating: ______

2. When I don't know the answer to a student's question, I should have known it.

Your rating: ______

3. When a lesson bombs, I think: "I'm a bad teacher."

Your rating: ______

4. When I need help with something, I struggle on my own rather than asking a colleague.

Your rating: ______

5. I believe good teachers should have it all figured out.

Your rating: ______

6. When I receive critical feedback, I feel defensive or attacked.

Your rating: ______

7. When I observe another teacher doing something better than me, I feel inadequate.

Your rating: ______

8. When I try a new strategy, and it doesn't work, I think: "I should just stick with what I know."

Your rating: ______

9. I compare myself to other teachers and feel like I'm not as good as they are.

Your rating: ______

10. I work late most nights trying to create perfect lessons.

Your rating: ______

Scoring:

40-50: Severe perfectionism. You're likely burning out. This chapter is critical for you.

30-39: Moderate perfectionism. You have perfectionistic tendencies that are holding you back.

20-29: Mild perfectionism. You're developing a growth mindset, but still have work to do.

10-19: Low perfectionism. You have a healthy relationship with mistakes and growth.

If you scored 30 or above, acknowledge it:

"I have internalized perfectionism. It's affecting my teaching and my well-being."

Journaling prompt:

"I notice that I'm perfectionistic about..."

"The voice in my head says..."

"This perfectionism costs me..."

Step Two: Examine Where the Belief Came From

Understanding the origin helps you question it.

Reflection questions:

1. When did you first learn that teachers should be perfect?
2. Who taught you that mistakes equal failure?
3. What experiences reinforced this belief?
4. Was there a specific moment when you learned to hide struggles?

Journaling prompt:

"I learned that teachers should be perfect when..."

"The message I absorbed was..."

"The cost I'm paying for this belief is..."

Example:

"I learned that teachers should be perfect when I was student teaching. My supervisor would sit in the back with a clipboard, writing down everything I did wrong. I was evaluated on my deficits, never my growth. The message I absorbed was: 'Mistakes mean you're failing.' The cost I'm paying is: I'm terrified of being observed, I don't try new things, and I'm burning out."

The insight:

This isn't the truth. It's a story you were taught. And you can unlearn it.

Step Three: Reframe Mistakes as Data—For Yourself

This is the core practice.

When you make a mistake, practice reframing:

Old response—Identity thinking:

"I explained that wrong. I'm so stupid. I should have known better. What kind of teacher makes that mistake? I'm a terrible teacher."

New response—Data thinking:

"I explained that wrong. Interesting. What happened? Why was my explanation unclear? What could I say differently next time? This is useful data about how to teach this concept better."

The process:

1. **Notice the identity thought**

"I'm a bad teacher."

2. **Pause**

Take a breath. Don't spiral.

3. **Ask: "Is this identity or data?"**

"Am I making this about who I am? Or about what I can learn?"

4. **Reframe**

"What's the data here? What can I learn from this?"

Practice scenarios:

Scenario 1: You explained a concept incorrectly

Identity response:

"I'm a terrible teacher. I should know this content inside and out. I can't believe I got that wrong in front of students."

Data response:

"My explanation was incorrect. What was my misconception? How can I re-teach this correctly? What will help me remember the correct explanation next time?"

Scenario 2: A student asks a question you don't know

Identity response:

"I should know this. I'm supposed to be the expert. They're going to think I'm incompetent."

Data response:

"I don't know the answer. That's okay. This is an opportunity to model research and inquiry. What resources can we use to find out together?"

Scenario 3: A lesson bombs

Identity response:

"I'm a failure. This lesson was terrible. I'm not good at planning. Other teachers can plan engaging lessons. Why can't I?"

Data response:

"That lesson didn't work. What specifically didn't work? Was it the pacing? The activity structure? Student confusion about the concept? What can I adjust for tomorrow?"

Scenario 4: You forget to grade assignments on time

Identity response:

"I'm so disorganized. I'm failing my students. I should be more on top of things. Good teachers don't fall behind like this."

Data response:

"I fell behind on grading this week. What got in the way? Too many commitments? Underestimated time required? What system do I need to stay on track? Grade as assignments come in? Block grading time on the calendar?"

The reframing process takes practice.

Be patient with yourself.

Each time you catch an identity thought and reframe it, you're rewiring your brain.

Step Four: Find One Safe Person to Be Vulnerable With

You don't have to do this alone.

Identify one colleague you trust:

Someone who:

Seems to have a growth mindset

Admits when they don't know something

Asks for help without shame

Talks about their teaching challenges openly

Reach out:

"I'm working on being more open about my mistakes and struggles as a teacher. I've realized I have perfectionist tendencies that are holding me back. Would you be willing to be a vulnerability buddy? We could check in once a week and share what's not working, what we're learning, what we need help with."

Why this works:

Accountability—you're more likely to practice vulnerability if someone's expecting you to share

Support—you're not alone

Perspective—they'll probably share that they struggle too

Connection—vulnerability builds relationships

Structure:

Weekly 15-minute check-in, in person, phone, or email:

Each person shares:

One thing that didn't work this week—a mistake, a failed lesson, a struggle

What you learned from it—the data

What you're trying next—the revision

One thing you need help with—ask for support

Example:

"This week, I tried a new discussion protocol, and it flopped. Students were confused about the structure. I learned that I need to model protocols before releasing students to try them. Next week, I'm going to do a fishbowl demonstration first. Can you help me think through how to structure that?"

Start with one person. As you get more comfortable, expand to a small group of 3-4 teachers. This becomes your lab team.

Step Five: Model Vulnerability in Low-Stakes Situations First

You don't have to start by sharing your biggest teaching failure.

Use the Vulnerability Ladder from Chapter 2:

Level 1—Low-stakes:

Admit a small mistake: "I misspelled a word on the board. Let me fix it."

Say "I don't know" to a factual question: "Good question. I don't know. Let's look it up."

Acknowledge minor forgetfulness: "I forgot to bring the handouts. My mistake."

Level 2—Medium-stakes:

Share when a lesson doesn't work: "That activity was confusing. Let me re-teach it differently."

Ask students for feedback: "What worked about today's lesson? What could I improve?"

Admit you're trying something new: "I've never taught this way before. I'm experimenting. Give me feedback as we go."

Level 3—High-stakes:

Share your learning journey: "I'm working on getting better at feedback. I'm reading a book about it. You'll notice me trying new things this semester."

Acknowledge gaps in your teaching: "I'm still learning the best way to teach this concept. Let's figure it out together."

Revise a decision based on reflection: "I graded that assignment too harshly. I reflected on it and realized my rubric wasn't clear. I'm re-grading it."

Start at Level 1.

Build confidence.

Move to Level 2, then Level 3.

Why this works:

Each small act of vulnerability:

Builds your courage

Shows you that students don't lose respect—they often gain respect

Normalizes mistake-making in your classroom

Makes bigger vulnerabilities easier

Step Six: Separate Your Identity From Your Performance

This is the deepest work.

Core practice:

When you make a mistake, say to yourself:

"I made a mistake. That doesn't mean I'm a mistake."

"My performance today does not equal my worth as a teacher."

"I'm a teacher who's learning. Just like my students."

Mantra to practice:

"I am not my mistakes."

"I am a learner."

"Mistakes are data, not identity."

Compassionate self-talk:

Instead of:

"I'm so stupid. I can't believe I did that. I'm a terrible teacher."

Try:

"I'm human. I made a mistake. What can I learn from this? How would I respond if a student made this mistake? I'd be kind and help them learn. I deserve the same kindness."

Self-compassion research—Kristin Neff:

Self-compassion has three components:

1. Self-kindness—treating yourself with care, not harsh criticism
2. Common humanity—recognizing everyone struggles; you're not alone.
3. Mindfulness—acknowledging your feelings without over-identifying with them

Practice:

When you make a mistake:

1. Self-kindness:

"It's okay. Everyone makes mistakes. I'm still a good teacher."

2. Common humanity:

"Other teachers make mistakes, too. This is part of being human."

3. Mindfulness:

"I feel embarrassed right now. That's a normal feeling. I don't have to spiral into shame."

Step Seven: Keep a "Teacher Lab Notebook"

Scientists keep lab notebooks documenting experiments—including failures.

You should, too.

What to document:

Each week, write:

1. One experiment I ran—a new strategy, lesson, or approach I tried
2. What happened—the data; did it work? Why or why not?
3. What I learned—the insight
4. What I'll try next—the revision

Example entry:

Date: October 10

Experiment: I tried using think-pair-share during the lecture instead of asking for volunteers.

What happened: More students participated. I heard more diverse ideas. But it took longer than I expected, and we didn't finish the content I planned.

What I learned: Think-pair-share increases engagement but requires more time. I need to plan fewer discussion questions or allocate more time.

What I'll try next: Use think-pair-share for 2-3 key questions instead of 5-6. Prioritize depth over breadth.

Why this works:

Reframes failures as experiments, not personal failures

Document learning—you can see your growth over time

Externalizes reflection—gets it out of your ruminating brain and onto paper

Model scientist mindset—you're treating your teaching like a lab

Bonus:

Share entries with your vulnerability buddy or lab team.

"Here's what I tried this week. Here's what I learned."

Part F: Real Teacher Stories

Let me show you what this looks like in practice.

Story One: The Veteran Teacher Who Believed She Should Know Everything

Sarah has been teaching for 15 years.

She thought: "By now, I should have it all figured out."

This year, she's struggling with classroom management in her 4th-period class.

Her internal dialogue:

"I've been teaching for 15 years. How am I still struggling with classroom management? What's wrong with me? Good teachers don't have these problems."

She's too embarrassed to ask for help.

She suffers in silence for 3 months.

Stress builds. She's snapping at students. She's dreading 4th period.

Finally, over lunch, she breaks down to a colleague:

"I feel like I should know how to handle this class by now. I've been teaching forever. I'm so frustrated with myself."

Her colleague says:

"Sarah, I've been teaching for 20 years, and I'm still learning classroom management. Every class is different. Every year, I have to adapt. This doesn't mean you're failing. Want to brainstorm together?"

That conversation changed everything.

Sarah realized:

Struggling doesn't mean she's failing. Veteran teachers don't have it all figured out. Asking for help is wisdom, not weakness.

They brainstormed strategies. Sarah tried them. Some worked, some didn't. She kept adjusting. By December, the 4th period was manageable.

What Sarah learned:

"I don't have to have it all figured out. I'm still allowed to learn. Experience doesn't mean I should be perfect—it means I know how to iterate and problem-solve."

Story Two: The First-Year Teacher Afraid of Looking Incompetent

Marcus is in his first year of teaching.

He's drowning.

Lesson planning takes 4 hours every night. Students are walking all over him. He has no idea how to manage behavior.

But he's terrified to ask for help.

He thinks:

"Everyone else seems fine. If I admit I'm struggling, they'll know I can't handle this. They'll regret hiring me."

One day, his mentor teacher stops by after school and finds Marcus near tears.

"What's wrong?"

Marcus breaks down:

"I feel like everyone else has it together and I'm the only one who's failing. I don't know what I'm doing."

His mentor laughs, not unkindly:

"Marcus, everyone is struggling. The first year is hell for everyone. We just don't talk about it."

She shares the mistakes she made in her first year.

She shares mistakes she made last year, in her 8th year of teaching.

She helps Marcus:

Build systems for lesson planning

Practice classroom management strategies

Observe her class and give feedback

Marcus still struggled. But he didn't feel alone.

What Marcus learned:

"Struggling doesn't mean I'm not cut out for teaching. It means I'm learning. Asking for help isn't weakness—it's how you get better."

Story Three: The Teacher Who Thought Admitting Mistakes Would Lose Student Respect

Jasmine believed: "If I admit I don't know something, students will lose respect for me."

She performed with expertise constantly.

One day, a student asked a science question she didn't know the answer to.

Her instinct: Deflect. But she decided to try something new:

"I don't know. That's a great question. Let's figure it out together."

They looked it up. They discussed it. Jasmine learned alongside students.

After class, a student came up to her:

"That was cool. I didn't know teachers could say they don't know stuff. I thought you had to know everything."

Jasmine realized:

Students didn't lose respect. They gained respect.

Because she was honest.

What Jasmine learned:

"Students don't need me to know everything. They need me to be real. Vulnerability builds trust."

Part G: The Work Starts With You

Here's the truth:

You can't build a Mistake Lab for students if you're still trapped in perfectionism.

Because students learn from what you model.

If you model:

Shame when you make mistakes
Hiding when you don't know
Performing expertise
Working alone, never asking for help

Students will learn:

Mistakes are shameful
Not knowing is a failure
Learning happens in private
Struggle should be hidden

If you model:

Analyzing mistakes as data
Saying "I don't know" and researching together
Sharing your learning process
Collaborating with colleagues

Students will learn:

Mistakes are learning opportunities
Not knowing is the start of inquiry
Learning is a visible, iterative process
Scientists collaborate

The Bottom Line

Before you build a Mistake Lab for students, you must become a scientist of your own teaching.

That means:

Acknowledging your perfectionism

Understanding where it came from

Reframing your mistakes as data

Finding support—vulnerability buddy

Practicing vulnerability—start small

Separating identity from performance

Documenting your experiments—teacher lab notebook

This is the foundation.

Do this work first.

Because everything else in this book depends on it.

Next: Building psychological safety for students.

But you can't build it for them until you've built it for yourself.

Let's continue.

REFLECTION QUESTIONS

Personal Reflection:

1. What was your score on the Teacher Perfectionism Self-Assessment? What does that tell you?
2. Which of the 6 sources of perfectionism resonates most with you? Training, first-year survival, culture, evaluation, societal expectations, impostor syndrome?
3. What's the cost you're paying for perfectionism right now? Burnout? Isolation? Anxiety? Not trying new things?
4. What would it feel like to let go of the belief that you should be perfect?

Identity Versus Data Practice:

Think of a recent mistake you made.

Write two responses:

Identity response:

"I made this mistake. This means I'm..."

Data response:

"I made this mistake. The data tells me..."

Notice the difference in how these feel.

Action Planning:

This week, choose one practice:

Complete the Teacher Perfectionism Self-Assessment

Journal: "I learned that teachers should be perfect when..."

Identify one colleague to be your vulnerability buddy

Practice reframing one mistake—identity to data

Model vulnerability in one low-stakes situation

Start a Teacher Lab Notebook—document one experiment

Practice self-compassion—next time you make a mistake, talk to yourself like you'd talk to a student

Further Exploration

Read:

- *Daring Greatly* by Brené Brown—on vulnerability and shame
- *The Gifts of Imperfection* by Brené Brown—on letting go of perfectionism
- *Self-Compassion* by Kristin Neff—on treating yourself with kindness
- *Radical Acceptance* by Tara Brach—on self-compassion and mindfulness
- *Mindset* by Carol Dweck—on growth mindset for yourself, not just students

Watch:

- Brené Brown's TED Talk: "The Power of Vulnerability"
- Brené Brown's TED Talk: "Listening to Shame"

Listen:

- "The Happiness Lab" podcast episode on self-compassion
- "WorkLife with Adam Grant" episode on impostor syndrome

This is the most important chapter in the book.

If you do the work in this chapter—confront your perfectionism, reframe your mistakes as data, practice vulnerability—everything else will follow.

If you skip this chapter, the rest of the book won't work.

Because you can't authentically teach students what you don't believe yourself.

Ready to continue?

CHAPTER 4

PSYCHOLOGICAL SAFETY FOR STUDENTS

Creating the Conditions Where Learning Out Loud Is Possible

Two classrooms. Same school. Same lesson on solving quadratic equations.

Classroom A: Low Psychological Safety

Ms. Thompson writes a problem on the board:

$x^2 + 5x + 6 = 0$

She calls on a student: "Marcus, solve this."

Marcus hesitates. He's not sure how to factor it.

After 10 seconds of silence, Ms. Thompson sighs:

"Anyone else? Come on, we learned this yesterday."

Three hands shoot up. She calls on Aisha, who solves it correctly.

Marcus sinks lower in his seat.

For the rest of class:

Marcus doesn't volunteer.

When he's called on again, he says "I don't know" without trying.

Other struggling students stay silent—don't want to be the next Marcus.

Only confident students participate.

What students learned:

"If you don't know the answer, don't volunteer. Being wrong in front of everyone is humiliating. It's safer to stay silent."

Classroom B: High Psychological Safety

Mr. Chen writes the same problem:

$x^2 + 5x + 6 = 0$

He says, "Turn to your partner. Try to solve this together. Make your thinking visible—show your work, even if you're not sure. You have 2 minutes."

Students work in pairs. Murmuring. Trying. Some struggling.

After 2 minutes:

Mr. Chen: "Who wants to share what you tried? Doesn't have to be correct—I want to see your thinking."

A student volunteers: "We tried to factor it. We got $(x + 2)(x + 3)$, but we're not sure if that's right."

Mr. Chen: "Walk me through how you got that. What were you thinking?"

Student explains.

Mr. Chen: "Excellent. You identified that you need to factor. Let's check your factors. If we expand $(x + 2)(x + 3)$, what do we get?"

Class works through it together. The factors are correct.

Mr. Chen: "Perfect. You got it. Who tried a different approach? Has anyone used the quadratic formula?" Another student shares.

What students learned:

"It's safe to share your thinking, even if you're not sure. The teacher values process, not just correct answers. We're learning together."

The Difference: Psychological Safety

Same problem. Different outcomes. The difference wasn't the content or the students' ability. The difference was psychological safety.

What Is Psychological Safety?

Definition—Amy Edmondson, Harvard researcher:

"Psychological safety is a belief that the team is safe for interpersonal risk-taking."

Translation for classrooms:

Students believe they can:

Admit confusion without being judged

Ask questions without being mocked

Make mistakes without being punished

Try new things without fear of failure

Share their thinking without embarrassment

What Psychological Safety Is Not

Lowering standards

Psychological safety does not equal low expectations.

You can have high standards and high safety.

Being nice all the time

You can give critical feedback in a psychologically safe environment.

Safety does not equal comfort. It means students can handle challenges without fear.

Avoiding hard conversations

Psychologically safe classrooms have honest conversations about mistakes, struggles, and growth.

What Psychological Safety Is

High expectations plus high support

"This is hard. You're capable of figuring it out. I'm going to help you. Mistakes are part of the process."

Honest feedback delivered with care

"This essay doesn't meet the standard yet. Here's specifically what needs to improve. Let's work on it together."

Mistakes treated as learning opportunities

"You got this wrong. Let's analyze why. What can we learn?"

Students feel safe being vulnerable

"I don't understand this part."

"Can you explain it differently?"

"I tried, but I'm stuck."

These statements are welcomed, not punished.

Why Most Classrooms Don't Have It

Classrooms are, by default, psychologically unsafe.

Why?

Threat One: Public Failure

Classrooms are public spaces.

When you answer a question in class:

25-30 peers are watching

Your answer is on display

If you're wrong, everyone knows

This is high-stakes.

Adolescent brains are especially sensitive to peer judgment.

Brain research shows:

The amygdala—threat detection—is hyperactive in adolescents

Peer judgment triggers the same brain regions as physical pain

Fear of social rejection is stronger in teens than in adults

Translation:

Being wrong in front of peers feels like a threat to survival, to a teenage brain.

When the brain perceives threat, → cortisol → learning is blocked.

Threat Two: Peer Judgment—Mockery, Eye Rolls, Whispers

Even if the teacher is supportive, peers might not be.

Scenario:

A student gives the wrong answer.

Teacher response: "Interesting. Walk me through your thinking."

Peer response: Eye roll. Whisper to a neighbor. Snicker.

What the student learns:

"Even though the teacher says mistakes are okay, my peers judge me. It's not safe."

Psychological safety requires peer norms, not just teacher support.

Threat Three: Grades as Punishment

If mistakes permanently lower your grade, the classroom isn't safe.

Why?

Because every assignment is high-stakes.

In a psychologically unsafe grading system:

Mistakes on practice assignments lower your grade

First drafts are graded—no revision allowed

Grades are averaged—early failures drag down your GPA forever

Message: "Don't make mistakes. They'll hurt you."

In a psychologically safe grading system:

Practice assignments equal feedback only—no grade

First drafts are not graded—only final drafts after revision

Grades reflect current mastery, not the average of all attempts

Message: "Mistakes during practice are expected. They don't hurt you."

We'll cover this in Chapter 10: Grading Revolution.

Threat Four: Teacher Responses—Criticism, Frustration, Impatience

How you respond to mistakes determines whether students feel safe.

Unsafe responses:

Sighing or showing frustration: Sigh. "We just went over this."

Criticism of the student, not just the work: "You're not trying hard enough."

Rushing past the mistake: "No, that's wrong. Anyone else?"

Expressing surprise, they don't know: "You don't know this? Really?"

Compared to other students: "Everyone else got this. What's wrong with you?"

Safe responses:

Curiosity: "Interesting. What made you think that?"

Analyzing the thinking: "Walk me through your reasoning."

Normalizing the mistake: "This is a common misconception. Let's explore why."

Separating person from problem: "Your thinking here is solid, but this part needs adjustment." Teacher tone matters as much as words.

Students can hear:

Frustration—unsafe

Judgment—unsafe

Curiosity—safe

Support—safe

Threat Five: Comparison Culture

When learning is competitive, the classroom isn't safe.

Comparison culture looks like:

Posting grades publicly—who got A's, who didn't

Ranking students—"Top 10 scorers."

Praising high achievers in ways that shame low achievers—"Why can't you be more like Sarah?"

Curving grades—your success depends on others' failure

What this creates:

Students aren't collaborators. They're competitors.

Message: "Your classmate's success is your failure. Don't help them."

In a psychologically safe classroom:

Grades are private

Students are compared to standards, not each other

Growth is celebrated—"You improved from 60% to 85%—that's 25% growth!"

Collaboration is encouraged—"Help each other. We all succeed together."

The result:

Most classrooms are psychologically unsafe by design.

Students learn early:

Don't volunteer—risk of public failure

Don't ask questions—peers will judge you

Don't admit confusion—grades will suffer

Pretend to understand—safer than being exposed

Why Psychological Safety Matters—The Research

Let me show you the evidence.

Research One: Amy Edmondson—Harvard Business School

Amy Edmondson has studied psychological safety for 25-plus years.

Her research, primarily in teams and organizations:

She studied hospital teams, asking:

"Which teams report more mistakes?"

Hypothesis:

High-performing teams make fewer mistakes.

Finding—surprising:

High-performing teams reported more mistakes.

Not because they made more errors.

Because they felt safe reporting them.

Low-performing teams:

Made mistakes but hid them

Feared blame

Low psychological safety

High-performing teams:

Made mistakes and reported them

Analyzed and learned from them

High psychological safety

Translation for classrooms:

Classrooms where students hide mistakes do not equal classrooms without mistakes.

They're classrooms where mistakes are hidden.

Classrooms where students share mistakes are equal classrooms where learning happens.

Research Two: Google's Project Aristotle

Google studied 180-plus teams asking: "What makes a team effective?"

They analyzed:

Team composition—who's on the team

Skills and experience

Leadership styles

Finding:

The number one predictor of team effectiveness: Psychological safety.

Not:

Who was on the team

How smart they were

How experienced they were

But:

Whether team members felt safe taking risks

Whether they felt comfortable being vulnerable

Whether mistakes were learning opportunities or punishments

Translation for classrooms:

The smartest students in a psychologically unsafe classroom will underperform.

Average students in a psychologically safe classroom will outperform their peers.

Because safety unlocks potential.

Research Three: Carol Dweck—Growth Mindset

Dweck's research shows:

Students with a growth mindset—who believe mistakes equal learning—outperform students with a fixed mindset—who believe mistakes equal evidence they're not smart.

But here's the key:

You can't develop a growth mindset in a psychologically unsafe environment.

Because:

If mistakes are punished—publicly shamed, graded harshly, mocked by peers:

→ Students learn: "Mistakes are dangerous."

→ Fixed mindset develops: "I'd better not try things I might fail at."

If mistakes are normalized, analyzed, learned from, and supported:

→ Students learn: "Mistakes are data."

→ Growth mindset develops: "I can learn from this."

Psychological safety is the prerequisite for a growth mindset.

The Four Pillars of Classroom Psychological Safety

To build a Mistake Lab, you need four pillars:

Pillar One: Teacher Modeling

You go first with mistakes.

This is Chapters 2-3.

If you hide mistakes, students will too.

If you admit mistakes and analyze them, students will too. Your vulnerability creates safety.

Pillar Two: Peer Norms

Students respond to each other's mistakes with curiosity, not mockery.

This is Chapter 9: Peer Culture.

It's not enough for you to be supportive.

Peers must be supportive too.

You have to teach students how to respond to each other.

Pillar Three: Mistake-Friendly Language

The words you use determine whether students feel safe.

This is Chapter 5: Language Shift.

Blame language creates a threat.

Learning a language creates safety.

Pillar Four: Separation of Learning From Grading

Practice is protected. Mistakes during learning don't lower grades.

This is Chapter 10: Grading Revolution.

If every mistake is graded, students won't take risks.

You need learning zones—safe to fail—and performance zones—demonstration of mastery.

These four pillars work together.

You can't have psychological safety with just one or two.

You need all four.

How to Build Psychological Safety—Week by Week

Here's the process:

Week One: Establish Lab Norms

Don't assume students know how to operate in a Mistake Lab.

You have to teach them.

Day 1 activity: Co-create lab norms

Ask students:

"For this classroom to be a place where we can make mistakes, learn from them, and grow, what do we need from each other?"

"What do you need from me, the teacher?"

"What do you need from each other?"

Students brainstorm in small groups, then share out.

Common responses:

"Don't laugh at each other's mistakes."

"Be respectful."

"Help each other."

"Don't judge."

"The teacher explains things in different ways if we don't understand."

You write these on chart paper.

Then you add:

"And here's what I commit to: I will make mistakes too. I will admit when I don't know something. I will never shame you for struggling. Mistakes are data in this classroom, not failures."

Post the norms. Reference them regularly.

"Remember our agreement? We don't laugh when someone makes a mistake. How should we respond instead?"

Week Two: Model Vulnerability Yourself

Students are testing to see if it's really safe.

They're watching you.

Show them it's safe by going first:

Admit a mistake: "I made an error on this slide. Can someone help me find it?"

Say "I don't know": "That's a great question. I don't know the answer. Let's research it together."

Acknowledge when a lesson doesn't work: "This activity isn't landing. Let me try explaining it differently."

Week 2 is when students learn:

"Oh, the teacher really means it. They actually admit mistakes. Maybe it is safe here."

Week Three-Four: Teach Students How to Respond to Each Other's Mistakes

Peer responses matter as much as teacher responses.

Explicit teaching:

You say:

"In a lab, scientists help each other. When someone's experiment doesn't work, we don't laugh. We get curious. We help analyze what happened. Let's practice."

Scenario:

"Imagine a student gives a wrong answer. How should we respond?"

Wrong responses—write these on the board:

Laughing

Eye rolling

Whispering, "I can't believe they said that."

"That's so wrong."

Right responses—practice these:

"I was thinking something similar."

"What made you think that?"

"I'm curious about your reasoning."

"Want to work through it together?"

Then practice:

The teacher intentionally gives the wrong answer.

Students practice responding with curiosity.

Reinforce this when it happens:

Scenario:

Student A gives the wrong answer. Student B starts to laugh.

You stop class immediately:

"Stop. In this classroom, we don't laugh at mistakes. Mistakes are how we learn. Student A just gave us valuable information about what we need to teach more clearly. Student B, how should you respond instead?"

Student B practices a curious response.

You move on.

This teaches:

Mockery is not tolerated. Curiosity is expected.

Ongoing: Check In Regularly

Psychological safety isn't "set it and forget it."

You have to maintain it.

Monthly check-in:

Give students the Psychological Safety Self-Assessment—see the tool below.

Ask:

Do you feel safe making mistakes in this class?

What's helping?

What's getting in the way?

Adjust based on feedback.

Practical Tool: Psychological Safety Self-Assessment—For Students

Give this to students anonymously once a month.

Rate each statement on a 1-5 scale:

1 = Strongly disagree

5 = Strongly agree

1. I feel safe asking questions in this class, even if they might sound "dumb."
2. I feel safe admitting when I'm confused or don't understand something.
3. I feel safe making mistakes in this class.
4. I feel safe trying new strategies, even if they might not work.
5. I feel safe asking for help when I need it.
6. I trust that my classmates won't laugh at me if I make a mistake.
7. I trust that the teacher won't judge me if I struggle.
8. I feel like I can be myself in this class—I don't have to pretend to understand when I don't.

Scoring—for you to interpret, not students:

32-40—High psychological safety:

Students feel very safe. Keep doing what you're doing.

24-31—Moderate psychological safety:

Students feel somewhat safe, but there are barriers.

Ask:

Which questions scored lowest?

What's getting in the way?

What needs to change?

8-23—Low psychological safety:

Students don't feel safe taking risks.

This is urgent. Address it immediately.

Ask:

What specific threats exist? Teacher responses? Peer mockery? Grading?

What needs to change first?

Use the data to adjust.

How to Respond When Students Mock Each Other

It will happen.

Especially early on, before peer norms are established.

When it happens, address it immediately.

Scenario One: Student Laughs at Another's Mistake

What happens:

Student A gives the wrong answer. Student B laughs.

Your response:

Stop class.

"Stop. We need to talk about this. In this classroom, we don't laugh when someone makes a mistake. Student A just gave us valuable information about what we need to teach more clearly. That's helpful, not funny."

"Student B, how do you think Student A feels right now?"

Student B reflects.

"How should you respond when someone makes a mistake?"

Student B practices a curious response: "I was thinking something similar. What made you think that?"

"Thank you. Let's continue."

Why this works:

Immediate—you don't let it slide

Teaches empathy—how does Student A feel?

Reinforces norms—we don't laugh.

Practice a new response—what should you do?

Moves on—doesn't over-dwell, which would embarrass Student A more

Scenario Two: Student Whispers to Neighbor After Someone's Mistake

What happens:

Student A gives the wrong answer. Student B whispers to Student C. They both smirk.

Your response:

Stop class.

"I saw whispering after Student A's answer. That's not how we respond in this lab. If you have something to say about the answer, say it to the whole class so we can learn together. Whispering makes it feel unsafe."

"Student B, what were you thinking?"

Student B might deflect or apologize.

"In this classroom, if you notice a mistake, we analyze it together. Out loud. Not in whispers. Let's practice. What did you notice about Student A's answer?"

Student B shares. You facilitate analysis.

Why this works:

It redirects whispers into public, collaborative analysis. It reinforces: We learn together, not in secret judgment.

Scenario Three: Student Says "That's So Wrong" in a Judgmental Tone

What happens:

Student A gives the wrong answer. Student B blurts out: "That's so wrong!"

Your response:

"Student B, you're right that the answer is incorrect. But the way you said that sounded judgmental. In a lab, we respond with curiosity, not judgment. How could you rephrase that?"

Student B practices: "I got a different answer. Want to compare our thinking?"

"Much better. Thank you."

Why this works:

Acknowledges Student B is correct—the answer is wrong.

But redirects the tone—curious rather than judgmental.

What to Do When You Accidentally Shame a Student

You're human. You'll mess up.

You might:

Respond with frustration when you're stressed

Rush past a student's confusion

Call on a student who isn't ready

Use a tone that sounds judgmental, even if you didn't mean it

When this happens:

Repair it immediately.

Example:

You sighed when a student gave the wrong answer. The student looks embarrassed.

Your repair:

"I'm sorry. I sighed just now, and that probably felt bad. I was frustrated with myself for not explaining that clearly; I wasn't frustrated with you. Your answer tells me I need to teach this differently. Thank you for helping me see that."

Why this works:

Acknowledges the harm—you don't pretend it didn't happen

Takes responsibility—not the student's fault

Reframes the mistake as data—your answer equals useful feedback

Models repair—shows students how to apologize and make things right

Real Scenarios: Building Psychological Safety

Let me show you what this looks like in practice.

Scenario One: Student Gives Wrong Answer in Class Discussion

What happens:

You're teaching photosynthesis. You ask: "What do plants take in during photosynthesis?" A student answers: "Oxygen."

Wrong.

Low psychological safety response:

"No, that's wrong. Plants take in carbon dioxide, not oxygen. Who knows the right answer?"

What student learns:

"I was wrong in front of everyone. I feel stupid. I'm not volunteering again."

High psychological safety response:

"Interesting! You said oxygen. What made you think that?"

Student explains: "Because we breathe oxygen, I thought plants do too."

"Ah, great connection. You're thinking about the relationship between plants and animals. Here's the twist: plants take in carbon dioxide and release oxygen. That oxygen is what we breathe. So you're right that oxygen is involved—but it's the output, not the input. Make sense?"

What student learns:

"My thinking was partially correct. The teacher explored my reasoning. I learned something. It's safe to think out loud here."

Scenario Two: Student Says "I Don't Understand"

What happens:

You just explained slope. A student raises their hand: "I don't understand."

Low psychological safety response:

"What don't you understand? I just explained it. Were you listening?"

What student learns:

"Asking for help gets me accused of not paying attention. I won't ask again."

High psychological safety response:

"Thank you for being honest. What part is confusing? The formula? The graph? How does it connect to Rise Over Run?"

Student: "The formula."

"Got it. Let me explain it a different way." Re-explains. "Does that help?"

What student learns:

"Admitting confusion is welcomed. The teacher will help me."

Scenario Three: Student Fails a Quiz

What happens:

You hand back quizzes. A student got 40%.

Low psychological safety response:

You write on the quiz: "See me after class."

After class: "You need to study more. This is unacceptable."

What student learns:

"I failed. I'm in trouble. I feel ashamed."

High psychological safety response:

You write on the quiz: "This shows me what you're still learning. Let's figure out what happened. See me after class."

After class: "This quiz tells me you're struggling with X and Y. What do you think happened?" Student shares. "Okay, here's what we're going to do. I'm going to re-teach X and Y differently. Then you can retake this quiz. Sound good?"

What student learns: "This quiz is feedback, not judgment. The teacher is going to help me. I can improve."

The Bottom Line

Psychological safety is the foundation of your Mistake Lab.

Without it:

Students won't share mistakes

They won't ask questions

They won't take risks

Learning slows down

With it:

Students share confusion openly

They ask for help

They experiment and iterate

Learning accelerates

Building psychological safety requires:
Teacher modeling—you go first with vulnerability
Peer norms—students respond to each other with curiosity, not judgment
Mistake-friendly language—your words create safety or threat
Separation of learning from grading—practice is safe; mistakes don't lower grades
You can't skip this.
If students don't feel safe, they won't engage with the rest of your Mistake Lab.
Build safety first. Everything else follows.

REFLECTION QUESTIONS

Personal Reflection:

1. Do students feel safe making mistakes in your classroom? How do you know?
2. What threatens psychological safety in your context? Public failure? Peer judgment? Grading? Your responses?
3. On a scale of 1-5, rate the psychological safety in your classroom. What evidence supports that rating?
4. What's one thing you could change this week to increase safety?

Scenario Practice:

Imagine this scenario:

A student gives the wrong answer in front of the class.

How do you respond?

Write two versions:

Version A—Low safety:

Version B—High safety:

What's the difference? How would the student feel in each scenario?

Action Planning:

This week, try one practice to build psychological safety:

Co-create classroom norms with students—What do we need from each other to feel safe making mistakes?

Model vulnerability—Admit one mistake, say "I don't know" once

Teach peer responses—Practice how to respond to each other's mistakes

Give students the Psychological Safety Self-Assessment—Collect data

Address one instance of peer mockery immediately—Reinforce norms

Repair one moment when you accidentally shamed a student—Model how to apologize

Further Exploration

Read:

- *The Fearless Organization* by Amy Edmondson—on psychological safety in teams
- *Culturally Responsive Teaching and the Brain* by Zaretta Hammond—on safety for marginalized students
- *The Culture Code* by Daniel Coyle—on building safe, high-performing cultures

Watch:

- Amy Edmondson's TEDx Talk: "Building a Psychologically Safe Workplace"
- Google's Project Aristotle research summary

Listen:

- "WorkLife with Adam Grant" episode on psychological safety

Psychological safety is the lab's protective equipment.

Without it, experiments are too dangerous to run.

With it, students can take risks, make mistakes, and learn.

Next: The Language Shift

The words you use either build safety or destroy it.

Let's make sure you're using the right ones.

Ready to continue?

CHAPTER 5

THE LANGUAGE SHIFT—FOR CLASSROOMS

The Words You Use Determine Whether Students See Mistakes as Data or Identity

Same mistake. Two teachers. Different words.

Scenario: A Student Struggles With Fractions

Student turns in homework. Gets 4 out of 10 problems correct.

Teacher A:

Writes on the paper: "You failed this. You need to study harder."

Hand it back in class.

The student sees the grade. Puts the paper in their backpack. Don't look at it again.

Teacher A's words:

"Failed"—identity judgment

"Need to study harder"—assumes lack of effort

What the student hears:

"I failed. I'm a failure at math. Trying harder won't help because I'm just not good at this."

Teacher B:

Writes on the paper: "You're still working on understanding equivalent fractions. Let's look at problem 3 together."

Hand it back. Pulls the student aside:

"I can see you understand how to find common denominators—problems 1, 2, 5, 8. You're still figuring out how to simplify: problems 3, 4, 6, 7, 9, and 10. Let's practice that. Can you stay for 5 minutes after class?"

Teacher B's words:

"Still working on"—growth mindset

"Let's look at this together"—support offered

"You understand X, still figuring out Y"—specific, diagnostic

What the student hears:

"I haven't mastered this yet. My teacher can help me. I'm making progress on some parts. I know what to work on next."

Same mistake. Different language. Different outcome.

The Power of Language

Words are not neutral.

The language you use shapes how students think about:

Mistakes—shameful versus informative

Intelligence—fixed versus growable

Themselves—smart or dumb versus a learner

Struggle—evidence of inability versus evidence of challenge

Blame language triggers:

Shame

Fixed mindset

Identity thinking—"I'm bad at this"

Avoidance—"I give up."

Learning language triggers:

Curiosity

Growth mindset

Data thinking—"What can I learn from this?"

Persistence—"I'll try a different approach."

Your words literally shape students' neural pathways.

Every time you say:

"You failed." → Reinforces: Mistakes equal identity

"You're not there yet." → Reinforces: Mistakes equal a temporary state

This chapter is about making the shift:

From blame language → To learning language

The Eight Language Shifts

Here are the most critical shifts you need to make:

Shift One: From "Failed" to "Not Yet" or "Still Learning"

Blame language:

"You failed the test."

"You failed this assignment."

"This is a failing grade."

Why this is harmful:

The word "failed" is a judgment of identity, not performance.

When you say "You failed," students hear: "You are a failure."

Learning language:

"You haven't mastered this yet."

"You're still learning this concept."

"You're not there yet, but you're making progress."

Why this works:

"Yet" implies: This is temporary. You're on a journey. Mastery is coming.

"Still learning" normalizes: Learning takes time. This is expected.

Examples in practice:

Instead of: "You failed the quiz."

Try: "You didn't pass the quiz yet. Let's figure out what you need to learn and try again."

Instead of: "You're failing math."

Try: "You haven't mastered fractions yet. We're going to work on that together."

Instead of: "This is a failing grade."

Try: "This grade shows me what you're still learning. Here's what we need to focus on."

Shift Two: From "Why Didn't You...?" to "What Happened?"

Blame language:

"Why didn't you study?"

"Why didn't you turn in your homework?"

"Why didn't you ask for help?"

Why this is harmful:

"Why" questions sound accusatory.

They imply: "You should have known better. You made a bad choice. You're at fault."

They trigger defensiveness, not reflection.

Learning language:

"What happened?"

"What got in the way?"

"What made this hard?"

Why this works:

"What" questions invite explanation, not defense.

They sound curious, not judgmental.

They open conversation, not shut it down.

Examples in practice:

Instead of: "Why didn't you study for the test?"

Try: "What got in the way of studying?"

A student might say, "I had soccer practice, and then I forgot."

Then you can problem-solve: "How can we help you remember next time? Calendar reminder? Study buddy?"

Instead of: "Why didn't you turn in your homework?"

Try: "What happened with the homework?"

A student might say: "I didn't understand it."

Then you help: "Next time you're confused, come see me before it's due. Let's work through it now."

Instead of: "Why didn't you ask for help?"

Try: "What made it hard to ask for help?"

A student might say: "I didn't want to look stupid."

Then you address the real issue: "Asking for help isn't stupid—it's what scientists do. Let me show you it's safe here."

Shift Three: From "You Need To..." to "What If We Tried...?"

Blame language:

"You need to try harder."

"You need to pay attention."

"You need to fix this."

Why this is harmful:

"You need to" sounds like a command.

It positions the student as deficient.

It doesn't offer support—just demands.

Learning language:

"What if we tried...?"

"Let's experiment with..."

"I wonder if... would help."

Why this works:

"What if we tried" is collaborative, not commanding.

It positions you and the student as lab partners.

It invites experimentation, not compliance.

Examples in practice:

Instead of: "You need to try harder."

Try: "What if we tried a different study strategy? Let's experiment with flashcards and see if that helps."

Instead of: "You need to pay attention."

Try: "I notice you're distracted. What if we tried sitting closer to the front? Or taking brain breaks every 15 minutes?"

Instead of: "You need to fix this essay."

Try: "Let's look at this paragraph together. What if we tried reorganizing it? Here's what I'm thinking..."

Shift Four: From "What's Wrong With You?" to "What Do You Need?"

Blame language:

"What's wrong with you?"

"Why can't you get this?"

"Everyone else understands. What's your problem?"

Why this is harmful:

This language says: "You're broken. You're the problem."

It triggers shame, not problem-solving.

Learning language:

"What do you need?" "What would help?" "What's hard about this?"

Why this works:

"What do you need?" positions the student as capable of identifying their needs.

It focuses on solutions, not deficits. It's empowering, not shaming.

Examples in practice:

Instead of: "What's wrong with you? Why can't you sit still?"

Try: "I notice you're having trouble sitting still. What do you need? A brain break? A fidget tool? To stand while you work?"

Instead of: "Everyone else gets this. What's your problem?"

Try: "You're working on something challenging. What would help you understand it better? A different explanation? An example? Time to practice?"

Instead of: "Why can't you follow directions?"

Try: "The directions aren't landing for you. What do you need? Written steps? A checklist? Should I model it first?"

Shift Five: From "This Is Unacceptable" to "This Didn't Work—Let's Try Again"

Blame language:

"This is unacceptable."

"This work is terrible."

"This is not good enough."

Why this is harmful:

"Unacceptable" is a judgment of worth.

It says: "You failed. This is bad." It doesn't give direction for improvement.

Learning language:

"This doesn't meet the standard yet."

"This didn't work. Let's figure out why and try again."

"Here's what needs to improve."

Why this works:

"Doesn't meet the standard yet" is diagnostic, not judgmental.

"Didn't work" frames it as an experiment rather than a failure. "Here's what needs to improve" gives clear direction.

Examples in practice:

Instead of: "This essay is unacceptable."

Try: "This essay doesn't meet the standard yet. Here's what needs to improve: Your thesis isn't clear—see highlighted section—and your evidence needs to be stronger—see my notes. Let's revise this together."

Instead of: "This is terrible work."

Try: "This experiment didn't work. Let's analyze what happened. What do you think went wrong? What can we try differently?"

Instead of: "This is not good enough."

Try: "This is a solid start, but it's not there yet. Here's what's working"—point out strengths. "Here's what needs work"—specific feedback. "Let's revise."

Shift Six: From "You're Struggling" to "You're Working on Something Hard"

Blame language:

"You're struggling."

"You're behind."

"You're weak in this area."

Why this is harmful:

"Struggling" implies: You're failing. You can't keep up.

It sounds like a deficit, not a challenge.

Learning language:

"You're working on something hard."

"This is challenging for you right now."

"You're developing this skill."

Why this works:

"Working on something hard" reframes struggle as effort applied to a challenge.

It normalizes difficulty.

It sounds temporary and conquerable.

Examples in practice:

Instead of: "You're struggling with fractions."

Try: "Fractions are hard. You're working through them. Let's practice together."

Instead of: "You're behind in reading."

Try: "You're developing your reading skills. Here's what we're working on next."

Instead of: "You're weak in math."

Try: "Math is challenging for you right now. That means your brain is growing. Let's build your skills."

Shift Seven: From "You're Smart" to "You Worked Hard" or "You Used a Great Strategy"

Blame language—yes, even praise can be harmful:

"You're so smart!"

"You're a natural at this."

"This is easy for you."

Why this is harmful:

Praising intelligence rather than effort creates a fixed mindset.

Research from Carol Dweck: When you praise intelligence—"You're smart"—students:

Avoid challenge—don't want to prove they're not smart

Give up when things get hard—if it's hard, I must not be smart after all

Attribute success to innate ability, not effort

Learning language:

"You worked hard on this."

"I love the strategy you used."

"You stuck with it even when it was hard."

Why this works:

Praising effort and strategy creates a growth mindset. Students learn: Success comes from work, not innate ability. They're more likely to persist when challenged.

Examples in practice:

Instead of: "You're so smart! You got an A!"

Try: "You worked really hard on this. Your effort paid off."

Instead of: "You're a natural at math."

Try: "I noticed you used a really efficient strategy to solve that problem. Can you show the class?"

Instead of: "This is easy for you."

Try: "You've practiced this a lot, so it's getting easier. That's how learning works—hard at first, easier with practice."

Shift Eight: From "Don't Make Mistakes" to "Mistakes Help Us Learn"

Blame language:

"Be careful. Don't make mistakes."

"Make sure you get this right."

"Check your work so you don't mess up."

Why this is harmful:

This language creates fear of mistakes.

Students internalize: Mistakes are bad. Avoid them.

Learning language:

"Mistakes help us learn."

"If you make a mistake, we'll figure out what happened."

"Try it. If it doesn't work, we'll adjust."

Why this works:

Normalizes mistakes as part of the process.

Reduces anxiety.

Encourages experimentation.

Examples in practice:

Instead of: "Be careful. Don't make any mistakes on this test."

Try: "Do your best. If you make mistakes, we'll learn from them, and you can retake it."

Instead of: "Make sure you get this right."

Try: "Try this strategy. If it doesn't work, we'll try a different one."

Instead of: "Check your work so you don't mess up."

Try: "Check your work to see if your answer makes sense. If you find a mistake, analyze it—that's valuable data."

The Language Shift Cheat Sheet

Print this. Post it. Reference it daily.

Instead of—Blame	Try—Learning
"You failed."	"You're not there yet."
"Why didn't you...?"	"What happened?"
"You need to try harder."	"What if we tried...?"
"What's wrong with you?"	"What do you need?"
"This is unacceptable."	"This didn't work. Let's try again."
"You're struggling."	"You're working on something hard."
"You're so smart!"	"You worked hard!" or "Great strategy!"
"Don't make mistakes."	"Mistakes help us learn."

Instead of—Blame	Try—Learning
"You should have known this."	"Let's review this concept."
"Everyone else understands."	"This is challenging. What would help?"
"You weren't paying attention."	"You missed this part. Let me re-explain."
"This is wrong."	"Let's look at what happened here."
"You can't do this."	"You can't do this yet."
"You're lazy."	"What got in the way of completing this?"
"This is easy. Why don't you get it?"	"This is hard for you right now. That's okay."

The Five Language Traps—And How to Avoid Them

Even well-meaning teachers fall into these traps:

Trap One: "I'm Disappointed in You"

Why this is a trap:

"I'm disappointed in you" makes it about identity rather than behavior.

The student hears: "I'm not good enough. I let my teacher down. I'm a disappointment."

What to say instead:

"I'm disappointed that this assignment didn't get turned in. What happened? How can I help?"

Focus on the action—assignment—not the person—you.

Trap Two: "You Just Need To..."

Why this is a trap:

"Just" minimizes the challenge.

"You just need to study more."

"You just need to pay attention."

"You just need to try harder."

Implies: This should be easy. If you're struggling, it's because you're not trying.

What to say instead:

Remove "just."

"Let's figure out what study strategies would help."

"What's making it hard to focus? What do you need?"

"What obstacles are you facing? Let's problem-solve."

Trap Three: Comparing to Other Students

Why this is a trap:

"Everyone else finished. Why didn't you?" "Sarah got it right. You should too."

This creates:

Shame—I'm not as good as others

Comparison culture—learning is competitive. Fixed mindset—some people are good at this, I'm not.

What to say instead:

Compare students to themselves, not others.

"You're working at your own pace. What do you need to finish?"

"Let's focus on your growth. Last week, you got 60%; this week, 75%. That's 15% growth!"

Trap Four: Vague Praise

Why this is a trap:

"Good job!"

"Nice work!"

"Great!"

Students don't know what they did well.

They can't replicate it.

What to say instead:

Be specific.

"I love how you used evidence from the text to support your claim."

"You tried three different strategies before finding one that worked. That's persistence."

"Your introduction really grabbed my attention. The question you asked made me want to keep reading."

Now they know what to do again.

Trap Five: Asking "Do You Understand?" After Explaining

Why this is a trap:

After you explain something, you ask: "Do you understand?"

Students will say: "Yes."

Even if they don't.

Why?

They don't want to look stupid

They don't want to hold up the class

They think they understand, but they don't

What to do instead:

Don't ask if they understand. Check.

"Show me how you'd solve the first problem."

"Turn to your partner and explain this in your own words."

"Write down one thing that's still confusing."

This gives you actual data, not false confirmation.

How to Practice the Language Shift

Language habits are hard to change.

You've been using blame language for years, probably because that's how you were taught.

Here's how to shift:

Step One: Record Yourself

Use your phone to record a lesson. Audio is fine.

Listen back. Notice:

How many times did you use blame language?

How many times have you learned a language?

What patterns do you notice?

No judgment. Just data.

Step Two: Choose One Shift to Focus On

Don't try to change everything at once.

Pick one shift from the list above.

Example:

"This week, I'm going to replace 'You failed' with 'You're not there yet.'"

Practice that one shift until it feels natural. Then add another.

Step Three: Post the Cheat Sheet

Print the Language Shift Cheat Sheet.

Post it somewhere you'll see it while teaching—on a desk, on a wall, near the board.

Glance at it when giving feedback.

Step Four: Notice and Repair

You'll slip up. You'll use blame language.

That's okay.

Notice it. Repair it in the moment.

Example:

You say: "Why didn't you study?"

You catch yourself.

You repair: "Actually, let me rephrase that. What got in the way of studying?"

Students will notice.

They'll learn: "Even the teacher catches and corrects their mistakes. Mistakes are okay."

Step Five: Teach Students the Language Shift

Don't just learn a language. Teach it. Show students the cheat sheet.

"Notice how I'm talking about mistakes? I'm saying 'not yet' instead of 'failed.' I'm asking 'what happened?' instead of 'why didn't you?' This language helps us think like scientists. Mistakes are data, not disasters."

Then teach students to use it with each other:

"When your partner makes a mistake, don't say 'That's wrong.' Say 'What were you thinking? Let's figure this out together."

Language Shift in Written Feedback

The language shift applies to written feedback, too.

On Assignments:

Instead of:

"Incorrect"—judgment

"No"—judgment

"This is wrong"—judgment

Try:

"Not quite. Let's look at this together."

"I see what you're thinking. Here's what to adjust..."

"This is close. What if you tried...?"

On Essays:

Instead of:

"Unclear"—vague, unhelpful

"Needs work"—vague

"Awkward"—vague

Try:

"I'm not sure what you mean here. Can you say this more directly?"

"This sentence is doing too much. What if you split it into two sentences?"

"This paragraph would be stronger if you added an example here. Like what?"

Specific. Actionable. Supportive.

On Tests and Quizzes:

Instead of:

Red X's everywhere—visual punishment

"-5 points"—focus on what's lost

Just a grade, no feedback

Try:

Checkmarks for correct answers—celebrate what's working.

"This shows me you understand X. You're still working on Y. Let's practice Y together."

Specific feedback plus opportunity to revise or retake

Real Scenarios: Language Shift in Action

Let me show you what this sounds like in real teaching moments:

Scenario One: Handing Back a Test

The student got 65%.

Old language—Blame:

"You failed this test. You need to study more."

Hands back test. Moves on.

New language—Learning:

"You didn't pass this test yet. But look—you mastered 65% of the content. That's solid. You're still working on these concepts."—circles specific sections. "Let's figure out what happened. Can we meet after school to review?"

Positions it as: Data to learn from, not evidence of failure.

Scenario Two: Student Didn't Turn In Homework

Old language—Blame:

"Why didn't you do your homework? This is the third time this week. You're going to fail this class if you keep this up."

New language—Learning:

"I noticed you didn't turn in homework again. What's going on? Is something getting in the way?"

A student might say: "I don't understand how to do it."

Then you help: "Okay, so the homework is too hard to do alone. Next time you're confused, see me before it's due, or email me. Let's work through it now so you understand it." Diagnostic. Problem-solving. Supportive.

Scenario Three: Student Shuts Down During Class

You're teaching. A student puts their head down.

Old language—Blame:

"Sit up. Pay attention. You need to participate."

New language—Learning:

After class, you pull them aside:

"I noticed you put your head down during class. What's going on? Are you feeling okay? Is the material too hard? Too easy? Are you tired?"

A student might say: "I'm just really confused and I don't want to look stupid."

Then you address it: "Being confused doesn't make you look stupid. It means you're working on something hard. Let me help. Here's what we're going to do..."

Curious. Caring. Solutions-focused.

Scenario Four: Student Says "I Can't Do This"

Old language—Blame or empty reassurance:

"Yes, you can. Just try harder."

"Of course you can. Don't say that."

New language—Learning:

"You can't do this yet. What specifically is hard? The first step? The middle part? The last part?"

Student identifies: "I don't know how to start."

Then you scaffold: "Okay, starting is hard. Let's do the first one together. Then you try the second one. I'll be right here if you get stuck." Reframes "I can't" as "I can't yet" plus provides support.

Scenario Five: Student Gives Up on a Challenging Problem

The student tries a problem, gets stuck, erases it, and pushes the paper away.

Old language—Blame:

"Don't give up. You need to keep trying."

New language—Learning:

"I see you tried this and got stuck. That's normal—this problem is hard. Let's look at what you did." Reviews their work. "You got this far correctly. Then you got stuck here. What were you thinking at this step?"

Student explains.

"Ah, I see. Here's what to try next." Guides them through the next step. "Now you try the next one." Normalizes struggle. Analyzes where they got stuck. Provides the next step.

The Bottom Line

Your words are powerful.

They shape how students think about:

Mistakes—shameful versus informative

Intelligence—fixed versus growable

Themselves—capable versus incapable

Learning—performance versus process

When you shift your language from blame to learning:

Students develop a growth mindset

Mistakes feel less threatening

Students ask for help more often

Persistence increases

Learning accelerates

The shift is a simple concept:

Replace judgment with curiosity.

Replace "you failed" with "not yet."

Replace "why didn't you?" with "what happened?"

But it takes practice. Your old language habits are deeply ingrained. Start with one shift. Practice it. Add another. Over time, learning a language will become automatic.

Your Mistake Lab depends on this. Because if your words say "mistakes are failures," students won't believe your actions that say "mistakes are data."

Language first. Everything else follows.

REFLECTION QUESTIONS

Personal Reflection:

1. Listen to yourself teach for 15 minutes—record yourself. How much blame language versus learning language did you use?
2. Which of the 8 language shifts is hardest for you? Why?
3. What blame language did you hear when you were a student? How did it affect you?
4. What's one phrase you want to eliminate from your teaching vocabulary this week?

Practice:

Rewrite these blame statements as learning statements:

1. "You failed the test."

Your rewrite:

2. "Why didn't you study?"

Your rewrite:

3. "This work is unacceptable."

Your rewrite:

4. "You're so smart!"

Your rewrite:

5. "You're struggling with this."

Your rewrite:

Action Planning:

This week, try one language shift:

Replace "failed" with "not yet"—every time

Replace "why didn't you?" with "what happened?"—every time

Replace "you need to" with "what if we tried?"—every time

Give specific praise—not "good job," but "I noticed you..."

Record yourself teaching and analyze your language. Post the Language Shift Cheat Sheet where you'll see it. Teach the language shift to students—show them the chart.

Further Exploration

Read:

- *Mindset* by Carol Dweck—on the power of "yet."
- *The Growth Mindset Coach* by Annie Brock & Heather Hundley—practical language strategies
- *Feedback That Moves Writers Forward* by Patty McGee—on learning-focused writing feedback

Watch:

- Carol Dweck's TED Talk: "The Power of Yet"
- Rita Pierson's TED Talk: "Every Kid Needs a Champion"—on language that builds students up

You've now learned:

Chapter 1: The science—why mistakes equal learning

Chapter 2: The teacher myth—hiding mistakes hurts students

Chapter 3: Your perfectionism—your relationship with failure

Chapter 4: Psychological safety—creating safe conditions

Chapter 5: Language shift—words that build versus words that harm

Next: Teaching students the core concept

Mistakes as Data, Not Identity

How to explicitly teach this to students so they internalize it?

Ready to continue?

CHAPTER 6

MISTAKES AS DATA, NOT IDENTITY

Teaching the Concept Explicitly to Students

First day of school. Mr. Chen's 7th-grade science class.

He doesn't start with classroom rules or a syllabus.

He starts with a lesson on learning.

Mr. Chen: "Before we learn science, we need to learn how to learn. I'm going to teach you the most important concept you'll learn all year. It's not about molecules or ecosystems. It's about mistakes."

He writes on the board:

MISTAKES = DATA

NOT

MISTAKES = IDENTITY

Mr. Chen: "Here's what I mean. When you make a mistake, your brain has two options for how to think about it."

He draws two columns:

IDENTITY THINKING	**DATA THINKING**
"I'm stupid."	"What can I learn?"
"I can't do this."	"I can't do this YET."
"I failed."	"This attempt didn't work. What's next?
WHO I AM	WHAT HAPPENED

Mr. Chen: "When you think with your identity brain, mistakes feel terrible. They feel like proof that you're not smart enough."

"But when you think with your data brain, mistakes feel useful. Their information. They tell you what to adjust." He pauses.

"Scientists make mistakes all the time. Thomas Edison tried 1,000 different materials before finding one that worked for the lightbulb filament. He didn't fail 1,000 times. He gathered 1,000 data points."

"That's what we're going to do in this class. We're going to make mistakes. We're going to treat them as data. We're going to learn from them."

"This is a lab. Experiments fail sometimes. That's expected. That's how science works."

A student raises their hand: "But what if we get a bad grade?"

Mr. Chen: "Great question. Here's how grading works in this class. When you're practicing—trying new things, experimenting—that's not graded. That's learning. I give you feedback. You revise. Then, when you demonstrate mastery, that's graded. And even then, if you don't pass, you can retake it after we reteach. Your grade reflects what you know now, not how many tries it took you to get there."

Another student: "So mistakes don't hurt our grade?"

Mr. Chen: "Not during practice. Mistakes during practice help you. They're data. They tell us both what you need to learn next."

By the end of Day 1, students understand:

Mistakes are data, not identity

This classroom is a lab—experiments sometimes fail

Practice is safe—not graded

Mastery is the goal—not perfection on the first try

This is explicit teaching of the core concept.

Mr. Chen didn't just say "mistakes are okay."

He taught students how to think about mistakes differently.

Why You Need to Teach This Explicitly

Most teachers assume students will just "get it" if we:

Hang growth mindset posters

Say encouraging things

Model vulnerability

But students have been trained for years to think:

"Mistakes equal I'm stupid."

"Getting it wrong equals I'm bad at this."

"Struggling equals I'm not smart enough." You can't undo years of conditioning with a poster.

You need to teach explicitly:

The neuroscience—your brain grows when you make mistakes

The distinction—identity thinking versus data thinking

How to shift—when you notice identity thinking, reframe it as data

What this looks like in practice—examples, practice, reinforcement

This chapter will show you how.

Part A: The Neuroscience Lesson—Age-Appropriate

Students need to understand that their brains are designed to learn from mistakes. Here's how to teach this at different grade levels:

For K-2: "Your Brain Is Like a Muscle"

The lesson:

Teacher: "Did you know your brain is like a muscle? When you use your muscles, they get stronger. When you use your brain, it gets stronger too."

"But here's the cool part: Your brain gets strongest when you make mistakes and fix them."

"When you get something wrong and then figure out how to get it right, your brain makes new connections. It's like building new pathways in your brain."

Show a visual:

Picture of a brain with pathways lighting up

Or: Two pictures of muscles—weak versus strong—next to two pictures of brains—learning versus not learning

Activity:

"Let me show you. Everyone, tie your shoe."

Students tie their shoes.

"That was easy, right? Because you've practiced it a lot. Your brain has a strong pathway for tying shoes."

"Now try tying your shoe with one hand."

Students struggle.

"This is hard! You're making mistakes. But guess what? Your brain is growing right now. Every mistake you make is building a new pathway."

The takeaway:

"Mistakes help your brain grow. When something is hard, and you make mistakes, your brain is getting stronger."

For 3-5: "Neurons That Fire Together Wire Together"

The lesson:

Teacher: "Your brain has billions of tiny cells called neurons. When you learn something new, neurons connect. The more you practice, the stronger the connections get."

"But here's the interesting part: Your brain learns the most when you make a mistake and correct it."

"Scientists have studied this. When you get something wrong, your brain releases a chemical called dopamine. Dopamine is like a signal that says: 'Pay attention! This is important! Remember this!"

Show a visual:

Diagram of neurons connecting

Or: Animation of brain pathways strengthening

Activity:

"Let's try an experiment. I'm going to teach you a word in another language. The word for 'hello' in Swahili is 'jambo.'" "Now, I'm going to quiz you. What's the word for 'hello' in Swahili?" Students answer correctly. "Great. But here's the thing: Because you got it right on the first try, your brain didn't have to work very hard. The connection is weak."

"Now let's try a different word. The word for 'thank you' in Swahili is..."—intentionally teaches it wrong—"'asante sana.'"

"Quiz: What's 'thank you' in Swahili?" Students answer. The teacher corrects if wrong. "Actually, I made an error. 'Asante' means thank you. 'Asante sana' means 'thank you very much.' Which one do you think you'll remember better tomorrow? The word you got right the first time, or the word you got wrong and corrected?"

Discuss. Students often remember the corrected mistake better.

The takeaway:

"Your brain learns more from mistakes than from getting things right the first time. Mistakes make your brain work harder, which makes the learning stick."

For 6-8: "The Science of Learning From Mistakes"

The lesson:

Teacher: "I want to teach you some neuroscience. When you make a mistake, here's what happens in your brain."

Step 1: Your brain makes a prediction

"Your brain is constantly predicting what's going to happen. When you solve a math problem, your brain predicts: 'If I do this operation, I'll get this answer.'"

Step 2: You get feedback

"You check your answer. It's wrong. Your brain's prediction was incorrect."

Step 3: Your brain processes the error

"This is the critical moment. When your brain realizes the prediction was wrong, it releases dopamine, a neurotransmitter. Dopamine tells your brain: 'Pay attention! This is important information!

Step 4: Your brain encodes the correct information

"Your brain updates its model. It makes a new, stronger neural pathway. The mistake actually made the learning stronger."

But—here's the catch:

"This only works if your brain feels safe. If you feel ashamed or threatened when you make a mistake, your brain releases cortisol instead—a stress hormone. Cortisol blocks learning. Your brain goes into survival mode instead of learning mode."

Show a visual:

Brain diagram with dopamine pathway—safe environment

Brain diagram with cortisol pathway—threatening environment

The takeaway:

"Your brain is designed to learn from mistakes. But only if you feel safe. That's why this classroom is a lab. Mistakes are expected. They're not shameful—they're how your brain grows."

For 9-12: "Prediction Error and Neuroplasticity"

The lesson:

Teacher: "Let's talk about how the brain learns. There's a concept in neuroscience called 'prediction error.' Your brain is essentially a prediction machine. It's constantly making predictions about the world."

"When your predictions are correct, your brain says: 'Good, my model of the world is accurate.' No learning happens—you already knew that."

"But when your predictions are wrong—when you make a mistake—that's when learning happens. That's called prediction error."

The neuroscience:

"When you make a mistake, your brain releases dopamine from the ventral tegmental area. Dopamine signals: 'This is a learning opportunity.' Your brain updates its model. New synaptic connections form. The neural pathway associated with the correct information gets stronger."

"This is called neuroplasticity—your brain's ability to reorganize itself based on experience."

The research:

"Scientists at MIT studied this. They found that students who made mistakes and corrected them showed more brain activity in the prefrontal cortex—the area responsible for learning—than students who got things right the first time."

"Translation: Making mistakes and correcting them is more effective for learning than getting things right on the first try."

The caveat:

"But there's a condition: You have to feel safe. If you feel threatened—if mistakes trigger shame or fear—your amygdala activates, cortisol is released, and the prefrontal cortex shuts down. You can't learn when you're in threat mode."

"That's why this classroom operates like a lab. We need psychological safety for your brain to learn from mistakes."

The takeaway:

"Mistakes aren't just 'okay.' They're necessary. Your brain is wired to learn from prediction error. Embrace it."

Part B: Teaching the Identity Versus Data Distinction

After students understand the neuroscience, teach them the distinction:

The Two Ways to Think About Mistakes

Create a visual—poster, slide, handout:

IDENTITY THINKING	DATA THINKING
About WHO I AM	About WHAT HAPPENED
"I'm bad at math."	"I haven't mastered fractions yet."
"I'm stupid."	"I made an error. What can I learn?"
"I failed."	"This attempt didn't work. What's next?"
"I can't do this."	"I can't do this YET."
FIXED MINDSET	GROWTH MINDSET
Mistakes = proof I'm not capable	Mistakes = information to improve

Walk through each row:

Row 1: "I'm bad at math" versus "I haven't mastered fractions yet"

Teacher: "Notice the difference. 'I'm bad at math' is about who you are. It's permanent. It's your identity."

"'I haven't mastered fractions yet' is about what you're learning. It's temporary. It's a skill you're developing."

"One makes you feel stuck. The other makes you feel like you can grow."

Row 2: "I'm stupid" versus "I made an error. What can I learn?"

Teacher: "When you think 'I'm stupid,' you're making a judgment about yourself. That's identity thinking."

"When you think, 'I made an error, what can I learn?' you're analyzing the situation. That's data thinking." "Scientists don't say 'I'm stupid' when an experiment fails. They say, 'Interesting. What happened? What do I need to adjust?"

Row 3: "I failed" versus "This attempt didn't work. What's next?"

Teacher: "The word 'failed' is loaded. It sounds final. It sounds like you are a failure."

"'This attempt didn't work' is about the action, not about you. And it's not final—it's one attempt. You can try again."

Row 4: "I can't do this" versus "I can't do this yet"

Teacher: "This is the power of one word: Yet."

"'I can't do this' is fixed. It says: This is beyond my ability."

"'I can't do this yet' is growth-oriented. It says, "I'm still learning." I'll get there."

Ask students:

"Which column sounds like how you usually think?"

Many will admit: Identity thinking. "That's normal. You've been trained to think that way. But we're going to practice shifting to data thinking."

Part C: Teaching Students to Catch and Reframe Identity Thoughts

The skill: When you notice identity thinking, reframe it as data thinking.

Step One: Teach Students to Notice Identity Thoughts

Teacher: "The first step is awareness. You need to catch yourself when you're thinking with your identity brain."

Common identity thoughts:

"I'm stupid."

"I'm bad at this."

"I failed."

"I can't do this."

"I'm not smart enough."

Activity:

"For the next week, every time you catch yourself thinking one of these thoughts, write it down. Just notice it. No judgment."

Give students a tracking sheet:

Date	Identity Thought I Noticed
Sept 10	"I'm bad at math."
Sept 11	"I can't do this."

Step Two: Teach Students to Reframe

Teacher: "Once you notice an identity thought, you can reframe it."

The reframing process:

1. Catch the thought

"I'm stupid."

2. Pause

"Wait. Is this identity thinking or data thinking?"

3. Ask: "What's the data?"

"What actually happened? Did I make a mistake? Am I struggling with a concept? Is this hard right now?"

4. Reframe

"I made a mistake on this problem. That's data. What do I need to learn? Who can help me?"

Practice with students:

Give them identity thoughts. Have them reframe.

Example 1:

Identity thought: "I failed the test."

Reframe: "I didn't pass the test yet. I'm still learning this material. What do I need to study?"

Example 2:

Identity thought: "I'm bad at writing."

Reframe: "I'm still developing my writing skills. This essay needs work on organization. What resources can help me?"

Example 3:

Identity thought: "Everyone else gets this. I'm the only one who doesn't."

Reframe: "This is hard for me right now. Other people might be struggling too, but hiding it. I'm going to ask for help."

Step Three: Practice Regularly

Make reframing a routine.

Weekly activity:

"Think of one time this week when you had an identity thought. Write it down. Then reframe it." Students share in pairs or write in journals.

Model it yourself:

When you make a mistake in front of students, verbalize your reframing:

"I just made an error on the board. My identity brain wants to say, 'I should have known better.' But my data brain says: 'I made a mistake. Let's find it and correct it.' See? I'm reframing too."

Part D: What This Looks Like at Different Grade Levels

The core concept—mistakes equal data, not identity—stays the same. The language and activities change by age.

K-2: Simple Language Plus Concrete Examples

Core message:

"Mistakes help your brain grow. When you make a mistake, it's not a bad thing. It means you're learning."

Activity: "Oops Board"

Create a bulletin board: "OOPS! Our Brains Are Growing!"

When students make mistakes and learn from them, they write them on the board:

"I spelled 'friend' wrong. Now I know it's F-R-I-E-N-D."

"I counted wrong. I practiced, and now I can count to 20."

Language:

"Your brain is growing!"

"Mistakes help us learn."

"Try again!"

"What did you learn?"

3-5: Introduce Growth Versus Fixed Mindset

Core message: "You can grow your brain. Mistakes make your brain stronger."

Activity: Growth versus Fixed Mindset Chart

FIXED MINDSET	GROWTH MINDSET
"I'm not good at this."	"I'm not good at this YET."
"I give up."	"I'll try a different strategy."
"I can't do it."	"I can't do it YET."
"This is too hard."	"This is hard, but I can learn it."

Students identify which mindset they're using and practice shifting to it.

Language:

"You're developing this skill."

"Your brain is making new connections."

"What strategy can you try?"

"Not yet, but you're getting closer."

6-8: Neuroscience Plus Identity Versus Data

Core message:

"Your brain learns from mistakes. Scientists make mistakes all the time—that's how discoveries happen."

Activity: Mistake Analysis Journal

Students keep a weekly journal:

Prompt:

"Describe one mistake you made this week. What did you learn from it? How did you adjust?"

Language:

"What's the data here?"

"This is a prediction error. Your brain is learning."

"What can you learn from this?"

"You haven't mastered this yet."

9-12: Deep Dive Into Neuroscience Plus Metacognition

Core message:

"Understanding how your brain learns gives you power over your learning. Mistakes are prediction errors—essential for neuroplasticity."

Activity: Metacognitive Reflection

After tests or major assignments:

Prompt:

"Analyze your mistakes. For each error: (1) What was your prediction? (2) What actually happened? (3) Why was your prediction wrong? (4) What will you do differently next time?"

Language:

"What was your hypothesis? What was the result?"

"Analyze the prediction error."

"What does this data tell you about your understanding?"

"How will you iterate?"

Part E: Addressing Resistance

Some students will resist this message.

Why?

They've been trained for years to fear mistakes

A fixed mindset is deeply ingrained

They don't trust that it's really safe

They're protecting themselves from disappointment

How to respond:

Resistance One: "But I'm Just Not Good at Math/Writing/Science"

Student says: "I'm just not a math person. I've never been good at it."

Your response:

"I hear you. You've struggled with math in the past. But here's what neuroscience tells us: There's no such thing as a 'math person' or 'not a math person.' Your brain can learn math. It might take more practice for you than for someone else, but you can learn it."

"What you're really saying is: 'I haven't mastered math yet.' And that's true. But yet means it's possible."

"Let's figure out where you're getting stuck and build from there."

Resistance Two: "I Don't Want to Look Stupid in Front of Everyone"

Student says: "I don't want to volunteer because if I'm wrong, everyone will think I'm dumb."

Your response:

"I get it. It feels risky to share your thinking publicly. But here's what I want you to know: In this classroom, mistakes don't make you look stupid. They make you look like a scientist who's testing a hypothesis."

"Let me prove it to you. Watch what happens when I make a mistake."

You intentionally make a small mistake. Students notice. You analyze it openly.

"See? I made a mistake. No one thinks I'm stupid. We just figured it out together."

"Your turn. Try it. I promise you're safe here."

Resistance Three: "Mistakes Hurt My Grade, So They're Bad"

Student says: "You say mistakes are okay, but they lower my grade. So mistakes are bad."

Your response:

"You're right to notice that. If mistakes during practice lower your grade, then it's not safe to take risks. That's why I've changed my grading system."

"Here's how it works: Practice assignments equal feedback only, no grade. You can make as many mistakes as you need. When you demonstrate mastery on the final assessment, that's graded. And even then, you can retake it if needed."

"Your grade reflects what you know now, not how many tries it took you to learn it."

"Does that make sense?"

Resistance Four: "I've Tried, and I Still Can't Do It"

Student says: "I've tried so many times and I still don't get it. Maybe I just can't."

Your response:

"I hear your frustration. You've tried a lot, and it still hasn't clicked. That's hard."

"But here's what I notice: You've tried the same strategy multiple times. When scientists run an experiment, and it doesn't work, they don't give up—they try a different approach."

"Let's try a different strategy. Maybe you need a visual. Maybe you need to work with a partner. Maybe you need me to explain it a different way. Let's experiment."

Part F: Reinforcing the Concept All Year

Teaching this concept once isn't enough.

You need to reinforce it constantly.

Strategy One: Reference It Regularly

When students make mistakes, reference the concept:

"Remember, mistakes are data. What's the data here?"

"Is this identity thinking or data thinking?"

"You're not there yet. What do you need to learn next?"

Strategy Two: Celebrate Mistakes Publicly

Highlight students who:

Share mistakes openly

Analyze their errors

Revise and improve

Help others learn from mistakes

Example:

"I want to celebrate Marcus today. He got problem 5 wrong on the quiz. But instead of just moving on, he came to me after class and said, 'Can we figure out what I did wrong? I want to understand it.' That's a scientist's mindset. That's what we're building here."

Strategy Three: Model It Yourself—Constantly

When you make mistakes, verbalize your thinking:

"I made an error on this slide. Let me reframe: Is this about my identity—' I'm bad at making slides'? Or is this data—' I need to proofread more carefully'? It's data. Let me fix it."

Strategy Four: Create Rituals Around Mistakes

"Favorite Mistake Friday"

Every Friday, students share:

One mistake they made this week

What they learned from it

What they'll do differently

"Mistake of the Week"—Teacher shares

Every Monday, you share a mistake you made last week and what you learned.

"Error Analysis Tuesday"

Students anonymously analyze common errors from the previous week's quiz. Treat it as a learning opportunity, not a shaming session.

Strategy Five: Anchor Charts and Posters

Keep the concept visible.

Post these in your classroom:

Poster 1:

MISTAKES = DATA

"What can I learn from this?"

Poster 2:

IDENTITY vs. DATA THINKING

Two-column chart from earlier

Poster 3:

THE POWER OF YET

~~I can't do this~~ → I can't do this YET

~~I'm bad at this~~ → I'm still learning this

~~I failed~~ → I haven't succeeded YET

Poster 4:

WHAT SCIENTISTS DO:

Make predictions

Test them

Analyze what happened

Revise and try again

THAT'S WHAT WE DO TOO.

The Bottom Line

Students won't internalize "mistakes equal data" unless you teach it explicitly.

You need to:

Teach the neuroscience—age-appropriately

Teach the distinction—identity versus data thinking

Teach the skill—catch and reframe identity thoughts

Practice regularly—activities, journals, discussions

Reinforce constantly—reference it, model it, celebrate it

This is foundational.

If students don't believe mistakes equal data, they won't engage with the rest of your Mistake Lab. Teach it. Practice it. Reinforce it.

Make it the operating system of your classroom.

REFLECTION QUESTIONS

Personal Reflection:

1. Have you ever explicitly taught students the difference between identity thinking and data thinking? If not, why not?
2. Which age-appropriate neuroscience lesson—K-2, 3-5, 6-8, 9-12—fits your students? What would you need to adapt?
3. How often do you reference "mistakes equal data" in your classroom? Daily? Weekly? Never?
4. What resistance do you anticipate from your students? How will you address it?

Planning:

Design your "Mistakes = Data" lesson:

1. What neuroscience will you teach? Choose an age-appropriate version.
2. How will you introduce identity versus data thinking? Visual? Chart? Examples?
3. What practice activity will you use? Journal? Reframing exercise? Mistake analysis?
4. How will you reinforce it all year? Rituals? Posters? Regular references?

Action Planning:

This week, try one practice:

Teach the neuroscience lesson—your brain learns from mistakes

Introduce the identity versus data chart—post it, reference it

Model reframing—when you make a mistake, verbalize your thinking

Have students practice reframing—give them identity thoughts, have them rewrite as data thoughts

Create a ritual—Favorite Mistake Friday, Mistake of the Week. Make posters—Mistakes = Data, Power of Yet.

Further Exploration

Read:

- *Mindset* by Carol Dweck—the research behind the growth mindset
- *Powerful Teaching* by Pooja Agarwal & Patrice Bain—on retrieval practice and productive failure
- *Make It Stick* by Peter Brown, Henry Roediger, Mark McDaniel—on how learning actually works

Watch:

- Carol Dweck's TED Talk: "The Power of Believing That You Can Improve"
- Khan Academy: "You Can Learn Anything"—great for students
- Sesame Street: "The Power of Yet"—for younger students

Listen:

- "Hidden Brain" podcast: "Getting Unstuck"—on growth mindset

END OF PART 1: THE FOUNDATION—LAB SAFETY & SETUP

Part 1 Recap

You've completed Part 1. Here's what you've learned:

Chapter 1: The Science of Learning From Mistakes

Your brain learns through prediction errors—mistakes

Dopamine in a safe environment versus cortisol in a threatening environment

Feedback research—Hattie, Wiliam

Motivation research—intrinsic greater than extrinsic

Equity research—psychological safety reduces achievement gaps

Chapter 2: The Infallible Teacher Myth

Students learn from what you model, not just what you say

Where the myth comes from—training, first-year survival, culture, evaluation, society, impostor syndrome

The cost of hiding mistakes—students absorb your perfectionism

The Fallibility Paradox—vulnerability builds credibility

How to model vulnerability—start small, build up

Chapter 3: Your Perfectionism Problem

You can't teach students mistake literacy if you haven't confronted your own perfectionism.

Where your perfectionism comes from—same 6 sources as the myth

The cost—shame, anxiety, burnout, isolation, can't model authentically

The shift—identity to data thinking, for you

How to make the shift—7 steps: acknowledge, examine origins, reframe, find support, model vulnerability, separate identity from performance, keep a lab notebook

Chapter 4: Psychological Safety for Students

Definition: Students feel safe taking interpersonal risks

Why most classrooms don't have it—public failure, peer judgment, grades as punishment, teacher responses, comparison culture

Research—Edmondson, Google, Dweck

Four pillars—teacher modeling, peer norms, mistake-friendly language, separation of learning and grading

How to build it—establish norms, model vulnerability, teach peer responses, check in regularly

Chapter 5: The Language Shift

Your words shape how students think about mistakes

8 language shifts—failed to not yet, why to what happened, you need to to what if we tried, what's wrong to what do you need, unacceptable to didn't work, struggling to working on something hard, you're smart to you worked hard, don't make mistakes to mistakes help us learn

Language traps to avoid—I'm disappointed in you; you just need to —comparing to others, vague praise. Do you understand?

Language shift cheat sheet—print it, post it, use it

Chapter 6: Mistakes as Data, Not Identity

Students need explicit teaching—not just posters

Teach the neuroscience—age-appropriately: K-2, 3-5, 6-8, 9-12

Teach the distinction—identity thinking versus data thinking

Teach the skill—catch and reframe identity thoughts

Reinforce constantly—reference it, model it, celebrate it

You've completed lab safety and setup.

You've built the foundation:

You understand the science

You've confronted your own perfectionism

You know how to build psychological safety

You're learning language

You've taught students the core concept

Now you're ready to build the lab culture.

That's Part 2.

Ready to continue?

PART 2

THE LAB CULTURE

Building a Mistake-Literate Learning Environment

You've completed the foundation. You've built lab safety:

The science—Chapter 1

Your own vulnerability—Chapters 2-3

Psychological safety—Chapter 4

Learning language—Chapter 5

The core concept—Chapter 6

Now it's time to build the lab itself.

Part 2 is about creating the structures, routines, and culture that make mistake literacy operational.

Not just talking about it. Actually doing it.

In Part 2, you'll learn:

Chapter 7: The First Week of School—Setting Up Your Lab

Chapter 8: Teacher as Co-Researcher—Not Just Expert

Chapter 9: Peer Culture—Lab Partners & Collaboration

Chapter 10: The Grading Revolution—Feedback, Not Judgment

Chapter 11: Equity in the Lab—Who Gets to Experiment Safely?

Think of this as building a functioning laboratory:

Chapter 7 equals lab setup—Day 1 protocols, establishing norms, first experiments

Chapter 8 equals your role—lead scientist, not sage on stage

Chapter 9 equals team dynamics—How Lab Partners Work Together

Chapter 10: Equal Assessment System—how you measure learning without punishing mistakes

Chapter 11: Equal Access and equity—ensuring all students can participate safely

By the end of Part 2, your classroom will operate like a lab:

Students experiment

Mistakes are documented and analyzed

Collaboration is the norm

Learning is separated from grading

Everyone has access to the culture

Let's build your lab.

CHAPTER 7

THE FIRST WEEK OF SCHOOL—SETTING UP YOUR LAB

How to Establish a Mistake-Literate Culture from Day 1

Two teachers. Same school. Different first weeks.

Teacher A: Traditional First Week

Day 1:

Seating chart

Go over syllabus—rules, grading policy, consequences

Icebreaker—name game

Homework: Read Chapter 1

Day 2-5:

Jump into content

Students take notes

Few students volunteer—too risky

Teacher lectures

By Week 2:

Students have learned:

The teacher is the expert—I receive knowledge

Don't make mistakes—they'll hurt your grade

Don't ask questions—you should already know

School is performance—execute, don't experiment

Culture established: Compliance, not collaboration. Performance, not learning.

Teacher B: Mistake Lab First Week

Day 1:

Brief intro, then: "Before we learn content, we learn how to learn."

Teach: Mistakes = Data, Not Identity—Chapter 6 lesson

Model vulnerability—share your own mistake

Co-create lab norms

First small experiment—low-stakes, everyone tries, mistakes expected

Day 2-5:

Continue building culture—not jumping straight into content

Practice mistake analysis

Establish routines—how we respond to mistakes, how we collaborate

Students already making mistakes publicly and analyzing them

By Week 2:

Students have learned:

The teacher is a co-learner—we figure things out together

Mistakes are expected—they're data, not disasters

Questions are valued—curiosity is the point

School is a lab—experiment, fail, learn, iterate

Culture established: Collaboration, experimentation, mistake literacy.

The difference?

Teacher A used Week 1 to establish control.

Teacher B used Week 1 to establish culture.

Why the First Week Matters

The first week sets the tone for the entire year.

Students are asking, consciously or unconsciously:

"What's expected here?"

"Is it safe to take risks?"

"What happens if I make a mistake?"

"What's the teacher's role? My role?"

Whatever you do in Week 1, students will assume that's how it works all year.

If Week 1 is:

Lecture-heavy → Students expect: I listen, teacher talks

Rule-heavy → Students expect: Compliance matters most

Jump-straight-to-content → Students expect: Speed matters, not depth

If Week 1 is:

Culture-building → Students expect: How we learn matters

Experimentation → Students expect: Trying things is valued

Mistake-friendly → Students expect: It's safe to be wrong here

You can't build a Mistake Lab in Week 10 if you've spent Weeks 1-9 establishing a performance culture.

Start Day 1.

The First Week Framework: Five Days to Build Your Lab

Here's the blueprint:

Day 1: Establish the Culture

Goal: Students understand this classroom is a lab. Mistakes are expected and valued.

Part 1: Opening—10-15 minutes

Don't start with:

Syllabus

Rules

Seating chart

Icebreaker

Start with: "Welcome. Before we learn [subject], we need to learn how to learn. This classroom is a lab. That means we experiment. Experiments sometimes fail. That's not just okay—that's expected. That's how science works. That's how learning works."

Part 2: Teach Mistakes = Data—20-30 minutes

Use the lesson from Chapter 6, age-appropriate version:

Teach the neuroscience—your brain learns from mistakes

Teach the distinction—identity versus data thinking

Show examples—Edison, scientists, etc.

Key message:

"In this room, mistakes are data, not identity. When you make a mistake, we're going to analyze it like scientists. What happened? Why? What can we learn? What's next?"

Part 3: Model Vulnerability—5-10 minutes

Share a real mistake you made, as a teacher or learner. Don't make it safe or small. Make it real.

Example:

"Last year, I tried a new teaching strategy. I thought it would be amazing. It completely flopped. Students were confused. I felt terrible. But here's what I learned from it..."

Share what you learned, what you adjusted, and how it got better. "That's what we're going to do here. Make mistakes. Learn from them. Get better."

Part 4: Co-Create Lab Norms—15-20 minutes

Don't hand students a list of rules. Co-create norms with them.

Ask: "For this classroom to be a place where we can make mistakes, learn from them, and grow, what do we need from each other?"

"What do you need from me, the teacher?"

"What do you need from each other?" Students brainstorm in small groups, then share out.

Common responses:

Don't laugh at mistakes

Be respectful

Help each other

Don't judge

The teacher explains things in different ways if we don't understand

You write these on chart paper.

Then you add your commitments:

"Here's what I commit to as your teacher:"

I will make mistakes. I will admit them and learn from them.

I will never shame you for struggling.

I will give you feedback to help you improve, not just a grade.

I will create space for safe practice—not everything will be graded.

I will ask for your feedback. You can tell me when something isn't working.

Post the norms. Everyone signs or adds their name.

Part 5: First Experiment—15-20 minutes

Give students a low-stakes task where mistakes are likely.

The goal: Normalize making mistakes on Day 1.

Examples by subject:

Math:

"Here's a problem we haven't learned yet. I want you to try solving it. You probably won't get it right—that's fine. I want to see your thinking. Try it. Make mistakes. We'll analyze them together."

Science:

"Here's a question: Why do ice cubes float? Make a hypothesis. Draw a diagram. You might be wrong—that's okay. Scientists make wrong predictions all the time. That's how they learn."

English:

"Here's a challenging sentence. Try to diagram it. Most of you will get stuck—that's expected. This is hard. Try it anyway."

Social Studies:

"Here's a primary source document from 1776. Read it. Try to summarize it. It's written in an old language. You'll struggle. That's normal. Just try."

After students try:

Debrief mistakes:

"Who made a mistake? Raise your hand."

Most hands go up.

"Perfect. Let's analyze one." Pick a student who volunteered. "What did you try? What happened? What did you learn?"

You model the Mistake Analysis Protocol—we'll cover this deeply in Chapter 12.

Key message: "See? We just made mistakes on Day 1. And we learned from them. That's how this class works."

Day 2: Practice Responding to Mistakes

Goal: Teach students how to respond to each other's mistakes—peer norms.

Part 1: Review Day 1 Norms—5 minutes

"Yesterday, we created lab norms. Let's review them. What did we agree on?"

Students recall.

Part 2: Teach Peer Responses—15-20 minutes

Scenario-based teaching.

"One of our norms is: Don't laugh at mistakes. But what should you do when someone makes a mistake?"

"Let's practice."

Role play:

You give a wrong answer intentionally.

"The capital of California is San Francisco."

Ask students: "What should you say?"

Wrong responses—list these:

Laughing

"That's so wrong."

Eye rolling

Whispering to neighbor

Right responses—practice these:

"I thought it was Sacramento. Want to check?"

"What made you think San Francisco?"

"I was thinking something similar."

Students practice in pairs:

Give them scenarios. They practice curious responses, not judgmental ones.

Part 3: Live Practice—20 minutes

Do an activity where students answer questions aloud.

When someone gives a wrong answer, the class practices responding.

You coach in real-time:

"Wait. Student A just gave an answer. How should we respond?"

Students practice: "What made you think that?" "I was wondering the same thing."

"Perfect. Now let's figure it out together."

Key message: "This is how we operate. We respond to mistakes with curiosity, not judgment."

Day 3: Introduce Lab Notebooks—Reflection Journals

Goal: Students start documenting their learning, including mistakes.

Part 1: Explain Lab Notebooks—10 minutes

"Scientists keep lab notebooks. They document experiments—what they tried, what happened, what they learned."

"You're going to do the same. This notebook isn't graded. It's for you. It's where you document your learning, including your mistakes."

Show an example:

Your own lab notebook entry, on projector or chart paper:

Date: September 3

Experiment: Tried a new way to explain fractions using pizza slices.

Result: Students were confused. The visual didn't match the numbers.

What I learned: I need to use the same visual for the whole unit, not switch mid-lesson.

Next time: Start with one visual and stick with it.

Part 2: Students Set Up Notebooks—10 minutes

Give students composition notebooks or have them create digital journals.

First entry—guided:

Prompt: "What's one thing you learned in the first two days of school? What surprised you? What's still confusing?"

Part 3: Establish Reflection Routine—5 minutes

"Every week, you'll write a reflection. It's not graded. I'll read it to understand how you're doing and what you need. You can share mistakes, confusions, questions—anything."

Make it routine:

End of Week Reflection—Fridays, last 10 minutes

Or: End of Lesson Reflection—last 3 minutes of class, daily

Day 4: Practice Mistake Analysis

Goal: Students practice using the Mistake Analysis Protocol.

Part 1: Introduce the Protocol—Simplified Version—10 minutes

"When you make a mistake, here's what you do:"

The 4-Step Student Mistake Analysis Protocol:

1. What happened? Describe the mistake
2. Why did it happen? Analyze the cause
3. What did I learn? Extract the lesson
4. What will I try next? Plan the revision. Post this. Reference it constantly.

Part 2: Model It—10 minutes

You analyze a mistake you made, teaching or personal. Walk through all 4 steps out loud.

Example:

1. What happened?

"I planned a 30-minute activity but it took 50 minutes. We didn't finish the lesson."

2. Why did it happen?

"I underestimated how long it would take. I didn't account for transition time."

3. What did I learn?

"I need to plan for transitions. Activities always take longer than I think."

4. What will I try next?

"Next time, I'll add 10 minutes of buffer time to my plan."

Part 3: Students Practice—20 minutes

Give students a practice scenario or have them use a real mistake from earlier in the week. They write through the 4 steps—share in pairs, then a few share with the whole class.

Day 5: Experiment, Fail, Learn, Celebrate

Goal: Students run a real experiment, make mistakes, analyze them, and celebrate the learning.

Part 1: The Challenge—20-30 minutes

Give students a challenging task in your subject. Make it hard enough that mistakes are likely.

Examples:

Math: Solve a multi-step problem you haven't taught yet.

Science: Design an experiment to test a hypothesis, using limited materials.

English: Write an argument with evidence on a complex topic.

Social Studies: Analyze a primary source and make inferences.

Students work in pairs or small groups. Emphasis: "Try things. Make mistakes. Document what happens."

Part 2: Mistake Analysis—15-20 minutes

Students use the 4-step protocol to analyze what didn't work. They write it in their lab notebooks.

Part 3: Share & Celebrate—10-15 minutes

Students share:

What they tried

What didn't work

What they learned

What they'll try next

You celebrate the mistakes: "I love that you tried this approach even though it didn't work. You learned something valuable. That's what scientists do."

Part 4: Week 1 Reflection—5-10 minutes

Prompt:

"What did you learn this week about how we learn?"

"What surprised you?"

"What are you nervous about?"

"What are you excited about?" Students write. Some share.

What You've Established by the End of Week 1

By the end of Week 1, students understand:

This classroom is a lab—experiments happen here

Mistakes are expected and valued—not shameful

The teacher makes mistakes too—vulnerability is modeled

We respond to each other's mistakes with curiosity—peer norms

We document our learning—lab notebooks

We analyze mistakes systematically—4-step protocol

Practice is safe—not everything is graded

We learn together—collaboration, not competition

You haven't taught much content yet. But you've built the culture that will make content learning more effective for the rest of the year.

Week 1 Mistakes to Avoid

Mistake One: Jumping Straight Into Content

What this looks like:

Day 1: Syllabus. Day 2: Chapter 1. Day 3: Notes.

The problem:

You've taught students: Content greater than culture. Speed greater than depth.

The fix:

Spend Week 1 on culture. Content can wait.

Mistake Two: Telling, Not Showing

What this looks like:

"In this class, mistakes are okay!"

Then you don't make any mistakes yourself.

The problem:

Students hear the words but see the opposite.

The fix:

Model it. Day 1. Publicly.

Mistake Three: Not Practicing Peer Responses

What this looks like:

You establish norms, but you don't practice what to do when mistakes happen.

The problem:

Students don't know how to respond. They default to old habits—mockery, judgment.

The fix:

Practice peer responses. Day 2. Explicitly.

Mistake Four: Grading Everything in Week 1

What this looks like:

Day 1 quiz. Day 3 homework graded. Day 5 test.

The problem:

Students learn: Everything counts. Mistakes hurt my grade.

The fix:

Week 1 equals no grades. Only feedback. Or completion-based points, not correctness-based.

Mistake Five: Being Vague About Grading

What this looks like:

"Don't worry about grades. Just learn!"

But you never explain how grading actually works.

The problem:

Students are anxious. They don't trust that it's safe.

The fix:

Be explicit about grading from Day 1. See Chapter 10.

"Here's how grading works: Practice equals feedback only. Demonstrations of mastery equals graded. You can revise or retake. Your grade reflects what you know now, not how many tries it took."

What Happens in Week 2 and Beyond

Week 1 established the culture.

Week 2 and beyond is about maintaining and deepening it.

Week 2: Deepen Culture, Introduce Content

Now you can start teaching content.

But continue reinforcing culture: Reference lab norms regularly

Continue modeling vulnerability

Use the Mistake Analysis Protocol when students make errors

Weekly lab notebook reflections

Week 3-4: Students Start Owning the Culture

Students start: Analyzing their own mistakes without you prompting

Responding to each other's mistakes with curiosity

Asking for help without shame

Revising their work without being told

This is when the culture starts to feel natural.

Month 2: The Culture Is Established

By Month 2:

Students know:

How this classroom works

Mistakes are data

It's safe to struggle

The teacher will help

We learn together

Now you can do deeper work—complex projects, challenging content, student-led inquiry.

Because the foundation is solid.

Age-Appropriate Adaptations

The core framework—5-day culture-building week—works for all ages.

But adapt the language and activities:

K-2:

Day 1: Mistakes help your brain grow—simple language

Day 2: Practice being kind when someone makes a mistake

Day 3: "Oops Board" instead of lab notebooks—post mistakes we learned from

Day 4: Simple protocol—What happened? What did you learn? What will you try?

Day 5: Fun experiment—building with blocks, trying to balance things, etc.

3-5:

Day 1: Mistakes = Data lesson—growth versus fixed mindset

Day 2: Practice peer responses—role play

Day 3: Lab notebooks—journals

Day 4: 4-step protocol

Day 5: Subject-based challenge—mistakes likely

6-8:

Day 1: Neuroscience of mistakes plus Identity versus Data

Day 2: Peer culture—practice responding

Day 3: Lab notebooks—metacognitive reflection

Day 4: Mistake Analysis Protocol

Day 5: Complex challenge—collaborative problem-solving

9-12:

Day 1: Deep dive into neuroscience—prediction error, neuroplasticity—plus Identity versus Data

Day 2: Peer norms plus academic discourse practices

Day 3: Metacognitive journals—sophisticated reflection

Day 4: Mistake Analysis Protocol plus application to their own learning

Day 5: Authentic challenge—research question, complex problem, project design

Real Teacher Story: First Week Transformation

Ms. Rivera teaches 6th-grade math.

Her first few years, she spent Week 1 on:

Syllabus

Rules

Classroom procedures

Jump into Chapter 1

Result:

Students were quiet. Compliant. But disengaged. When they didn't understand something, they didn't ask. When they made mistakes, they hid them.

Year 4, she tried something different.

She spent Week 1 building culture:

Day 1: Taught Mistakes = Data. Shared her own math mistakes from when she was a student.

Day 2: Students practiced responding to each other's mistakes.

Day 3: Introduced math journals—not graded, just reflection.

Day 4: Taught the 4-step protocol. Students analyzed mistakes from a sample problem.

Day 5: Gave students a challenging problem they hadn't learned yet. Students tried, failed, analyzed, and learned.

By Week 2:

Students were asking questions. Students were volunteering even when unsure.

Students were saying: "I don't get this part. Can you explain it differently?"

By Month 2:

Students were analyzing their own mistakes without being prompted. Students were helping each other. Students were revising their work.

Ms. Rivera reflected:

"I used to think Week 1 was 'wasted' if we weren't covering content. Now I know: Week 1 is the most important week of the year. If I build the culture right, everything else flows. If I skip it, I'm fighting the culture all year."

The Bottom Line

The first week sets the tone for the entire year.

Use Week 1 to:

Establish this is a lab—not a performance stage

Teach mistakes = data—explicitly

Model vulnerability—go first

Co-create norms—with students

Practice peer responses—how we treat each other's mistakes

Introduce lab notebooks—documentation

Teach the Mistake Analysis Protocol—systematic approach

Run experiments—low-stakes, mistakes likely, learning valued

Content can wait. Culture can't. Spend Week 1 building the lab. Everything else will follow.

REFLECTION QUESTIONS

Personal Reflection:

1. How have you typically spent Week 1 in the past? Syllabus? Content? Culture?
2. What would it feel like to spend an entire week on culture before diving into content?
3. What resistance do you anticipate—from yourself, students, admin, parents—to spending Week 1 this way?
4. What's one element from the 5-day framework that excites you? Scares you?

Planning:

Design your Week 1:

Day 1:

How will you introduce "mistakes = data"? What mistake will you share?

How will you co-create norms? What first experiment will you run?

Day 2:

How will you teach peer responses? What scenarios will you use for practice?

Day 3:

Physical or digital lab notebooks? What will the first reflection prompt be?

Day 4:

How will you teach the 4-step protocol? What mistake will you model analyze?

Day 5:

What challenge will you give students? How will you celebrate their mistakes?

Action Planning:

If it's mid-year—not Week 1:

Do a "culture reset"—one week focused on re-establishing mistake-literate norms

Introduce one element at a time—this week: lab notebooks, next week: peer responses, etc.

Name it: "We've been operating one way. I want to shift. Here's why..."

If it's summer—planning for next year:

Design your full Week 1 plan—use the 5-day framework

Create materials—norms chart, protocol poster, lab notebook template

Practice your Day 1 vulnerability—what mistake will you share?

Further Exploration

Read:

- *The First Days of School* by Harry Wong—classic on establishing routines, adapt with mistake literacy lens
- *The Culture Code* by Daniel Coyle—on building strong team cultures

Watch:

- Ron Berger: "An Ethic of Excellence"—on building a culture of quality through revision

You've set up your lab. Culture established. Norms in place. Students ready.

Next: Your role as lead scientist, not sage on stage.

That's Chapter 8. Ready?

CHAPTER 8

TEACHER AS CO-RESEARCHER—NOT JUST EXPERT

Shifting from Sage on the Stage to Lead Scientist

Two classrooms. Same lesson on ecosystems.

Classroom A: Teacher as Expert

Ms. Anderson stands at the front.

She has a PowerPoint. 42 slides. She's prepared.

She lectures:

"Ecosystems have producers, consumers, and decomposers. Producers make their own food through photosynthesis. Consumers eat other organisms. Decomposers break down dead material."

Students take notes.

She asks: "Any questions?"

Silence.

"Good. Let's move on."

45 minutes later:

Students have filled out notes. They've copied diagrams. They've listened.

But they haven't:

Asked authentic questions

Explored ideas

Made discoveries

Seen the teacher think through anything

What students learned:

"The teacher knows everything. I receive knowledge. My job is to absorb and repeat."

Classroom B: Teacher as Co-Researcher

Mr. Davis sits with students at a table.

He has a terrarium in front of them—soil, plants, insects, and moisture.

He asks:

"What do you notice?"

Students observe. Share observations.

"Here's what I'm curious about: How does this whole system stay alive? Nothing comes in or out. No one feeds the insects. But they're still living. Why?"

Students hypothesize.

One student says, "The plants make food?"

Mr. Davis: "Interesting. How?"

Another student: "From the sun?"

Mr. Davis: "Let me think about that. The sun provides energy. But how do plants turn sunlight into food? I learned this once, but let me remember... I think it's called photosynthesis. Let's look it up together to make sure I'm remembering correctly."

He pulls up a resource. They read together.

"Okay, so plants use sunlight to make glucose. That's their food. So what eats the plants?"

Students: "The insects?"

Mr. Davis: "Right. So the insects are... what would we call them? If the plants make food, and the insects eat the plants...?"

Students work through it.

"Consumers?"

Mr. Davis: "Exactly. I didn't tell you that word—you figured it out. That's what scientists do. They observe, hypothesize, research, and build understanding."

What students learned:

"The teacher doesn't know everything. We figure things out together. Questions drive learning. Thinking is more valuable than memorizing."

The Difference: Role of the Teacher

Same content. Different approach.

Ms. Anderson's role: Sage on the stage—expert who delivers knowledge

Students' role: Passive recipients—absorb and repeat

Mr. Davis's role:

Lead scientist—co-researcher, guide, facilitator

Students' role:

Junior scientists—observe, question, hypothesize, discover

This chapter is about shifting your role.

From an expert who has all the answers → to lead scientist who learns alongside students.

Why the Shift Matters

When you position yourself as the all-knowing expert:

Students think: "I should already know this."

Students hide their confusion—don't want to look ignorant

Students don't develop thinking skills—just memorize what you said

Curiosity dies—there's nothing to wonder about; the teacher has the answers

Students can't model your learning—because you're not learning

When you position yourself as a co-researcher:

Students think: "We're figuring this out together."

Students share confusion—it's part of the process

Students develop thinking skills—they have to think, not just absorb

Curiosity thrives—questions drive the learning

Students see what learning looks like—you model thinking, questioning, and revising.

In a Mistake Lab, the teacher is not the expert with all the answers.

The teacher is the lead scientist who:

Designs experiments

Asks questions

Models thinking

Admits uncertainty

Researches alongside students

Facilitates discovery

What "Lead Scientist" Looks Like in Practice

Let me show you what this role shift looks like across different teaching moments:

Scenario One: Student Asks a Question You Don't Know

Old role—Expert:

Student: "Why is the sky blue?"

Teacher, panics internally: "Great question. Look it up for homework."

Never brings it up again.

What student learned:

"Teachers should know everything. If I don't know, I should hide it."

New role—Lead Scientist:

Student: "Why is the sky blue?"

Teacher: "I don't know. I've heard something about light scattering, but I don't remember the details. Let's research it together."

Pulls it up on the projector. Reads together. Discusses.

"So it's because blue light scatters more than other colors. I didn't know that detail. Thanks for asking—we both learned something."

What student learned:

"Not knowing is the start of inquiry. Scientists say 'I don't know' all the time. Then they research."

Scenario Two: Explaining a Concept

Old role—Expert:

Teacher: "Here's how photosynthesis works." Explains clearly and confidently. "Any questions?"

New role—Lead Scientist:

Teacher: "Let's figure out how photosynthesis works. Here's what I know: Plants need sunlight, water, and carbon dioxide. Somehow they turn that into food—glucose—and release oxygen."

"But here's what I'm curious about: How? What's the process? Let's look at a diagram together and see if we can figure it out."

Projects diagram. Thinks aloud.

"Okay, I see chloroplasts here. Those must be important. And there's light energy coming in. What do you notice?"

Students observe. You facilitate their discovery.

What students learned:

"Learning is about figuring things out, not just being told."

Scenario Three: When a Lesson Doesn't Work

Old role—Expert:

Activity flops. Students are confused.

Teacher, internal: "This isn't working. But I can't let them see that."

Pushes through. Finishes the lesson. Doesn't acknowledge it.

New role—Lead Scientist:

Activity flops. Students are confused.

Teacher, out loud: "This isn't working. I can see you're confused. Let me think about what's not landing."

Pauses. Thinks.

"I think the problem is I gave you too many steps at once. Let me try breaking it down differently. Here's what I'm going to do..."

Adjusts in real-time.

"Is this clearer?"

What students learned:

"When an experiment doesn't work, you adjust. You don't just push through."

Scenario Four: Introducing New Content

Old role—Expert:

Teacher: "Today I'm going to teach you about the water cycle."

Lectures for 30 minutes.

New role—Lead Scientist:

Teacher: "Today, we're going to investigate a question: Where does water go when it evaporates? Let's start with observations." Shows a time-lapse of a puddle evaporating.

"What do you notice? Where did the water go?" Students hypothesize.

"Let's test these hypotheses. Here's an experiment we can run..."

Students design an experiment, collect data, and draw conclusions. "So based on our data, what can we conclude about where water goes?" Students build understanding through inquiry.

What students learned:

"We can figure things out through observation and experimentation. We don't need to be told everything."

Scenario Five: When You Make a Mistake

Old role—Expert:

You solve a problem wrong on the board. Teacher, internal: "Oh no. I messed up. Erase it quickly. Hope no one noticed."

New role—Lead Scientist:

You solve a problem wrong on the board. Teacher, out loud: "Wait. I made an error. Can someone help me find it?"

Student: "I think you added instead of subtracted."

Teacher: "You're right. Let me fix that. Thanks for catching it. This is exactly what scientists do—check each other's work. I make mistakes. You make mistakes. We help each other find them."

What students learned:

"Everyone makes mistakes. Finding them is collaborative, not shameful."

The Key Practices of a Lead Scientist

Here are the specific practices that shift you from expert to co-researcher:

Practice One: Think Aloud—Make Your Thinking Visible

What this is: Verbalizing your thought process as you work through problems, analyze texts, or solve challenges.

Why it matters: Students can't see inside your head. If you just give them the answer, they don't learn how you got there.

How to do it:

Example—Math:

Instead of: "The answer is 42."

Try:

"Let me think this out loud. First, I need to figure out what the question is asking. It says 'how many total.' So I'm adding or multiplying. Let me look at the numbers... Okay, I see 6 groups of 7. That's multiplication. So 6 times 7. Let me calculate... 6 times 7 is... 42. So the answer is 42."

Example—Reading:

Instead of: "The theme is perseverance."

Try:

"Let me think about what this story is really about. The character keeps failing, but she doesn't give up. She tries different strategies. Even when people tell her it's impossible, she keeps going. So I'm thinking... this is about not giving up. What's the word for that? Perseverance? Determination? Yeah, I think the theme is perseverance."

Example—Science:

Instead of: "The hypothesis is that plants need sunlight to grow."

Try:

"Okay, we want to test whether plants need sunlight. So I'm thinking... if plants do need sunlight, then a plant without sunlight should not grow as well. So our hypothesis could be: 'If we deprive a plant of sunlight, it will grow more slowly than a plant with sunlight.' Does that make sense as a testable hypothesis?"

The key:

Don't just show the answer. Show the thinking that gets you there.

Practice Two: Say "I Don't Know"—And Research Together

What this is: Admitting when you don't have an answer, then modeling how to find it.

Why it matters: Students need to see that not knowing is normal—and that research is the response.

How to do it: When a student asks something you don't know:

"I don't know the answer to that. But I know how to find out. Let's look it up."

You and the students research together.

"Here's what I found." Share source. "What do you notice?"

Make it routine:

Once a week, model researching something you genuinely don't know.

"I've always wondered why [topic]. Let's investigate together this week."

The key:

"I don't know" is followed by "Let's find out," not silence or deflection.

Practice Three: Ask Questions—Don't Just Answer Them

What this is:

Instead of delivering information, ask questions that guide students to discover it.

Why it matters:

Questions engage thinking. Answers shut down thinking.

How to do it:

Instead of telling, ask:

Instead of: "The capital of France is Paris."

Try: "What's the capital of France? How could we find out?"

Instead of: "Photosynthesis happens in chloroplasts."

Try: "Where in the plant do you think photosynthesis happens? What evidence do you see in this diagram?"

Instead of: "The theme is friendship."

Try: "What do you think this story is really about? What keeps coming up again and again?"

Types of questions to ask:

Observational: "What do you notice?"

Predictive: "What do you think will happen?"

Analytical: "Why do you think that happened?"

Reflective: "What did you learn from that?"

Metacognitive: "What strategy did you use? How did you know to try that?"

The key:

Questions before answers. Discovery before delivery.

Practice Four: Wonder Out Loud

What this is:

Sharing your genuine curiosity about topics, even ones you're teaching.

Why it matters:

Curiosity is contagious. When students see you wondering, they start wondering too.

How to do it:

Example:

"I've always wondered why leaves change color in the fall. I know it has something to do with chlorophyll breaking down, but I don't fully understand the process. Want to investigate this with me?"

"Here's something that's always confused me about fractions: Why does multiplying fractions make them smaller, but multiplying whole numbers makes them bigger? Let's explore that."

"I'm curious: Why did the author choose to write this from the first-person perspective? What would change if it were in the third person? Let's think about that together."

The key:

Model curiosity. Share what you wonder about. Investigate together.

Practice Five: Learn New Things Publicly

What this is:

Learning content you don't already know—in front of students.

Why it matters:

Students need to see what learning looks like—struggle, confusion, and breakthrough.

How to do it:

Teach something you're learning:

"I'm learning how to code. I'm going to share my screen, and we're going to learn Python together. I'll make mistakes. We'll debug together. You'll see what learning looks like."

Learn something students request:

"You asked about [topic I don't know]. I don't know much about it, but I'm curious too. Let's research it together this week."

Document your learning:

"I'm reading a book about [topic]. Here's what I'm learning. Here's what's confusing me. Here's what I'm trying next."

The key:

Don't just teach content you've mastered. Learn new things publicly, so students see the process.

Practice Six: Invite Students to Teach You

What this is:

Positioning students as experts and asking them to teach you.

Why it matters:

Reverses the traditional hierarchy. Values student knowledge.

How to do it:

When students know something you don't:

"You know way more about [video games/social media/current music] than I do. Can you teach me how it works?"

When students solve problems differently: "You solved that differently than I would have. Show me your strategy. I want to learn from you."

When students have expertise: "You play soccer. I don't. Can you explain the rules to the class? You're the expert here."

The key:

Students have knowledge. Value it. Learn from them.

Practice Seven: Design Experiments—Not Just Lessons

What this is:

Framing lessons as experiments to be run, not information to be delivered.

Why it matters:

Experiments have uncertain outcomes. Lessons have predetermined endpoints. Experiments invite discovery.

How to do it:

Instead of: "Today I'm going to teach you about density."

Try:

"Today we're going to investigate a question: Why do some objects float and others sink? Here's our experiment..."

Students test objects, collect data, and draw conclusions.

Instead of: "Here's how to write a strong thesis statement."

Try:

"Let's experiment with different thesis statements and see which ones are most effective. Here are three versions. Which is strongest? Why? Let's test our theories by analyzing them."

The key:

Frame learning as investigation, not delivery.

How to Shift Your Role—Step-by-Step

This is a big shift.

If you've been "sage on the stage" for years, you can't flip a switch.

Here's how to transition:

Step One: Start Small—Pick One Practice

Don't try to implement all 7 practices at once.

Pick one:

This week, I'll think aloud when I solve problems.

This week, I'll say "I don't know" at least once and research with students.

This week, I'll ask questions before giving answers.

Master one. Then add another.

Step Two: Plan for It

Add it to your lesson plans.

Example:

In your plan, write:

"When I solve this problem, I think aloud. Don't just write the answer."

"When students ask about X, say 'I don't know' and research together."

If you don't plan for it, you'll default to old habits.

Step Three: Narrate the Shift

Tell students what you're doing and why.

"I'm trying something different this year. Instead of just telling you answers, I'm going to think out loud so you can see how I problem-solve. I'm also going to say 'I don't know' more often and research with you. This is how scientists work—we figure things out together."

This helps students understand the shift and be patient when it feels different.

Step Four: Practice in Low-Stakes Moments

Don't start with your most important lesson.

Start with:

Warm-ups

Review problems

Discussions

Informal moments

Build confidence. Then apply to bigger lessons.

Step Five: Reflect After Lessons

After class, ask yourself:

Did I think aloud today?

Did I say "I don't know" when I didn't know?

Did I ask questions or just give answers?

Did I model curiosity?

Did I position myself as an expert or a co-learner? Adjust for tomorrow.

What This Looks Like at Different Grade Levels

K-2: Teacher as "Lead Explorer"

Language:

"Let's explore this together."

"I wonder why... What do you think?"

"Let's find out!"

Activities:

Wonder walls—what we're curious about

Think-alouds during read-alouds—"Hmm, I'm wondering why the character did that..." Science observations—"What do you notice? I notice... What else?"

3-5: Teacher as "Lead Investigator."

Language:

"Let's investigate this question."

"I'm curious about..." "Let's test that hypothesis."

Activities:

Inquiry-based projects—students design investigations

Think-alouds when solving problems

Shared research—teachers and students research new topics together

6-8: Teacher as "Lead Researcher."

Language:

"Let's research this together."

"I don't fully understand this. Let's dig deeper."

"What's your hypothesis? Mine is..."

Activities:

Student-led research projects

The teacher models researching a new topic

Socratic seminars—teacher asks questions, students build understanding collaboratively

9-12: Teacher as "Lead Scientist/Scholar."

Language:

"Let's analyze this primary source together."

"I'm still working through this concept. Here's where I'm stuck..."

"Let's co-construct understanding."

Activities:

Teacher learns new content publicly—e.g., a new programming language or literary theory.

Students present original research—teacher learns from them

Philosophical discussions—teacher doesn't have "the answer"; class explores together

Common Fears—And Why They're Unfounded

Fear One: "Students Will Think I'm Incompetent"

You think:

"If I say 'I don't know,' students will lose respect for me."

Reality:

Students respect honesty and curiosity more than false expertise.

Remember: The Fallibility Paradox, Chapter 2.

Vulnerability equals credibility.

Fear Two: "We Won't Cover Enough Content"

You think:

"If I stop lecturing and start facilitating discovery, we'll never get through the curriculum."

Reality:

Students retain more when they discover than when they're told.

Research:

Active learning is greater than passive learning—retention, transfer, engagement.

You might cover less. But students will learn more.

Fear Three: "I'll Lose Control of the Class"

You think:

"If I'm not the expert directing everything, chaos will ensue."

Reality:

Co-learning does not equal no structure.

You're still designing the experiments, asking guiding questions, and facilitating.

You're shifting from controller to facilitator.

Students are more engaged, not less, when they're co-constructing understanding.

Fear Four: "What If Students Ask Something I Truly Don't Know?"

You think:

"What if I can't answer? What if I look foolish?"

Reality:

"I don't know" followed by "Let's find out" is the most powerful teaching move.

You're modeling:

Intellectual humility

Curiosity

Research skills

Lifelong learning. This is the goal.

The Bottom Line

In a Mistake Lab, the teacher is not the sage on the stage.

The teacher is the lead scientist who:

Thinks aloud—makes thinking visible. Says "I don't know"—and researches with students. Asks questions—before giving answers. Wonders out loud—models curiosity. Learns new things publicly—shows the process. Invites students to teach—values their expertise. Design experiments—not just lessons

This shift:

Models what learning looks like—struggle, curiosity, discovery. Develops students' thinking skills—not just content knowledge. Normalizes not knowing—the start of inquiry. Positions students as co-constructors of knowledge—not passive recipients

You don't have to know everything. You have to model how to learn everything.

That's the role of a lead scientist.

REFLECTION QUESTIONS

Personal Reflection:

1. On a scale of 1-5, where are you currently?

1 = Sage on the stage—expert, deliverer of knowledge

5 = Lead scientist—co-learner, facilitator of discovery

Your rating: _____

What would it take to move one point higher?

2. Which of the 7 practices feels most natural to you? Most uncomfortable?

Natural:

Uncomfortable:

3. When was the last time you said "I don't know" to a student? What happened?
4. What would your students say your role is? Expert? Guide? Co-learner?

Scenario Practice:

Imagine:

A student asks: "Why do we have to learn this? When will we ever use it?"

How would you respond as:

Expert:

Lead scientist:

Action Planning:

This week, try one practice:

Think aloud when solving one problem—make your thinking visible

Say "I don't know" once and research with students

Ask 5 questions before giving any answers in one lesson

Share something you're curious about and investigate it with students

Learn something new publicly—show students your learning process

Ask a student to teach you something they know

Frame one lesson as an experiment—not delivery of information

Further Exploration

Read:

- *Make Just One Change* by Dan Rothstein & Luz Santana—on teaching through questions
- *Inquiry and the National Science Education Standards*—on inquiry-based teaching
- *Visible Learning for Teachers* by John Hattie—on effective teaching strategies

Watch:

- Dan Meyer's TED Talk: "Math Class Needs a Makeover"—on problem-based learning
- Any video of Socratic seminars—students co-constructing understanding

You've shifted your role from expert to co-researcher.

Next: Building the peer culture

How do students support each other as lab partners?

Ready?

CHAPTER 9

PEER CULTURE—LAB PARTNERS & COLLABORATION

How Students Support Each Other's Learning

Two classrooms. Same lesson on solving systems of equations.

Classroom A: Competitive Culture

Ms. Thompson gives a problem:

Solve:

$2x + y = 10$

$x - y = 2$

She says: "First person to solve it gets extra credit."

What happens:

Three students race to solve it

One student shouts: "I got it!"

Ms. Thompson checks. "Correct! Nice work, Marcus."

The rest of the class puts down their pencils

What students learned:

"Learning is a race. Someone won. I lost. Why keep trying?"

"Marcus is smart. I'm not."

"We're competing, not collaborating."

Classroom B: Collaborative Culture

Mr. Chen gives the same problem.

He says: "Turn to your lab partner. Work together. You have 3 minutes. I want to hear your thinking—it doesn't have to be correct yet."

What happens:

Students work in pairs

They talk through strategies

Some make mistakes, catch them together

Mr. Chen circulates, listens

After 3 minutes:

"Who wants to share what you tried? Remember, we're interested in your thinking, even if you didn't get the answer yet."

A pair shares: "We tried substitution but got stuck."

Mr. Chen: "Interesting. Where did you get stuck? Let's troubleshoot together."

Another pair: "We got $x = 4$ and $y = 2$."

Mr. Chen: "How did you get that? Walk us through your strategy."

They explain. Class discusses.

What students learned:

"We're in this together. We help each other. Sharing thinking—even when stuck—is valued. We all get smarter when we collaborate."

The Difference: Peer Culture

Same problem. Different culture.

Classroom A:

Competition—someone wins, others lose

Isolation—work alone

Public ranking—who's smartest?

Shame—I didn't get it first equals I'm not smart

Classroom B:

Collaboration—we're lab partners

Partnership—work together

Shared thinking—all perspectives valued

Safety—it's okay to be stuck. This chapter is about building Classroom B's peer culture.

Why Peer Culture Matters

You, the teacher, can model vulnerability all day.

But if peers mock mistakes, the classroom isn't safe.

Research—Amy Edmondson:

Psychological safety is a team dynamic, not just a leader dynamic.

Translation for classrooms:

Safety requires:

Teacher modeling—Chapters 2-3

Plus peer norms—this chapter

Both are necessary. Neither is sufficient alone.

Why?

Students spend more time with each other than with you.

Group work

Pair work

Hallway conversations

Lunchtime

Between classes

If peers judge mistakes, students will hide them—even if you model vulnerability.

You need to teach students:
How to respond to each other's mistakes
How to give feedback—curious, not judgmental
How to collaborate, not compete
How to be lab partners—support each other's learning

The Five Pillars of Collaborative Lab Culture

Pillar One: Peer Norms—How We Treat Each Other's Mistakes

This is foundational.
Students need explicit teaching on: What to do when someone makes a mistake
What not to do
How to respond with curiosity, not judgment

How to teach this:

Step 1: Name the Old Norms—What Doesn't Work

"In many classrooms, here's what happens when someone makes a mistake:"
List on board:
People laugh
People whisper to each other
Someone says, "That's so wrong."
People roll their eyes
The person who made the mistake feels embarrassed and never volunteers again.
"Has anyone experienced this?"
Students nod.
"That's not how scientists work. In a lab, when an experiment doesn't work, the team asks: 'What happened? What can we learn?' They don't mock each other."

Step 2: Co-Create New Norms

"So in this lab, here's how we respond when someone makes a mistake. What should we do?"
Students brainstorm. You write:
Ask: "What were you thinking?"—curiosity
Say: "I was thinking something similar."—solidarity
Offer: "Want to work through it together?"—support
Share: "I made that same mistake. Here's what I learned."—normalizing
Don't: Laugh, judge, whisper, mock
Post these norms. Reference them constantly.

Step 3: Practice the Norms

Don't just post norms and hope students follow them.

Practice.

Activity: Norm practice

You give a wrong answer intentionally.

"The capital of the United States is New York."

Ask students: "How should you respond?"

Wrong responses:

Laughter

"No, that's wrong."

"Everyone knows it's Washington, D.C."

Right responses:

"I thought it was Washington, D.C. Want to double-check?"

"What made you think of New York?"

"I was confused about that too at first."

Students practice in pairs.

Give them scenarios. They practice responding.

Step 4: Reinforce in the Moment

When students violate norms:

Address it immediately.

Example:

Student A gives the wrong answer. Student B laughs.

You stop class:

"Stop. Student B, we don't laugh at someone when they make a mistake. How should you have responded?"

Student B practices a curious response.

"Thank you. Let's continue."

When students follow norms:

Celebrate it.

"I love how Student C responded to Student D's mistake. Did you hear what they said? 'I was thinking that too. Let's figure it out together.' That's exactly how lab partners support each other."

Pillar Two: Structured Collaboration—Not Just "Work Together"

Simply saying "work in groups" doesn't create collaboration.

You need structures.

Why structure matters:

Without structure:

One student does all the work

Others disengage

No real collaboration happens

With structure:

Everyone has a role

Everyone participates

True collaboration happens

Effective collaboration structures:

Structure One: Think-Pair-Share

How it works:

1. Think—individual: Students think alone, 30 seconds to 1 minute
2. Pair—partner: Students discuss with a partner, 1-2 minutes
3. Share—whole class: Pairs share with the class

Why it works:

Everyone thinks—not just fast processors

Everyone talks—in pairs, not just volunteers

Mistakes happen in pairs first—lower stakes than whole class

Example:

"Here's the question: Why did the author choose this setting? Think for 30 seconds. Then pair with your partner and discuss. Then we'll share."

Structure Two: Numbered Heads Together

How it works:

1. Students work in groups of 4. Number off—1, 2, 3, 4.
2. The teacher gives a question.
3. Groups work together. Everyone must understand the answer.
4. Teacher calls a random number: "Number 3s, share your group's answer."

Why it works:

Everyone must understand—anyone could be called

Groups teach each other—peer explanation

Accountability—can't hide

Example:

"In your groups, solve this equation. Make sure everyone understands how to solve it. I'm going to call on Number 2s to explain."

Structure Three: Jigsaw

How it works:

1. Home groups: Students start in groups of 4.
2. Expert groups: Students regroup by number—1s together, 2s together, etc. Each expert group learns one piece of content.
3. Home groups: Students return to home groups. Each person teaches their piece.

Why it works:

Everyone is an expert in something

Everyone teaches—deepens understanding

Interdependent—need each other to learn the whole topic

Example:

"We're learning about ecosystems. Expert group 1: Producers. Expert group 2: Consumers. Expert group 3: Decomposers. Expert group 4: Energy flow. Learn your piece, then teach your home group."

Structure Four: Reciprocal Teaching

How it works:

Students take turns playing 4 roles:

Questioner—asks questions about the text

Clarifier—identifies confusing parts, clarifies them

Summarizer—summarizes the main points

Predictor—predicts what comes next

Why it works:

Metacognitive—students think about their thinking

Everyone participates—roles rotate

Deepens comprehension

Example—reading:

"As we read this chapter, take turns: Questioner asks a question. Clarifier addresses confusion. Summarizer summarizes. Predictor predicts. Then switch roles."

Structure Five: Peer Review/Error Analysis Partners

How it works:

Students swap work. Partners:

Identify strengths

Identify errors or areas for improvement

Give specific feedback

Discuss together

Why it works:

Students learn from analyzing others' work

Feedback is peer-to-peer—not just teacher-to-student

Normalizes mistakes—everyone sees everyone's rough drafts

Example—writing:

"Swap essays with your partner. Read their intro paragraph. Identify: (1) What's working well? (2) What could be clearer? Write feedback, then discuss."

The key:

Don't just say "work together."

Use structured protocols that ensure real collaboration.

Pillar Three: Teaching Students to Give Feedback—Not Just Criticism

Students don't automatically know how to give good feedback.

They default to:

"This is good."—vague, unhelpful

"This is wrong."—judgmental, unhelpful

Silence—afraid to give feedback at all

You need to teach feedback skills.

The Feedback Framework—For Students

Teach students this structure:

Step 1: Notice—What's working

"I notice that..."—specific strengths

Examples:

"I notice your thesis is clear."

"I notice you used evidence from the text."

"I notice you showed your work step-by-step."

Step 2: Wonder—What could improve

"I wonder if..."—specific, curious questions

Examples:

"I wonder if this paragraph could be reorganized?"

"I wonder if you could add more detail here?"

"I wonder if this step is where the error happened?"

Step 3: Suggest—Optional

"What if you tried..."—concrete suggestion

Examples:

"What if you tried starting with the evidence, then the claim?"

"What if you tried solving it this way?"

"What if you added a transition sentence here?"

Practice this framework:

Model it:

Show student work—anonymously or with permission.

"I notice the introduction grabs my attention. I wonder if the thesis could be more specific. What if you tried adding what you're arguing about the topic?"

Students practice:

Give students sample work. They practice giving feedback using the framework.

Then apply:

Students give each other feedback on real work.

Why this works:

"I notice" equals starts with strengths—builds confidence

"I wonder" equals sounds curious, not judgmental

"What if you tried" equals offers concrete suggestions, not just criticism

Pillar Four: Celebrating Peer Support—Not Just Individual Achievement

If you only celebrate individual achievement, students compete.

If you celebrate peer support, students collaborate.

What to celebrate:

When a student helps another student:

"I love how Marcus helped Sarah understand this concept. That's what lab partners do."

When a student asks for help:

"Maria asked for help when she was stuck. That's exactly what scientists do. Asking for help is smart."

When a group solves a problem together:

"Table 3 worked together to solve this. They tried three different strategies before finding one that worked. That's persistence and collaboration."

When a student shares a mistake that helps others:

"James shared his mistake, and we all learned from it. That's a valuable contribution to our lab."

What not to celebrate:

"Emma finished first!"—creates a race mentality

"Who's the smartest?"—ranking

"Let's see who got 100%."—public comparison

Instead:

"Look how much we learned together today."

"I saw so many examples of students helping each other."

"Our collaboration is getting stronger."

Pillar Five: Making Collaboration the Norm—Not the Exception

If students work alone 90% of the time and collaborate 10%, they'll think:

"Collaboration is a special activity. The real work is done alone."

If collaboration is routine:

Students think: "We learn together. That's how this works."

How to make collaboration routine:

1. Daily pair work

Every day, students work with a partner at some point.

"Turn to your partner and..."

2. Weekly group projects

At least once a week, students work in small groups on a task.

3. Peer feedback is built into every assignment

Before submitting work:

Students get peer feedback

Students revise based on feedback

Then submit

This teaches:

Collaboration improves work

First drafts aren't final

Peers are resources

4. Collaborative problem-solving

When you introduce new, challenging content:

Don't lecture. "Here's the problem. Work in groups to solve it. I'll circulate and support." Students figure it out together.

The key:

Collaboration isn't a special event. It's how the lab operates.

How to Assign Lab Partners

Random pairs don't always work.

Strategic pairing matters.

Options:

Option 1: Teacher-Assigned Pairs—Strategic

You pair students based on:

Complementary skills—one strong in X, one strong in Y. Similar skill levels—both working on the same concept. Personality compatibility—who works well together

Pros:

You can ensure productive pairs

You can avoid problematic pairs

Cons:

Takes time to plan

Students might resist

Option 2: Random Pairs—Rotating

Students work with different partners regularly, in a daily or weekly rotation.

How:

Draw names

Number off

Deck of cards—match suits

Pros:

Students learn to work with everyone

No cliques

Cons:

Some pairs won't work well together

Takes time to build rapport

Option 3: Student Choice—Within Structure

Students choose partners from a constrained set.

Example: "Choose someone you haven't worked with this month."

"Choose someone who's working on the same skill as you."

Pros:

Student agency

Comfort—students choose who they work with

Cons:

Cliques can form

Some students are always left out

Recommendation:

Use a mix.

Monday/Wednesday: Teacher-assigned—strategic

Friday: Student choice—within constraints

Rotate every 2-4 weeks—so students don't get stuck with a difficult partner forever.

What to Do When Collaboration Goes Wrong

Not all groups work well together.

Here's how to address common problems:

Problem One: One Student Dominates, Others Disengage

What it looks like:

One student does all the work. Others sit back.

How to fix it:

Use roles:

Assign specific roles to each student:

Facilitator—keeps group on task

Recorder—writes down ideas

Researcher—looks up info

Reporter—shares with the class

Everyone has a job. Everyone participates.

Or use structures like Numbered Heads Together:

"I'll call on random numbers, so everyone needs to understand the answer."

This creates accountability.

Problem Two: Students Mock Each Other's Mistakes

What it looks like:

One student makes a mistake. Partner laughs or criticizes.

How to fix it:

Stop the group. Address it publicly if needed, or privately.

"I saw Student A laugh when Student B made a mistake. That's not how we operate in this lab. Student A, how should you have responded?"

The student practices a curious response.

"Thank you. Let's continue."

Reinforce norms immediately.

Problem Three: Students Won't Talk to Each Other

What it looks like:

You say, "discuss with your partner." Students sit in silence.

How to fix it:

Provide sentence stems:

"When you discuss with your partner, start with: 'I think... because...' or 'I noticed...'"

Give a specific task:

"Don't just discuss. I want each of you to share one idea. Partner A, you go first."

Model it:

"Let me show you what productive discussion looks like."

You and a student model a discussion.

Problem Four: One Student Is Completely Lost, Partner Can't Help

What it looks like:

Student A doesn't understand. Student B tries to explain, but it's not helping. Frustration builds.

How to fix it:

Teach students to ask for teacher help when peer help isn't enough:

"If you try to explain and your partner is still stuck, raise your hand, and I'll come help both of you."

This teaches:

Peer help first

The teacher helps when needed

It's okay to need extra support

Problem Five: Students Copy Instead of Collaborate

What it looks like:

Student A solves the problem. Student B just copies the answer.

How to fix it:

Change the task structure:

Instead of: "Solve this problem together."

Try: "Each person solves the problem independently. Then compare your answers. If they're different, figure out why."

Or:

"Partner A, explain your thinking. Partner B, summarize what Partner A said. Then switch."

This ensures both people are thinking, not just copying.

Teaching Students to Be Good Lab Partners

Explicitly teach the skills of partnership.

Skill One: Active Listening

What it looks like:

Eye contact

Nodding

Asking clarifying questions—"Can you say more about that?"

Summarizing—"So you're saying..."

Not:

Interrupting

Looking at the phone

Thinking about what to say next instead of listening

How to teach it:

Model it:

"Watch me listen to this student. Notice what I do."

You demonstrate active listening.

"What did you notice?"

Students identify: eye contact, nodding, asking questions.

Practice it:

Students practice active listening in pairs.

One person talks for 1 minute. Partner listens actively. Then summarizes.

Skill Two: Asking Clarifying Questions—Not Just Saying "I Don't Get It"

Instead of:

"I don't get it."

Teach:

"I don't understand [specific part]. Can you explain that part again?"

"I'm confused about [specific step]. What did you do there?"

"I followed you up to [point]. Then I got lost. Can you slow down?"

Why this works:

Specific questions are easier to answer than vague ones.

Skill Three: Explaining Without Just Giving the Answer

Instead of:

"The answer is 42. Write that down."

Teach:

"Let me show you my thinking. First, I... Then I... What would you do next?"

Or:

"What have you tried so far? Where did you get stuck? Let's start there."

Why this works:

Explanation builds understanding. Answers don't.

Skill Four: Encouraging Each Other

Teach students to: "You're getting closer."

"That's a smart strategy."

"Keep trying. You'll get it."

"I made that same mistake. Here's what helped me."

Not:

"That's wrong."

"This is easy. Why don't you get it?"

"Just do it this way."

The Bottom Line

Psychological safety requires peer norms, not just teacher modeling.

To build a collaborative lab culture:

Teach peer norms explicitly—how to respond to mistakes

Use structured collaboration—not just "work together."

Teach feedback skills—I notice, I wonder, What if...

Celebrate peer support—not just individual achievement

Make collaboration routine—the norm, not the exception

When peer culture is strong:

Students help each other

Mistakes are normalized—peers respond with curiosity

Learning is collaborative, not competitive

Students feel safe—teacher plus peers create safety

Your Mistake Lab depends on this.

Build the peer culture. Everything else flows from it.

REFLECTION QUESTIONS

Personal Reflection:

1. Is your classroom culture more competitive or collaborative? What evidence supports your answer?
2. How do students currently respond to each other's mistakes? Mockery? Silence? Curiosity?
3. Do you celebrate individual achievement or collaborative support more? How do students know what you value?
4. What collaboration structures do you currently use? How often?

Observation:

Watch one group work session. Notice:

Who talks? Who doesn't?

How do students respond to each other's mistakes?

Are they really collaborating, or is one person doing all the work?

What norms are operating, even if unstated?

What did you notice?

Action Planning:

This week, try one practice:

Teach peer norms explicitly—how to respond to mistakes

Practice peer responses—role play, scenario practice

Use one collaboration structure—Think-Pair-Share, Numbered Heads, Jigsaw

Teach the feedback framework—I notice, I wonder, What if

Celebrate peer support—publicly recognize students helping each other

Make collaboration routine—daily pair work

Assign strategic lab partners—thoughtful pairing

Further Exploration

Read:

- *Cooperative Learning* by Spencer Kagan—structures for collaboration
- *Mathematical Mindsets* by Jo Boaler—collaborative math classrooms
- *The Power of Protocols* by Joseph McDonald—structured collaboration

Watch:

- Videos of Socratic seminars—student-led collaborative discussion
- Kagan Cooperative Learning structures—demonstrations

You've built the peer culture.

Students know how to support each other as lab partners.

Next: The grading revolution

How do you assess learning without punishing mistakes?

That's Chapter 10—the longest and most important chapter in Part 2.

Ready?

CHAPTER 10

THE GRADING REVOLUTION

Why Traditional Grading Kills Learning—And What to Do About It

Two teachers. Same unit on persuasive writing. Different grading systems.

Teacher A: Traditional Grading

Week 1:

Assignment: Rough draft of persuasive essay—graded

Student writes rough draft. Teacher grades it: C-

Comments: "Weak thesis. Needs more evidence. Organization unclear."

Student's reaction:

"I got a C-. I'm bad at writing. Why bother revising? The grade is already in the gradebook."

Week 2:

Assignment: Peer review—graded on participation

The student goes through the motions. Doesn't really engage.

Week 3:

Assignment: Final draft—graded

The student makes minimal changes. Submits.

Grade: C

Final grade for the unit: Average of rough draft C- and final C equals C-

What the student learned:

"My rough draft grade dragged down my final grade. Mistakes during learning hurt me. I should only submit work when I'm sure it's perfect. I'm not a good writer."

Teacher B: Learning-Focused Grading

Week 1:

Assignment: Rough draft of persuasive essay—feedback only, no grade

Student writes rough draft. Teacher gives feedback:

"Your argument has potential, but your thesis needs to be clearer. Here's what I mean: [specific example]. Try rewriting your thesis using this structure: [provides template]. Your evidence is strong in paragraph 2, but missing in paragraph 3. What evidence could you add there?"

Student's reaction:

"Okay, my thesis is unclear, and I need more evidence in paragraph 3. I can fix that. This is just a draft—it's supposed to be rough."

Week 2:

Assignment: Peer review—feedback practice, not graded

The student gives and receives feedback. Learns what makes arguments strong.

Week 3:

Assignment: Revised draft—this is what's graded

Student revises based on feedback. The thesis is clearer. Evidence is stronger.

Grade: B+

Final grade for the unit: B+—based on what the student knows now, not the average of the rough draft plus the final

What the student learned:

"Rough drafts are supposed to be rough. Feedback helps me improve. Revision is part of the process. My grade reflects what I can do now, not how many tries it took me. I'm developing as a writer."

The Difference: Grading Philosophy

Same content. Different grading systems. Different outcomes.

Teacher A—Traditional:

Grades everything—rough drafts, practice, final

Averages all grades—early mistakes hurt the final grade

No revision—once graded, it's done

Message: Don't make mistakes. They'll lower your grade permanently.

Teacher B—Learning-focused:

Feedback on practice—rough drafts, peer review

Grades only demonstrations of mastery—final draft

Revision expected—based on feedback

Message: Mistakes during practice are expected. Revise. Your grade reflects current mastery.

This chapter is about why traditional grading is incompatible with mistake literacy—and what to do about it.

The Problem: Traditional Grading Kills Mistake Literacy

Here's the brutal truth:

You cannot have a mistake-literate classroom with traditional grading.

They are fundamentally incompatible.

Why?

Problem One: Traditional Grading Punishes Mistakes Permanently

Traditional grading averages all attempts.

Example:

Quiz 1: The student doesn't understand yet. Gets 40%.

Quiz 2 after reteaching: Student now understands. Gets 90%.

Traditional grading: Average equals 65%

The 40% haunts them forever.

What this teaches:

"Early mistakes are permanent. I'm being punished for not knowing something I hadn't learned yet."

In a Mistake Lab:

Quiz 1: Diagnostic—feedback only, shows what the student needs to learn

Quiz 2: Assessment—graded, shows current mastery

Grade: 90%—reflects what the student knows now

What this teaches:

"My grade reflects what I know now, not how long it took me to learn it."

Problem Two: Traditional Grading Makes Every Mistake High-Stakes

If everything is graded, every assignment is high-stakes.

Every mistake lowers your grade.

Result:

Students don't take risks—they only do what they're sure they can do

Students don't try new strategies—might fail

Students hide confusion—asking for help feels risky

Students focus on grade, not learning—"What's this worth?"

In a Mistake Lab:

Practice does not equal performance

Practice equals feedback only—safe to fail

Performance equals graded—demonstration of mastery

Result:

Students take risks during practice—failure is expected

Students try new strategies—experimentation is valued

Students ask for help—it won't hurt their grade

Students focus on learning—"What am I learning?"

Problem Three: Traditional Grading Gives Grades Without Actionable Feedback

Traditional grading:

"You got a 75%. Good job."

Student thinks: "Okay, I got a 75%. But what do I need to improve? What did I do wrong?"

No guidance. Just a number.

Research—Ruth Butler, 1988:

When you give grades plus feedback, students focus on the grade and ignore the feedback.

When you give feedback only, no grade, students use the feedback and improve.

In a Mistake Lab:

Feedback first.

Grades later, or only when necessary.

Problem Four: Traditional Grading Promotes Fixed Mindset

When grades are averaged, and mistakes are permanent:

Students develop a fixed mindset.

"I got a bad grade. I'm bad at this. I can't improve."

Research—Carol Dweck:

When students believe grades measure innate ability, not effort or growth, they:

Avoid challenge

Give up when things get hard

See mistakes as evidence they're not smart

In a Mistake Lab:

Grades reflect growth and current mastery, not averages.

Students develop a growth mindset.

"I didn't know this before. Now I do. My grade reflects that."

Problem Five: Traditional Grading Focuses on Compliance, Not Learning

Traditional grading often includes:

Participation points—showing up, raising a hand

Homework completion—did you do it? not "did you learn?"

Extra credit—unrelated to learning objectives

Penalties—late work equals automatic deduction

What this teaches:

"Grades measure compliance and work ethic, not learning."

In a Mistake Lab:

Grades measure mastery of learning objectives. Period.

Not:

How many times have you raised your hand

Whether you brought supplies

Whether you turned work in on time

How much effort do you put in

But:

Can you demonstrate understanding of the concept?

Can you apply the skill?

Have you mastered the objective?

The Solution: Learning-Focused Grading Systems

There are several alternatives to traditional grading.

I'll show you three main approaches:

Standards-Based Grading—most comprehensive shift

Specifications Grading—clear standards, pass/fail on tasks

Hybrid Approach—keeps letter grades but shifts philosophy

You don't have to implement all three. Pick the approach that fits your context.

Approach One: Standards-Based Grading (SBG)

Core idea:

Students are graded on mastery of specific standards, not on the average of all assignments.

How It Works:

Step 1: Identify Learning Standards

Instead of grading "Unit Test" as a single grade, you break it down into specific standards.

Example—Math:

Instead of: "Chapter 5 Test equals 85%."

Your grade:

Standard 5.1: Solving linear equations equals 3/4—Proficient

Standard 5.2: Graphing linear equations equals 4/4—Advanced

Standard 5.3: Writing equations from word problems equals 2/4—Developing

Step 2: Use a Proficiency Scale—Not Percentages

Instead of 0-100%, use a 1-4 scale:

4 equals Advanced—exceeds standard

3 equals Proficient—meets standard

2 equals Developing—approaching standard

1 equals Beginning—not yet demonstrating understanding

Step 3: Grade Current Mastery—Not Averages

Traditional grading:

Student gets 2/4 on Standard 5.3 on the first attempt.

After reteaching, the student gets 4/4 on the second attempt.

Average: (2 + 4) / 2 equals 3/4

Standards-based grading:

Student gets 2/4—first attempt equals diagnostic.

After reteaching, the student gets 4/4 on the second attempt.

Grade: 4/4—reflects current mastery, not average.

Step 4: Allow Reassessment

Students can retake assessments or do alternative demonstrations until they demonstrate mastery. This is built into the system, not an exception.

Step 5: Separate Practice from Performance

Practice work—homework, rough drafts, formative quizzes: Feedback only, no grade

Performance—tests, final drafts, demonstrations: Graded on standards

What This Looks Like in a Gradebook:

Traditional gradebook:

Assignment	Grade
Homework 1	85%
Homework 2	90%
Quiz 1	60%
Quiz 2	85%
Test	78%
Final Grade	80%

Standards-based gradebook:

Standard	Current Level
Standard 5.1: Solve linear equations	3/4—Proficient
Standard 5.2: Graph linear equations	4/4—Advanced
Standard 5.3: Write equations from word problems	3/4—Proficient
Overall	**3.3/4-Proficient**

Advantages of SBG:

Grades reflect learning, not averages

Students and parents know exactly what's mastered and what's not

Encourages revision and retakes—built into the system

Separates practice from performance—practice is safe

Promotes a growth mindset—you can improve your grade by learning more

Challenges of SBG:

Requires significant system change—new gradebook setup, new reporting

Parents may not understand it initially—requires clear communication

Takes time to set up—identifying standards, creating proficiency scales

May not be supported by your school's grading system—some systems require percentages

Approach Two: Specifications Grading

Core idea:

Students earn grades by completing work to a specified standard.

Pass/Fail on each assignment—meets standard or doesn't.

No partial credit. No averaging.

How It Works:

Step 1: Define Clear Specifications for Each Assignment

Example—Essay:

To pass, your essay must:

Have a clear thesis statement

Include at least 3 pieces of evidence

Cite sources correctly

Be 800-1000 words

Be free of major grammatical errors

If the essay meets all specs: Pass

If it doesn't: Not Yet—revise and resubmit

Step 2: Bundle Assignments Into Grade Levels

To earn a B in this class:

Complete 8/10 assignments to specification.

To earn an A:

Complete 10/10 assignments to specification, plus 1 extension project.

To earn a C:

Complete 6/10 assignments to specification.

Step 3: Allow Revisions

If a student doesn't meet specs on the first try:

They revise and resubmit—within a deadline.

No penalty for revising.

Step 4: Use Tokens for Flexibility

Give students "tokens"—2-3 per semester—they can use to:

Get an extension on a deadline

Revise an assignment after the deadline

Miss one assignment without penalty

This builds in grace for life circumstances—illness, emergencies—without making excuses the norm.

What This Looks Like:

Assignment tracker:

Assignment	Status	Revisions
Essay 1	✓ Pass	1 revision
Essay 2	✓ Pass	0 revisions
Essay 3	Not Yet	Revising
Essay 4	✓ Pass	2 revisions

Current standing: 3/4 passed—on track for B

Advantages of Specs Grading:

Crystal clear expectations—students know exactly what's required

No mystery grades—either meets specs or doesn't

Encourages revision—built into the system

No partial credit—eliminates negotiating over points

Simpler than SBG—easier to implement

Challenges of Specs Grading:

Requires extremely clear specifications—if specs are vague, students get frustrated

Can feel binary—pass/fail doesn't show gradations of quality

Requires revision infrastructure—need time built in for revisions

Approach Three: Hybrid Approach—Keep Letter Grades, Shift Philosophy

If your school requires traditional letter grades and you can't fully adopt SBG or Specs Grading:

You can still shift your philosophy within the traditional system.

How It Works:

Shift One: Separate Practice from Performance

In your gradebook, create two categories:

1. Practice—Formative—10-20% of grade

Homework

Rough drafts

Formative quizzes

In-class practice

Graded on: Completion/effort—did you try?, not correctness

2. Performance—Summative—80-90% of grade

Tests

Final drafts after revision

Projects

Demonstrations of mastery

Graded on: Mastery of content

Why this works:

Practice is low-stakes—mistakes won't tank your grade.

Performance is high-stakes—but you've had time to practice.

Shift Two: Weight Recent Grades More Heavily

Instead of: All quizzes count equally—Quiz 1 equals 40%, Quiz 5 equals 90%, average equals 65%

Try: Recent quizzes count more—Quiz 5 equals 90%, earlier quizzes count less or drop.

Why: Your grade reflects current understanding, not how long it took you to learn.

How to implement in a traditional gradebook:

Option A: Drop the lowest scores

"I drop your two lowest quiz grades."

Option B: Weight later assessments more

Quiz 1-3: 10% each

Quiz 4-5: 20% each

Shift Three: Allow Retakes/Revisions

Build revision into your grading policy:

"You can retake any test/quiz after:"

Completing test corrections

Attending reteaching session

Showing evidence of studying

New grade replaces old grade—or you average them, if required; but replacing is better

Shift Four: Give Feedback Before Grades

On major assignments:

Draft 1: Feedback only—no grade

Draft 2 after revision: Graded

Students submit drafts → receive feedback → revise → and then are graded.

Why this works:

Students focus on feedback, not grades, during Draft 1.

Final grade reflects work after improvement.

Shift Five: Eliminate or Minimize Grading for Compliance

Traditional systems include:

Participation points

Homework completion—regardless of learning

Extra credit—unrelated to learning

Late penalties—automatic deductions

Shift to:

Grade only learning.

Participation:

Don't grade it. Or if you must, define it clearly:

"Participation equals contributing to class discussions, helping peers, asking questions"—engagement in learning

Not: "Sitting quietly, raising hand X times"—compliance

Homework:

Grade on completion/effort—did you try?, not correctness.

Or: Don't grade homework. Use it diagnostically—who needs help?

Extra credit:

If you use it, make it learning-related.

Not: "Bring in tissues for extra credit."

But: "Demonstrate mastery of an additional standard for extra credit."

Late work:

Traditional: Automatic 10% deduction per day.

Better: Accept late work without penalty—within reason.

Why: We care about learning, not arbitrary deadlines.

If you must have consequences for late work:

"Late work accepted up to 1 week after due date. After that, we move on."

Consequence equals you miss the learning window, not a point deduction

Advantages of Hybrid Approach:

Works within traditional grading systems—no need for school-wide change

Easier to implement—small shifts, not full overhaul

Parents understand letter grades—familiar system

Challenges of Hybrid Approach:

Still uses percentages—which can feel arbitrary

Not as transparent as SBG—students don't know exactly what they've mastered

Requires discipline—to weigh formative lightly and allow revisions consistently

Grading Policies That Support Mistake Literacy

Regardless of which system you use, these policies are essential:

Policy One: Retakes/Revisions Allowed

State clearly: "You can retake any assessment. Your grade reflects what you know now, not how many tries it took."

How to manage it:

Require:

Test corrections—analyze mistakes first

Reteaching session—come to office hours or tutoring

Evidence of additional study/practice

Then: Allow retake—alternate version of test

Concern: "Students won't study the first time if they can retake."

Response:

True. Some won't.

But:

They'll learn eventually—through retakes

First attempt equals diagnostic—shows what they need to learn

This mirrors real life—you can learn from failures and try again

The goal is learning, not one-shot performance.

Policy Two: Feedback Before Grades—When Possible

On major assignments:

Submit draft → receive feedback → revise → submit final—graded

On tests/quizzes:

Option A: Ungraded practice quiz → feedback → graded quiz

Option B: Graded quiz → feedback → retake option

Policy Three: Late Work Accepted—With Boundaries

Instead of: "Late work equals 10% off per day."

Try:

"I accept late work up to [1 week/end of unit/end of semester]. After that, the learning window has closed, and we've moved on."

Rationale:

We care about learning, not arbitrary deadlines.

But: There are boundaries—you can't turn in work from September in May.

Concern: "Students will procrastinate."

Response:

Some will.

But:

Arbitrary deadlines don't teach time management—real consequences do—missing the learning window is a real consequence.

Punishing late work with grade deductions conflates learning with compliance.

Better approach:

Teach time management explicitly. Build in checkpoints. Support students who struggle with executive function.

But don't lower grades for learning because of late submission.

Policy Four: Practice Does Not Equal Performance

Be explicit:

"In this class, we have two types of work:"

1. Practice—Formative:

Homework

Rough drafts

Practice quizzes

In-class work

Graded on: Completion/effort—or not graded at all, just feedback

Purpose: Learning, experimenting, making mistakes

2. Performance—Summative:

Tests

Final drafts

Projects

Demonstrations

Graded on: Mastery

Purpose: Showing what you've learned

Make this distinction clear from Day 1.

Policy Five: Grades Reflect Learning, Not Compliance

State clearly:

"Your grade reflects what you've learned, not:"

How many times have you raised your hand

Whether you brought supplies

Whether you turned work in on time

How much effort do you put in

Your grade reflects:

Mastery of learning objectives

Demonstration of skills

Evidence of understanding

Concern: "But effort matters!"

Response:

Yes, effort matters for learning.

But grades should reflect learning outcomes, not effort.

Otherwise: Student A works incredibly hard, doesn't master the content → gets a good grade for effort → is unprepared for the next level.

Student B doesn't work hard, masters the content easily → gets a bad grade for low effort → is bored and disengaged.

Better: Grade learning. Address effort separately—in comments, conferences, etc.

How to Communicate Your Grading System

Parents and students will have questions.

Especially if your system is different from traditional grading.

Here's how to communicate it:

To Students—Day 1:

"Let me explain how grading works in this class."

"In many classes, every assignment is graded, and mistakes lower your grade. That makes it risky to try new things or make mistakes."

"In this class, we separate practice from performance."

Practice equals safe to make mistakes—feedback only, or graded on effort

Performance equals demonstrations of what you've learned—graded on mastery

"You can also retake tests and revise work. Your grade reflects what you know now, not how many tries it took." "Questions?"

To Parents—Back-to-School Night/Email:

Sample email/letter:

Subject: How Grading Works in [Your Class]

Dear Families,

I want to explain my grading philosophy, so you understand how your student's grade is determined.

In this class, grades reflect learning, not compliance or averages.

Here's how it works:

1. Practice vs. Performance

Not all work is graded the same way: Practice work—homework, rough drafts, formative quizzes—is graded on completion/effort or given feedback only. This is where students experiment and make mistakes. Performance work—tests, final drafts, projects—is graded on mastery of learning objectives.

2. Revisions and Retakes

Students can revise major assignments and retake assessments after receiving feedback and engaging in additional learning. Final grades reflect current understanding, not averages of all attempts.

3. Late Work

I accept late work [within reason/up to one week/until the end of the unit] because learning is more important than arbitrary deadlines. However, there are boundaries—work cannot be turned in after [specified time].

4. What Grades Measure

Grades measure mastery of learning objectives, not:

Participation points

Effort

Timeliness

These things matter for learning, but grades specifically reflect what your student has learned.

Why This Approach?

Research shows that when students can learn from mistakes without permanent grade penalties, they:

Learn more deeply

Take more intellectual risks

Develop growth mindsets

Focus on learning, not just grades

I'm happy to answer questions. Please don't hesitate to reach out.

Sincerely,

[Your Name]

When Parents Push Back:

Common concerns and how to respond:

Concern One: "This doesn't prepare them for the real world. In the real world, you don't get retakes."

Response:

"Actually, the real world is full of revisions and iterations." Writers revise drafts—multiple times

Engineers redesign prototypes—after testing

Scientists revise hypotheses—based on data

Professionals learn from failures and try again

"What doesn't happen in the real world: one-shot, high-stakes performances with no chance to improve."

"This system teaches resilience, revision, and growth—skills they'll need."

Concern Two: "Won't students slack off if they can retake?"

Response:

"Some might initially. But:"

First attempt is diagnostic—it shows what they need to learn

Retakes require work—test corrections, reteaching sessions, and additional studying

Students who retake are actually engaging more with learning, not less

"And honestly: If a student didn't master content the first time, do we want them to move on without understanding? Or do we want them to learn it?"

"Our goal is mastery, not speed."

Concern Three: "My child got a bad grade on a test. Shouldn't that count?"

Response:

"The test showed what your child didn't know yet. That's valuable information."

"They can retake it after additional learning. The retake grade will replace the original, because we care about what they know now, not what they didn't know before."

"Would you rather your child's grade reflect temporary confusion, or their actual understanding after learning?"

Concern Four: "Colleges want to see grades. How will this work on a transcript?"

Response:

"Your child will still receive letter grades [or GPA, depending on your system]. But those grades will reflect actual learning, not averages that include early mistakes."

"Colleges want students who can think, learn, and grow—not students who memorize for tests and forget everything."

"Our system produces deeper learning, which better prepares students for college."

Implementing a New Grading System: Step-by-Step

Don't try to overhaul everything at once.

Here's a gradual implementation plan:

Year 1: Start Small

Pick one shift:

Separate practice—formative—from performance—summative—in your gradebook

Allow one retake per quarter

Give feedback before grades on one major assignment per unit

Master that shift. Build confidence.

Year 2: Expand

Add another shift:

Weight recent assessments more heavily—or drop the lowest scores

Accept late work without penalty—within boundaries

Eliminate grading homework for correctness—completion/effort only

Year 3: Full Implementation

By Year 3, you might be ready for:

Full standards-based grading

Or full specifications grading

Or a robust hybrid system with all the shifts integrated

The key:

Gradual change. Don't overwhelm yourself or your students.

Real Teacher Stories

Story One: Ms. Garcia—Standards-Based Grading in High School Math

Ms. Garcia taught Algebra 1.

For years, she used traditional grading:

Homework equals 20%

Quizzes equals 30%

Tests equals 50%

She noticed:

Students who struggled early couldn't recover—averages haunted them

Students focused on points, not learning—"Is this extra credit?"

Students didn't revise or reflect—once graded, they moved on

Year 5, she switched to standards-based grading:

Her system:

Identified 8 standards per semester

Graded each standard on a 1-4 scale

Allowed reassessment at any time

Practice work equals feedback only

Results:

Students retook assessments—they cared about mastery, not just passing

Grades reflected learning—a student who struggled early but mastered content by the end of the semester got high grades

Students asked better questions—"I don't understand Standard 3.2. Can you reteach it?"—rather than "How many points is this worth?"

Test scores improved—students actually learned the content instead of memorizing and forgetting.

Ms. Garcia reflected:

"The first semester was rocky. Students were confused. Parents had questions. But by the second semester, students got it. They understood: grades reflect learning. And they started actually learning."

Story Two: Mr. Johnson—Specifications Grading in English

Mr. Johnson taught 11th-grade English. He was drowning in grading: 120 essays to grade. Each essay took 20-30 minutes, trying to justify every point deduction.

Students argued about points—"Why did I get an 87 instead of 90?"

He switched to specifications grading:

His system:

Each essay had clear specifications—5-7 criteria

Pass/Fail—meets all specs equals Pass, doesn't equal Revise

Students could revise until they passed

Results:

Grading took less time—check specs, write feedback, mark Pass or Revise

No more point negotiations—either meets specs or doesn't

Students revised—50% of students revised at least once; previously, almost no one revised

Quality improved—students worked until they met the standard, not just "good enough for a B."

Mr. Johnson reflected:

"I was skeptical. But this has been the best change I've made in 15 years of teaching. Students care about quality now, not points. And I'm not drowning in grading."

Story Three: Ms. Patel—Hybrid Approach in Middle School Science

Ms. Patel's school required traditional letter grades.

She couldn't do full SBG or Specs Grading.

But she made shifts within the traditional system:

Her shifts:

Practice equals 10% of the grade—completion only

Tests equals 90% of the grade—mastery

Retakes allowed—after test corrections plus reteaching. Feedback on lab reports before grading—draft → feedback → final

Results:

Students took risks in labs—practice was low-stakes

Students retook tests—grades improved

Students used feedback—lab reports improved from draft to final

Ms. Patel reflected:

"I couldn't change the whole system. But I could change my philosophy within it. And it made a huge difference."

The Bottom Line

Traditional grading is incompatible with mistake literacy.

You cannot have both.

To build a Mistake Lab, you must shift your grading system to:

Reflect current mastery—not averages

Separate practice from performance—practice is safe

Allow revisions/retakes—learning takes time

Give feedback before grades—focus on improvement

Measure learning, not compliance—grades equal mastery

Three approaches:

1. Standards-Based Grading—most comprehensive
2. Specifications Grading—clear standards, pass/fail
3. Hybrid Approach—shifts within the traditional system.

Pick one. Start small. Build gradually. Your grading system will either support or sabotage your Mistake Lab. Choose wisely.

REFLECTION QUESTIONS

Personal Reflection:

1. How does your current grading system support or undermine mistake literacy?
2. What percentage of your grade is practice vs. performance? Is practice high-stakes or low-stakes?
3. Do your grades reflect current mastery or averages? Can students recover from early mistakes?
4. Do you allow revisions/retakes? Why or why not?
5. What would you need to change to make your grading system more learning-focused?

Gradebook Audit:

Look at your current gradebook. Ask:

How many assignments are graded? Could some be feedback-only?

Do early low grades drag down students' final grades? Could you weigh recent work more heavily?

Do students revise work? Could you build revision into assignments?

Do grades reflect learning or compliance? Are you grading participation, timeliness, and effort instead of mastery?

Action Planning:

This semester/year, try one shift:

Separate practice from performance—practice equals 10-20%, performance equals 80-90%

Allow one retake per unit—after test corrections, plus reteaching

Give feedback before grades on one major assignment

Drop the lowest quiz/test scores—or weight recent assessments more

Accept late work without a grade penalty—within boundaries

Stop grading homework for correctness—completion/effort only

Research SBG or Specs Grading—plan for bigger shift next year

Further Exploration

Read:

- *Grading for Equity* by Joe Feldman—a comprehensive guide to equitable grading
- *Specifications Grading* by Linda Nilson—how to implement specs grading
- *Standards-Based Learning in Action* by Tom Schimmer—SBG implementation
- *Fair Isn't Always Equal* by Rick Wormeli—grading and differentiation

Watch:

- Rick Wormeli: "Redos, Retakes, and Do-Overs"—YouTube
- Joe Feldman talks on grading for equity

Listen:

- Cult of Pedagogy podcast episodes on alternative grading

You've revolutionized grading.

Practice is safe. Performance reflects current mastery. Revisions are expected.

Next: Equity in the Lab

Who gets to experiment safely? How do we ensure all students have access to mistake literacy?

That's Chapter 11—the final chapter of Part 2.

Ready?

CHAPTER 11

EQUITY IN THE LAB—WHO GETS TO EXPERIMENT SAFELY?

Ensuring All Students Have Access to Mistake Literacy

Two students. Same classroom. Different experiences.

Student A: Emma—White, Middle-Class, No Learning Disabilities

Week 1:

Emma makes a mistake in class. Gives a wrong answer.

Teacher responds: "Interesting thinking. What made you say that?"

Peers respond: Curious. Supportive.

Emma thinks: "It's safe to be wrong here. I can take risks."

Week 3:

Emma struggles with a concept. Asks for help.

Teacher responds: "Great question. Let's work through this together."

Emma gets extra support. Improves. Succeeds.

End of semester:

Emma has taken risks, made mistakes, and learned from them.

Her experience of the Mistake Lab: Safe, supportive, effective.

Student B: Jamal—Black Male, Low-Income, Twice-Exceptional

Week 1:

Jamal makes a mistake in class. Gives a wrong answer.

Teacher responds: "Interesting thinking. What made you say that?"

But Jamal hears it differently.

Jamal thinks: "She's asking because she's surprised I don't know. She expects less from me. Everyone's looking at me. I'm confirming the stereotype."

He feels: Stereotype threat. Not curiosity. Threat.

Week 3:

Jamal struggles with a concept. He wants to ask for help.

But he thinks: "If I ask, they'll think I'm not smart enough to be in this class. I'm the only Black student here. I can't confirm stereotypes."

He doesn't ask. He falls further behind.

End of semester:

Jamal has not taken risks. He's hidden struggles. He's disengaged.

His experience of the Mistake Lab: Threatening, not safe.

The Problem: Mistake Literacy Is Not Equally Accessible

Same teacher. Same classroom. Same "mistake-literate" culture.

Different experiences.

Why?

Because the perfectionist culture doesn't harm all students equally.

And mistake literacy, if not designed with equity in mind, doesn't help all students equally.

This chapter addresses:

How the culture of perfectionism disproportionately harms marginalized students

Why "colorblind" or "neutral" approaches to mistake literacy don't work

How to build an equity-centered Mistake Lab where all students can experiment safely

Part A: Who Perfectionism Culture Harms Most

Perfectionism culture is harmful to everyone.

But it's most harmful to:

Students of color—especially in majority-white spaces

Students with learning disabilities

Students from low-income backgrounds

English learners-Students at the intersection of multiple marginalized identities. Why?

Harm One: Stereotype Threat—Students of Color

Research: Claude Steele

Stereotype threat: When you're aware of a negative stereotype about your group, and you fear confirming it, your performance drops.

Example:

Black student in a majority-white AP class.

Negative stereotype: "Black students aren't as academically capable."

When taking a test—especially if told it's measuring intelligence:

The student is aware of the stereotype.

They feel pressure: "If I fail, I confirm the stereotype."

Result:

Anxiety increases

Cognitive load increases—the brain is managing anxiety and solving problems

Performance drops

This happens with mistakes too:

When a Black student makes a mistake in front of the class:

They might think:

"Everyone's judging me."

"They think I don't belong here."

"I'm confirming stereotypes."

Even if the teacher and peers respond supportively, the student experiences a sense of threat.

Translation for Mistake Labs:

If you tell students "mistakes are okay" but don't address stereotype threat:

Students of color may still feel unsafe making mistakes publicly.

Why?

Because mistakes feel like they have higher stakes:

"If I'm wrong, people will think all students like me are not capable."

"I can't afford to mess up. I'm representing my whole group." This is exhausting. And it blocks learning.

Harm Two: "Deficits" Framing—Students with Learning Disabilities

Students with learning disabilities have been told they're "broken" their whole lives.

IEP language:

"Student struggles with..."

"Student is below grade level in..."

"Areas of weakness include..."

Message absorbed: "I'm deficient. I'm not capable. There's something wrong with me."

When these students make mistakes:

They think:

"See, I can't do this. It's because of my disability."

"This proves I'm not smart enough."

"Other students don't struggle like this."

Even in a Mistake Lab that says "mistakes are okay":

Students with disabilities may internalize:

"Mistakes are okay for other students. But my mistakes are proof of my deficits."

Translation for Mistake Labs:

Telling students with disabilities "mistakes are learning opportunities" isn't enough.

You need to reframe explicitly:

"Your brain works differently. That's not wrong—it's just different. Everyone's brain has strengths and areas that need support. Mistakes don't mean you're incapable. They mean you're learning."

Harm Three: Scarcity Plus Instability—Students from Poverty

Students from low-income backgrounds often experience:

Scarcity—not enough resources, time, stability

Unpredictability—housing instability, food insecurity, family stress

Research—Ruby Payne, Zaretta Hammond:

Chronic stress from poverty affects the brain:

Amygdala—threat detection—is hyperactive

Prefrontal cortex—higher-order thinking—is suppressed

Students are in survival mode

When these students make mistakes:

If they've experienced mistakes at home as having serious consequences—punishment, instability, loss—mistakes at school feel threatening.

Even if the teacher says "mistakes are okay":

The student's nervous system might not believe it.

Brain thinks: "Mistakes equal danger. Protect yourself."

Translation for Mistake Labs:

Students from poverty need:

Predictability—routines, clear expectations

Stability—consistent responses to mistakes

Explicit safety—"You are safe here. Mistakes won't hurt you here."

Not just permission to fail. Active reassurance that failure is safe.

Harm Four: Language Plus Cultural Barriers—English Learners

English learners make mistakes in two domains:

Content—like all students

Language—pronunciation, grammar, vocabulary

Perfectionism culture conflates these:

"You got the answer wrong because your English isn't good enough."

Message absorbed: "I can't succeed until I master English perfectly."

When EL students make mistakes:

They might think:

"Is this a language mistake or a content mistake?"

"People will judge my English."

"I should stay quiet until I can say it perfectly."

Translation for Mistake Labs:

You need to separate content mastery from language proficiency. "Your thinking is strong. Let's work on expressing it in English. Language mistakes are part of learning a new language—they're expected."

And provide language scaffolds: Sentence stems.

Word banks

Option to respond in the home language first, then translate

Harm Five: Intersectionality—Multiple Marginalized Identities

Students who hold multiple marginalized identities experience compounded harm.

Example:

Black female student with a learning disability from a low-income background.

She experiences: Stereotype threat—race plus gender

Deficit framing—learning disability

Scarcity/instability—poverty

Each layer adds pressure:

"I can't make mistakes because..."

"...people already doubt my intelligence because I'm Black and female."

"...people think my disability means I can't learn."

"...I can't afford to fail this class."

Translation for Mistake Labs:

You must design for the students with the most barriers.

If mistake literacy works for them, it works for everyone.

Part B: Why "Colorblind"/"Neutral" Approaches Don't Work

Some teachers think:

"I treat all students the same. I don't see color. Mistakes are okay for everyone in my class." This doesn't work.

Why?

Problem One: "Same" Does Not Equal "Equitable"

Treating everyone the same assumes everyone starts from the same place.

They don't.

Example:

Two students make the same mistake.

Student A—white, middle-class:

No stereotype threat

No deficit framing

Stable home environment

Confident academic identity

Experiences the mistake as: Low-stakes. A learning opportunity.

Student B—Black, low-income:

Stereotype threat

Possible history of being labeled "behind." Unstable home environment

Fragile academic identity

Experiences the mistake as: High-stakes. Potentially confirming stereotypes.

"Treating them the same" means: Responding the same way to both.

But they need different support:

Student A: Standard feedback, encouragement.

Student B: Plus explicit reassurance—"This mistake doesn't define you. You're capable."

Plus acknowledgment of barriers—"I know you're juggling a lot. How can I support you?"

Plus extra scaffolding—if needed due to gaps in prior learning

Equity does not equal sameness.

Equity equals giving each student what they need to succeed.

Problem Two: "Colorblind" Ignores Real Barriers

Saying "I don't see color" means: "I don't see the barriers students of color face."

Those barriers are real:

Stereotype threat

Microaggressions

Lower expectations from other teachers

Less access to resources

Systemic racism

Ignoring them doesn't make them go away.

Better approach:

"I see you. I see the barriers you face. And I'm going to actively work to remove them."

Problem Three: "Neutral" Language Can Still Harm

Even well-meaning, "neutral" language can trigger marginalized students.

Example:

The teacher says to the whole class, "You need to try harder."

Intent: Encourage effort.

White student hears: "I should put in more effort."

A Black student might hear: "She thinks I'm lazy. That's the stereotype. She has low expectations of me."

Why the difference?

Because Black students have a history of being labeled "lazy" or "not trying hard enough" as a way to dismiss systemic barriers.

The "neutral" phrase isn't neutral in context.

Better approach:

Be specific. Avoid language that can be interpreted as confirming stereotypes.

Instead of: "You need to try harder."

Try: "I see you're working hard. Let's figure out what's getting in the way. What specific support do you need?"

Part C: Equity-Centered Practices for Mistake Labs

Here's how to design your Mistake Lab so all students—especially marginalized students—can experiment safely.

Practice One: Explicitly Name and Reduce Stereotype Threat

Don't pretend stereotype threat doesn't exist.

Address it.

How:

Step 1: Acknowledge It—Without Reinforcing It

Don't say: "Some of you might feel stereotype threat because of your race."

This reinforces the stereotype.

Instead, say:

"In many schools, some students have been told—explicitly or implicitly—that they don't belong in rigorous classes. That's wrong. You all belong here. You're all capable. And I'm going to support you."

Step 2: Emphasize Growth—Not Innate Ability

Research—Aronson, Steele:

When you emphasize that intelligence is growable, rather than fixed, stereotype threat decreases.

How:

"Intelligence isn't fixed. Your brain grows when you work hard and learn from mistakes. Everyone in this room can get smarter."

This reduces stereotype threat because:

It shifts focus from "Am I smart?"—identity—to "Am I growing?"—effort.

Step 3: Provide Critical Feedback with High Expectations Plus High Support

Research—Geoffrey Cohen:

"Wise feedback" reduces stereotype threat.

Wise feedback structure:

"I'm giving you this feedback because I have high expectations for you, and I know you can meet them. Here's specifically what you need to work on. I'm going to support you."

Example: "This essay doesn't meet the standard yet. But I'm giving you this feedback because I believe you can write at a high level. Here's what needs to improve: [specific feedback]. Let's work on this together."

Why this works:

It signals:

High expectations—I believe in you

Support—I'll help you

Growth is possible—you can meet the standard

This reduces fear that feedback equals "You don't belong here."

Step 4: Create Affinity Spaces—If Possible

Affinity spaces: Safe spaces for students who share an identity to connect, support each other, and discuss shared experiences.

Example:

Students of color affinity group

LGBTQ+ affinity group

EL students affinity group

Why this helps:

Students can:

Share experiences of navigating predominantly white spaces

Support each other

Build solidarity

Reduce isolation

In these spaces, students can process:

"I felt stereotype threat today when..."

And realize: "I'm not the only one."

If you can't create formal affinity spaces:

At minimum:

Don't isolate students—ensure they're not the only student of color in a class

Connect students to mentors who share their identity

Acknowledge their experiences

Practice Two: Reframe "Deficits" as "Developing Skills"—Students with Disabilities

Stop using deficit language.

Instead of:

"Student struggles with reading comprehension."

"Student is below grade level in math."

"Areas of weakness include..."

Try:

"Student is developing reading comprehension skills."

"Student is working toward grade-level proficiency in math."

"Areas of growth include..."

Why this matters:

Words shape identity.

"Struggling" equals identity—I am a struggling reader

"Developing" equals process—I'm becoming a better reader

In your Mistake Lab:

When a student with a disability makes a mistake:

Don't say: "You're struggling with this because of your disability."

Instead: "Your brain works differently. That means some strategies that work for other students might not work for you. Let's find strategies that do work for your brain." Reframe disability as difference, not deficit.

Practice Three: Provide Trauma-Informed Support—Students from Poverty/Unstable Homes

Students who've experienced trauma need explicit safety cues.

How:

Predictable Routines

Students from chaotic home environments need predictability at school.

Example:

Same warm-up every day—Monday

Same lesson structure—I do, we do, you do

Same response to mistakes—always curious, never punitive

Why this helps:

When routines are predictable, students can relax. Their amygdala—threat detection—calms down.

Calm, Consistent Responses to Mistakes

Never:

Yell

Show visible frustration

Give sudden, unexpected consequences

These trigger students with trauma.

Their brain thinks: "Danger. Fight/flight/freeze."

Always:

Calm tone

Consistent response—every time, same curiosity

Clear expectations—students know what will happen

Why this helps:

Consistency equals safety. Students learn: "Mistakes won't result in unpredictable bad things happening."

Explicit Statements of Safety

Don't assume students feel safe.

Say it explicitly:

"You are safe here."

"Mistakes will not hurt you in this class."

"I will not yell at you or punish you for making mistakes."

Repeat regularly.

Why this helps:

Students with trauma need explicit reassurance, not just implied safety.

Practice Four: Separate Language from Content—English Learners

English learners are learning two things:

Content—math, science, history

Language—English

Don't conflate them.

How:

Provide Language Scaffolds

Sentence stems:

"I think... because..."

"I notice... I wonder..."

"This reminds me of..."

Word banks—key vocabulary with definitions. Visuals—diagrams, images to support understanding

Allow Home Language Use—When Appropriate

Example:

"If you're stuck explaining something in English, you can explain it in [home language] first. Then we'll work on translating it together."

Why this helps:

Separates content mastery from language proficiency. A student might know the concept but struggle to express it in English.

Give Feedback on Content Separately from Language

When grading writing:

Feedback on content: "Your argument is strong. You provided solid evidence."

Feedback on language: "Let's work on grammar. Here are some patterns I notice..."

Grade content, not language—or grade them separately.

Why this helps:

Student knows: "My thinking is valued, even if my English isn't perfect yet."

Practice Five: Be Aware of Scrutiny Bias—Marginalized Students Are Watched More Closely

Scrutiny bias: Marginalized students—especially Black students—are monitored more closely and disciplined more harshly for the same behaviors as white students.

Research:

Black students are suspended at 3 times the rate of white students—for the same infractions. Teachers call on Black students less often.

Teachers interpret the same behavior differently based on race—Black student equals "defiant," white student equals "spirited."

In Mistake Labs:

Be aware:

Are you calling on all students equally?

Are you responding to mistakes the same way, regardless of students' identities?

Are you quicker to judge certain students' mistakes as "not trying" versus "still learning"? Check yourself.

Track:

Who you call on—keep a tally

Who you give feedback to—are you giving rich feedback to all students?

Whose mistakes you celebrate versus correct quickly

Practice Six: Model Vulnerability from Your Position of Privilege—If Applicable

If you hold privilege—white, cisgender, able-bodied, native English speaker, etc.: Use your privilege to model vulnerability.

Why this matters:

When a person with privilege admits mistakes, it signals:

"Even people with societal advantages make mistakes. Mistakes aren't about your identity or worth."

Example:

White teacher in a majority-white school with a few students of color:

"I made a mistake yesterday. I assumed something about a student's background, and I was wrong. I apologized to them. I'm learning to check my assumptions. This is part of my growth."

These models:

Mistakes happen to people with privilege, too

Admitting mistakes is courageous

Growth is ongoing—even for adults, even for people with privilege

Practice Seven: Recruit and Retain Diverse Educators

Students need to see themselves reflected in their teachers.

Research:

Students of color have better outcomes when they have teachers who share their racial/ethnic background. LGBTQ+ students benefit from LGBTQ+ teachers/mentors.

Students with disabilities benefit from teachers with disabilities.

Why?

Representation signals: "People like me belong here. People like me succeed here."

If you're a school leader:

Recruit diverse teachers.

Support them—don't ask them to carry the burden of "representing" their group or educating staff on diversity.

Retain them—create inclusive environments where they want to stay.

If you're a teacher:

Connect students to mentors who share their identities—even if they're not at your school —such as community mentors, virtual mentors, etc.

Practice Eight: Address Microaggressions Immediately

Microaggressions: Small, everyday slights—often unintentional—that communicate bias.

Examples:

"You're so articulate!"—to a Black student, implies surprise that they speak well.

"Where are you really from?"—to an Asian American student, implies they're not American

"You don't look autistic."—to a student with autism; implies there's a "look."

These happen in mistake-literate classrooms too.

When you witness a microaggression:

Address it.

Don't ignore it—ignoring signals: "This is acceptable."

How to address:

In the moment—if appropriate:

"Wait. Let's pause. That comment might have been unintentional, but it could be hurtful. Here's why..."

Or privately—if addressing publicly would embarrass the student who said it:

"I noticed you said [comment]. Can we talk about why that might be hurtful?"

Why this matters:

If students experience microaggressions without intervention:

They learn: "This space isn't actually safe for me."

Even if you're saying, "mistakes are okay."

Part D: Assessing Equity in Your Mistake Lab

How do you know if your Mistake Lab is equitable?

Ask these questions:

Question One: Who Participates?

Look at your classroom data: Who volunteers to answer questions?

Who shares mistakes publicly?

Who asks for help?

Who takes intellectual risks?

If it's mostly white, middle-class, able-bodied students:

Your Mistake Lab isn't equitable yet.

Marginalized students aren't experiencing it as safe.

Question Two: Who Succeeds?

Look at grades/outcomes:

Are there patterns by race, income, language, and disability status?

Do students from marginalized groups have lower grades?

Are they disproportionately "not yet" meeting standards?

If yes:

Something in your system is creating barriers.

Could be:

Grading policies—traditional grading harms marginalized students more

Lack of scaffolds

Unaddressed stereotype threat

Implicit bias in how you give feedback

Investigate. Adjust.

Question Three: Who Feels Safe?

Give students an anonymous survey:

"Do you feel safe making mistakes in this class?"

"Do you feel like you belong here?"

"Do you feel like the teacher believes in you?"

Disaggregate responses by demographic groups.

If students of color, EL students, and students with disabilities report feeling less safe:

Your Mistake Lab has equity gaps.

Question Four: Whose Mistakes Are Celebrated?

Reflect:

Whose mistakes do you highlight as "learning opportunities"?

Whose mistakes do you quietly correct?

Are you celebrating mistakes from students with privilege more than mistakes from marginalized students?

Implicit bias shows up here. Check yourself.

Real Teacher Story: Ms. Johnson's Equity Journey

Ms. Johnson, a white teacher, taught 9th-grade English in a diverse urban school.

70% students are of color. 40% EL students. 30% students with IEPs.

Year 1 of her Mistake Lab:

She implemented everything: Taught mistakes equals data

Modeled vulnerability

Built psychological safety

Changed grading to SBG

But after one semester, she noticed: White students were thriving—taking risks, revising work, engaging

Students of color were quiet—not volunteering, not sharing mistakes

EL students were disengaged

Students with disabilities were falling behind

She thought: "I'm treating everyone the same. Why isn't this working for everyone?"

Then she read about stereotype threat and equity-centered teaching.

She realized: "I need to do more than just say 'mistakes are okay.' I need to dismantle barriers actively."

Year 2 shifts:

1. She explicitly addressed stereotype threat:

"Some of you have been told you don't belong in rigorous classes. That's wrong. You belong here. I believe in your intelligence. And I'm going to support you."

2. She gave "wise feedback" to students of color:

Instead of just: "This needs revision."

She said: "I'm giving you this feedback because I have high standards for you and I know you can meet them. Here's what to revise. Let's work on this together."

3. She provided language scaffolds for EL students:

Sentence stems

Word banks

Option to write in home language first, then translate

4. She reframed disability:

Instead of: "You're struggling because of your disability."

She said, "Your brain works differently. Let's find strategies that work for you."

5. She tracked who she called on:

Realized she was calling on white students more.

Adjusted: Used equity sticks—popsicle sticks with names to ensure everyone gets called on.

Results—Year 2:

Students of color started volunteering more

EL students engaged—language scaffolds helped

Students with disabilities showed growth—reframing plus support

Achievement gaps narrowed

Ms. Johnson reflected:

"Year 1, I thought equity meant treating everyone the same. In Year 2, I learned equity means giving each student what they need. That's harder. But it works."

The Bottom Line

Mistake literacy isn't equally accessible to all students.

Marginalized students face additional barriers:

Stereotype threat—students of color

Deficit framing—students with disabilities

Trauma/instability—students from poverty

Language barriers—EL students

"Colorblind" or "neutral" approaches don't work.

You must actively design for equity:

Name and reduce stereotype threat

Reframe deficits as developing skills

Provide trauma-informed support—predictability, calm consistency, explicit safety

Separate language from content—EL students

Be aware of scrutiny bias—monitor your own patterns

Model vulnerability from privilege—if applicable

Recruit diverse educators

Address microaggressions immediately

Equity-centered Mistake Labs ensure:

All students—not just privileged students—can experiment, fail, learn, and grow.

REFLECTION QUESTIONS

Personal Reflection:

1. What identities do you hold? Race, class, ability, language, etc. How might your privilege or marginalization affect how you experience/teach mistake literacy?
2. Who participates most in your classroom? Who volunteers, shares mistakes, and asks for help? Are there patterns by race, class, ability, language?
3. Have you witnessed stereotype threat in your classroom? What did it look like?
4. Do you use deficit language when talking about students with disabilities or students who are "behind"? How could you reframe?

Equity Audit:

Collect data on:

Participation: Who volunteers? Who shares mistakes publicly?

Outcomes: Are there achievement gaps by race, income, disability, or language?

Safety: Do all students feel equally safe? Anonymous survey

Your patterns: Who do you call on? Who do you give rich feedback to?

What patterns do you notice?

Action Planning:

This week/month, try one equity-centered practice:

Explicitly address stereotype threat—growth mindset message plus "you belong here."

Give "wise feedback" to a marginalized student—high expectations plus high support.

Reframe deficit language—change IEP language from "struggles with" to "developing skills in."

Provide predictable routines—for students with trauma

Add language scaffolds—sentence stems, word banks for EL students

Track who you call on—equity sticks, tally marks

Address one microaggression—don't let it slide

Survey students on safety—disaggregate by demographics

Further Exploration

Read:

- *Whistling Vivaldi* by Claude Steele—stereotype threat
- *Culturally Responsive Teaching and the Brain* by Zaretta Hammond—equity plus neuroscience
- *For White Folks Who Teach in the Hood* by Christopher Emdin—equity-centered teaching
- *Grading for Equity* by Joe Feldman—equitable grading practices
- *The Danger of a Single Story* by Chimamanda Ngozi Adichie—stereotypes plus identity

Watch:

- Claude Steele's talks on stereotype threat
- Zaretta Hammond's talks on culturally responsive teaching

Listen:

- "Code Switch" podcast—race, identity, culture
- "Cult of Pedagogy" episodes on equity

PART 2 RECAP

You've completed Part 2. Here's what you've built:

Chapter 7: The First Week of School

Week 1 sets the tone for the entire year

5-day framework: culture first, content second

Day 1: Mistakes equal data lesson, plus model vulnerability, plus co-create norms

Days 2-5: Practice peer responses, introduce lab notebooks, teach mistake analysis protocol, run experiments

Chapter 8: Teacher as Co-Researcher

Shift from sage on stage to lead scientist

7 practices: think aloud, say "I don't know," ask questions, wonder out loud, learn publicly, invite students to teach, design experiments

Students learn from what you model, not just what you teach

Chapter 9: Peer Culture—Lab Partners

Psychological safety requires peer norms, not just teacher modeling

5 pillars: peer norms, structured collaboration, feedback skills, celebrate peer support, make collaboration routine

Teach students how to respond to each other's mistakes with curiosity

Chapter 10: The Grading Revolution

Traditional grading is incompatible with mistake literacy

3 approaches: Standards-Based Grading, Specifications Grading, Hybrid

Core principles: grade current mastery, not averages, separate practice from performance, allow revisions, feedback before grades, measure learning, not compliance

Chapter 11: Equity in the Lab

Mistake literacy isn't equally accessible to all students

Marginalized students face additional barriers: stereotype threat, deficit framing, trauma, and language barriers. Equity-centered practices: address stereotype threat, reframe deficits, trauma-informed support, language scaffolds, and address microaggressions. You've built the lab culture. Students know how to learn from mistakes. Peers support each other. Grading supports growth. Equity is centered.

Next: Part 3—Lab Protocols

The systematic tools students use to analyze their own mistakes.

Ready to continue?

PART 3

LAB PROTOCOLS

Teaching Students to Analyze and Learn From Their Own Mistakes

You've built the foundation—Part 1—and the culture—Part 2.

Now it's time to give students the tools to become independent mistake analysts.

Part 3 is about protocols:

Systematic, repeatable processes students use to:

Analyze their mistakes

Extract learning

Revise their work

Develop metacognition. Build agency

In Part 3, you'll learn:

Chapter 12: The Mistake Analysis Protocol—The Core Tool

Chapter 13: Error Pattern Recognition—Finding Trends

Chapter 14: Revision as Learning—Not Just "Fixing"

Chapter 15: Student-Led Conferences—Owning Your Learning

Chapter 16: Student Voice and Choice—Agency in the Lab

Think of this as equipping students with scientific instruments:

Chapter 12 equals the microscope—examining individual mistakes closely

Chapter 13 equals the data tracker—identifying patterns across multiple mistakes

Chapter 14 equals the iteration cycle—using data to improve experiments

Chapter 15 equals the lab report presentation—communicating findings

Chapter 16 equals designing your own experiments—student agency

By the end of Part 3, students will:

Analyze their own mistakes systematically—without you. Identify patterns in their errors—metacognition. Revise their work strategically—targeted improvement. Articulate their learning—to you, peers, parents

Take ownership of their learning—agency. Let's start with the core tool: The Mistake Analysis Protocol.

CHAPTER 12

THE MISTAKE ANALYSIS PROTOCOL

Teaching Students to Analyze Their Own Mistakes Systematically

Two students. Same mistake on a math test.

Student A: No Protocol

Mistake: Solved $2x + 5 = 15$ incorrectly. Got $x = 10$—correct answer: $x = 5$.

Teacher writes: "Incorrect. See me."

Student's response:

"I got it wrong. I'm bad at algebra." Crumples paper. Doesn't look at it again.

What the student learned:

Nothing. The mistake was wasted.

Student B: Uses Mistake Analysis Protocol

Same mistake: Solved $2x + 5 = 15$ incorrectly. Got $x = 10$.

Teacher writes: "Your answer is incorrect. Use the Mistake Analysis Protocol to figure out what happened."

Student uses the 4-step protocol:

Step 1: What happened?—Describe the mistake

"I got $x = 10$. The correct answer is $x = 5$."

Step 2: Why did it happen?—Analyze the cause

"Let me retrace my steps..."

"$2x + 5 = 15$"

"$2x = 10$"—I subtracted 5 from both sides; correct

"$x = 10$"—Wait, I forgot to divide both sides by 2

"Oh! I stopped too early. I should have divided by 2."

Step 3: What did I learn?—Extract the lesson

"I learned: After isolating the variable term, I need to divide by the coefficient. I can't stop until the variable is completely alone."

Step 4: What will I do differently next time?—Plan the revision

"Next time: Check if the variable is completely isolated—x = [number], not 2x = [number]."

"I'll add a checkpoint: 'Is the coefficient 1?' If not, divide."

What the student learned:

Exactly why the mistake happened. Exactly how to prevent it. A strategy to use next time. The mistake became a learning opportunity.

The Difference: Systematic Analysis

Same mistake. Different outcomes.

Student A: Mistake → Shame → Avoidance

Student B: Mistake → Analysis → Learning → Growth

The difference is the protocol.

A systematic, repeatable process for analyzing mistakes.

What Is the Mistake Analysis Protocol?

The Mistake Analysis Protocol is a 4-step process students use every time they make a mistake.

It transforms mistakes from shameful failures into data points.

The 4 steps:

1. What happened?—Describe the mistake
2. Why did it happen?—Analyze the cause
3. What did I learn?—Extract the lesson
4. What will I do differently next time?—Plan the revision

This works for any subject:

Math—calculation errors, conceptual misunderstandings

Writing—grammar, organization, argument

Science—experimental design, data interpretation

History—analysis, evidence, argument

Language—vocabulary, grammar, pronunciation

The protocol is:

Systematic—same steps every time

Student-driven—students analyze their own mistakes

Metacognitive—students think about their thinking

Actionable—results in clear next steps

Why Students Need a Protocol

Without a protocol, students don't know how to analyze mistakes.

They default to:

Shame—"I'm stupid."

Vague explanations—"I don't know what I did wrong."

Surface fixes—"I'll try harder next time."

Avoidance—"I'll never look at this again."

None of these leads to learning.

With a protocol:

Students have a process.

They know what to do when they make a mistake.

This:

Reduces anxiety—there's a clear path forward

Builds metacognition—thinking about thinking

Creates actionable insights—specific strategies to try

Develops independence—students can do this without you

The 4-Step Protocol—Detailed

Let me walk you through each step in detail.

Step 1: What Happened?—Describe the Mistake

Purpose: State the facts. No judgment. Just describe what occurred.

Guiding questions:

What was the task/question/problem?

What did I produce/answer?

What was expected/correct?

Where specifically did I go wrong?

Example—Math:

"The problem was: Solve 3x - 7 = 14."

"I got x = 7."

"The correct answer is x = 7."

"Wait—I need to check my work more carefully..."

Re-solves.

"Actually, I got x = 3. The correct answer is x = 7. So my answer was wrong."

Example—Writing:

"The task was: Write a thesis statement for my persuasive essay."

"I wrote: 'School uniforms are good.'"

"Teacher feedback: 'This is too vague. What specifically are you arguing about school uniforms?"

"So my thesis was too general."

Example—Science:

"The task was: Design an experiment to test which material insulates best."

"I tested foam, cotton, and newspaper by wrapping them around cups of hot water."

"But I used different amounts of each material."

"The feedback: 'Your experiment isn't controlled. You need to use the same amount of each material."

Key:

No judgment yet. Just facts.

Not: "I'm so stupid, I can't believe I got this wrong."

But: "I got x = 3. The correct answer is x = 7. Let me figure out why."

Step 2: Why Did It Happen?—Analyze the Cause

Purpose: Identify the root cause. Not just "I made a mistake," but why.

Guiding questions:

What was my thinking?

Where did my thinking go wrong?

What concept am I misunderstanding?

What skill am I still developing?

Did I misread the question?

Did I rush?

Did I skip a step?

Types of causes:

Cause Type One: Conceptual Misunderstanding

"I don't understand the underlying concept."

Example:

"I thought when you multiply fractions, you add the denominators. But you actually multiply both numerator and denominator. I had a conceptual misunderstanding."

Cause Type Two: Procedural Error

"I understand the concept, but I made an error in the process/steps."

Example:

"I understand how to solve equations. But I forgot to divide both sides by 3 in this problem. I skipped a step."

Cause Type Three: Careless Mistake

"I understand it and know how to do it, but I made a simple error—misread, miscalculated, rushed."

Example:

"I can do long division. But I miscalculated 7 × 8 = 54 instead of 56. Careless arithmetic error."

Cause Type Four: Misread the Question

"I answered a different question than what was asked."

Example:

"The question asked for the area. I calculated the perimeter. I misread."

Cause Type Five: Incomplete Work

"I started correctly but didn't finish."

Example:

"I wrote a good intro paragraph, but I never finished the body paragraphs. I ran out of time or got stuck."

The key:

Be specific. "I don't know" is not an analysis.

Retrace your steps. Go back through your work and find exactly where it went wrong.

Example—Math:

Student retraces:

"3x - 7 = 14"

"Step 1: I added 7 to both sides. 3x = 21. Correct."

"Step 2: I divided both sides by... wait. I divided by 7, not 3. That's the error."

"Why did I divide by 7? Because 7 was the number I just worked with. I wasn't thinking about the coefficient of x."

"Root cause: I didn't identify the coefficient correctly. Procedural error."

Step 3: What Did I Learn?—Extract the Lesson

Purpose: Turn the mistake into a takeaway. What knowledge or strategy did you gain?

Guiding questions:

What do I now understand that I didn't before?

What concept is clearer now?

What strategy can I use in the future?

What will I remember because of this mistake?

Examples:

Example—Math:

"I learned: When solving equations, always divide by the coefficient of the variable—the number in front of x—not whatever number you just worked with."

Example—Writing:

"I learned: A thesis needs to be specific. Instead of 'School uniforms are good,' I should say 'School uniforms reduce bullying and increase focus, and should be required in all public schools.'"

Example—Science: "I learned: In an experiment, you can only change one variable at a time. Everything else needs to be controlled—kept the same. Otherwise, you don't know what caused the results."

Example—History:

"I learned: Citing a source isn't just putting the author's name. I need: author, title, publication, year, and page number for quotes. I was missing publication and year."

The key:

Articulate the lesson clearly. You should be able to teach this to someone else.

Step 4: What Will I Do Differently Next Time?—Plan the Revision

Purpose: Create a concrete action plan. How will you prevent this mistake in the future?

Guiding questions:

What specific strategy will I use next time? What checkpoint can I add to catch this error? What resources or support do I need?

How will I practice this skill?

Examples:

Example—Math:

"Next time I solve an equation:"

"Strategy: After isolating the variable term—like 3x = 21—I'll ask: 'What's the coefficient?' Then divide by that number."

"Checkpoint: Before I finish, I'll check: Is x completely alone—x = [number]? If not, keep going."

Example—Writing:

"Next time I write a thesis:"

"Strategy: Use this template: '[Topic] is important because [reason 1], [reason 2], and [reason 3].'"

"Checkpoint: Ask: Does my thesis answer 'So what? Why does this matter?"

Example—Science:

"Next time I design an experiment:"

"Strategy: Make a chart with columns: Independent Variable—what I'm changing, Dependent Variable—what I'm measuring, Controlled Variables—what stays the same."

"Checkpoint: Before I start the experiment, ask: Am I only changing one thing?"

The key:

Be specific. "I'll try harder" is not a plan.

Create checkpoints—questions you ask yourself to catch errors.

Identify resources if needed: "I'll ask the teacher to reteach fractions" or "I'll watch a Khan Academy video on this."

Age-Appropriate Versions of the Protocol

The core 4 steps work for all ages, but the language changes.

K-2: Simplified Protocol

4 steps:

1. What happened?

"I made a mistake. What was it?"

2. Why did it happen?

"Why did I get it wrong?"

3. What did I learn?

"What do I know now?"

4. What will I try next time?

"What will I do differently?"

Example—1st grade math:

1. What happened?

"I counted the dots and said 12. The right answer is 10."

2. Why?

"I counted too fast. I counted some dots twice."

3. What did I learn?

"I need to count slowly and touch each dot, so I don't count it twice."

4. Next time?

"I'll point to each dot while I count."

3-5: Basic Protocol

4 steps—same structure, slightly more sophisticated:

1. Describe the mistake
2. Figure out why
3. What I learned
4. My plan for next time

Provide sentence stems:

"I made a mistake when..."

"I think it happened because..."

"I learned that..."

"Next time I will..."

6-8: Standard Protocol

Use the full 4-step protocol as written:

1. What happened?
2. Why did it happen?
3. What did I learn?
4. What will I do differently next time?

Add:

Categorizing mistake types—conceptual, procedural, careless, and misread

Tracking patterns—keeping a log of mistakes to identify trends; covered in Chapter 13

9-12: Advanced Protocol

Same 4 steps, but add:

Metacognitive reflection:

What was my thinking process?

What assumptions did I make?

How does this connect to other concepts?

Transfer:

How does this mistake apply to other contexts?

What broader principle does this reveal?

Example—high school physics:

The student makes a mistake calculating force—F = ma.

Advanced analysis:

"I confused mass and weight. I used 100 lbs instead of converting to kg first. This reveals that I don't fully understand the difference between mass—the amount of matter—and weight—the force due to gravity. This matters in any physics problem involving force. I need to review the relationship between mass, weight, and gravity."

How to Teach the Protocol

Don't just hand students a worksheet and expect them to use it.

Explicitly teach the protocol. Model it. Practice it. Reinforce it.

Step 1: Introduce the Protocol—Day 1 or Week 1

Explain why:

"When scientists make mistakes in the lab, they don't just throw out the experiment and give up. They analyze what happened. They figure out why. They learn from it. Then they revise."

"That's what you're going to do in this class. Every time you make a mistake, you'll use this 4-step protocol to analyze it."

Show the 4 steps on a poster or slide. Explain each step briefly.

Step 2: Model the Protocol—With Your Own Mistake

Use a real mistake you made—teaching mistake or content mistake.

Walk through all 4 steps out loud.

Example:

Yesterday I tried a new activity in class. It flopped. Students were confused. Let me analyze that mistake using our protocol."

1. What happened?

"I tried a group discussion activity. Students didn't know what to discuss. They sat in silence."

2. Why did it happen?

"I didn't give them clear questions to discuss. I just said, 'discuss the reading.' That was too vague."

3. What did I learn?

"I learned: Students need specific discussion questions, not just 'discuss the topic.' Vague prompts don't work."

4. What will I do differently?

"Next time I do a discussion, I'll give 2-3 specific questions to start with. I'll also model what a good discussion looks like."

Students see:

The teacher uses the protocol too. Mistakes are analyzed, not hidden.

Step 3: Guided Practice—Whole Class

Give students a sample mistake—not their own yet; lower stakes.

Walk through the protocol together.

Example—Math class:

Show a sample problem with a mistake:

Problem: $4x - 6 = 10$

Student work—wrong:

$4x = 4$

$x = 1$—incorrect; correct answer is $x = 4$

Guide students through analysis:

1. What happened?

"The student got $x = 1$. The correct answer is $x = 4$."

2. Why did it happen?

"Let's retrace the steps. They wrote $4x = 4$. But if you add 6 to both sides of $4x - 6 = 10$, you get $4x = 16$, not $4x = 4$. They added wrong. They added 6 to 10 and got 4 instead of 16. Arithmetic error."

3. What did the student learn?

"They need to double-check arithmetic when adding/subtracting."

4. What should they do next time?

"Use a checkpoint: After adding or subtracting, verify the arithmetic before moving to the next step." Students practice thinking through the protocol.

Step 4: Individual Practice—Low-Stakes

Give students a small quiz or problem set—formative, ungraded, or graded only for completion. When they make mistakes, they use the protocol to analyze them.

You circulate and coach: "You described what happened. Now dig deeper—why did it happen?" "Good analysis. Now, what's your specific plan for next time?"

Step 5: Make It Routine

Anytime students make mistakes—on quizzes, tests, or assignments—they use the protocol. Build it into your feedback: Instead of just: "Incorrect. See me."

Write: "Use the Mistake Analysis Protocol to figure out what happened."

Over time, Students internalize the protocol. They start doing it automatically. "I made a mistake. Let me figure out why..."

Tools to Support the Protocol

Tool One: Mistake Analysis Template

Create a template that students fill out.

Mistake Analysis Protocol

Name: ________________ Date: ________________

Assignment/Test: ______________________________

1. What happened?—Describe the mistake

2. Why did it happen?—Analyze the cause

☐ Conceptual misunderstanding

☐ Procedural error

☐ Careless mistake

☐ Misread the question

☐ Incomplete work

Explanation:

3. What did I learn?—Extract the lesson

4. What will I do differently next time?—Plan

Strategy:

Checkpoint I'll use:

Resource/support I need:

Students complete this for each significant mistake.

Tool Two: Mistake Log—Ongoing Tracker

Students keep a running log of mistakes.

Format:

Date	Mistake	Why?	What I Learned	Next Steps
9/15	Got x = 3 instead of x = 4 on equation	Arithmetic error adding	Double-check arithmetic	Use a calculator to verify
9/20	Thesis too vague	Didn't include a specific argument	The thesis needs a specific claim	Use the thesis template

This becomes powerful in Chapter 13—Error Pattern Recognition.

Students can look back and see:

"I keep making arithmetic errors. That's a pattern. I need to focus on that."

Tool Three: Mistake Analysis Checklist—For You

When reviewing student work, check:

☐ Did the student describe the mistake clearly?

☐ Did they identify the root cause—not just "I got it wrong"?

☐ Did they extract a clear lesson?

☐ Did they create a specific action plan—not vague "try harder"?

If any box is unchecked:

Give feedback: "Go deeper on Step 2. Why did this happen? What was your thinking?"

What to Do When Students Resist

Some students will resist the protocol at first.

Resistance One: "This Takes Too Long"

Student: "I don't have time to analyze every mistake. Just tell me the answer."

Your response:

"I could tell you the answer. You'd write it down. Then you'd forget it."

"Or you could spend 5 minutes analyzing the mistake yourself. You'll remember it because you figured it out."

"Which approach actually saves time in the long run?"

Also, you don't analyze every mistake. Focus on significant ones—tests, major assignments, repeated errors.

Resistance Two: "I Don't Know Why I Got It Wrong"

Student: "I don't know. I just got it wrong."

Your response:

"Let's figure it out together. Show me your work. Let's retrace your steps."

Guide them through the analysis—at first, they'll need coaching.

Sentence stems help:

"I think I got it wrong because..."

"Looking back, I see that I..."

Resistance Three: "I Just Made a Dumb Mistake"

Student: "It was just a dumb mistake. I won't do it again."

Your response:

"Maybe. But let's analyze it anyway. Even 'dumb mistakes' have causes."

"Why did you make this 'dumb mistake' and not a different one? What were you thinking?"

Often, "dumb mistakes" reveal patterns:

Rushing

Not reading carefully

Skipping steps

Identifying the pattern helps prevent it.

Resistance Four: "This Is Embarrassing"

Student: "I don't want to write about my mistakes. It's embarrassing."

Your response:

"This is private. It's for you, not for me to judge you."

"The protocol helps you learn. Scientists document failures all the time—it's how they get smarter."

"Your mistakes are data. That's all."

If needed:

Students can keep their Mistake Analysis private—not shared publicly.

But:

Over time, as the culture builds, students become more comfortable sharing.

Real Teacher Story: Mr. Davis's Mistake Analysis Transformation

Mr. Davis taught 8th-grade math.

For years, he handed back tests with:

Red X's

Correct answers written in

Grade at the top

Students looked at the grade, then threw the test away.

In Year 6, he introduced the Mistake Analysis Protocol.

New system:

1. Hand back tests with mistakes marked—but no correct answers written in.
2. Students use the protocol to analyze 3 significant mistakes.
3. Students can schedule a retake after completing their analysis.

The first quarter was rough.

Students complained:

"This takes too long."

"Just tell me the answer."

"I don't know why I got it wrong."

Mr. Davis persisted.

He modeled the protocol with his own mistakes.

He coached students through their analyses.

He provided sentence stems and templates.

By the second quarter:

Students were analyzing mistakes without prompting.

By the end of the year:

Results:

Test scores improved—students were learning from mistakes, not repeating them

Students asked better questions—"I keep making this type of mistake. Can you reteach this concept?"

Retakes were more effective—students had diagnosed their errors before retaking

Students developed metacognition—"I notice I rush through multi-step problems. I need to slow down."

Mr. Davis reflected:

"The protocol felt like extra work at first. But it saves time in the long run. Students don't make the same mistakes over and over. They actually learn from them."

The Bottom Line

The Mistake Analysis Protocol is the core tool of your Mistake Lab.

It transforms mistakes from wasted failures into learning opportunities.

The 4 steps:

1. What happened?—Describe
2. Why did it happen?—Analyze
3. What did I learn?—Extract
4. What will I do differently?—Plan

To implement:

Introduce the protocol explicitly—Day 1 or Week 1

Model it with your own mistakes. Practice together—guided, then independent

Make it routine—use it on every significant mistake. Provide tools—templates, logs, checklists.

Address resistance—coach students through it. When students master the protocol:

They become independent analysts of their own learning.

They don't need you to tell them what went wrong. They can figure it out themselves. That's the goal.

REFLECTION QUESTIONS

Personal Reflection:

1. Do your students currently analyze their mistakes? Or do they just look at the grade and move on?
2. When you were a student, did you analyze your mistakes? Why or why not?
3. What would change if students systematically analyzed every significant mistake?
4. What barriers might prevent students from using the protocol? How will you address them?

Practice:

Think of a mistake you made recently—teaching or personal.

Use the 4-step protocol to analyze it:

1. What happened?
2. Why did it happen?
3. What did you learn?
4. What will you do differently next time?

How did it feel to use the protocol? What did you notice?

Action Planning:

This week/month:

☐ Introduce the Mistake Analysis Protocol to students—explain the 4 steps
☐ Model the protocol with your own mistake—show students how it works
☐ Create a Mistake Analysis template—for students to fill out
☐ Practice the protocol together—whole-class guided practice with a sample mistake
☐ Have students analyze one mistake—low-stakes assignment
☐ Make it routine—build it into feedback on every test/quiz
☐ Create a Mistake Log—for students to track mistakes over time

Further Exploration

Read:

- *Visible Learning for Teachers* by John Hattie—on feedback and error analysis
- *Make It Stick* by Brown, Roediger, McDaniel—on retrieval practice and learning from mistakes
- *Powerful Teaching* by Agarwal & Bain—on using errors productively

Students now have the core tool: The Mistake Analysis Protocol.

Next: Error Pattern Recognition

How do students identify trends in their mistakes, not just individual errors?

That's Chapter 13.

Ready?

CHAPTER 13

ERROR PATTERN RECOGNITION

Teaching Students to Find Trends in Their Mistakes

Two students. Both make mistakes regularly. Both use the Mistake Analysis Protocol.

Student A: Analyzes Mistakes in Isolation

September:

Makes a mistake on a math test—forgets to distribute the negative sign.

Uses the protocol. Learns from it. Moves on.

October:

Makes a mistake on a different math test—forgets to distribute the negative sign again. Uses the protocol. Learns from it—moves on.

November:

Makes the same mistake again—forgets to distribute the negative sign. Uses the protocol again.

Thinks: "Why do I keep making this mistake?"

Has no answer. Doesn't see the pattern.

Student B: Tracks Patterns

September:

Makes a mistake—forgets to distribute the negative sign. Uses the protocol. Logs it in her Mistake Tracker:

Date	Mistake	Type	Pattern?
9/15	Didn't distribute negative	Procedural	Negative signs

October:

Makes the same type of mistake again. Uses the protocol. Logs it:

Date	Mistake	Type	Pattern?
9/15	Didn't distribute negative	Procedural	Negative signs
10/8	Forgot the negative when simplifying	Procedural	Negative signs

Notices: "Wait. I've made two mistakes with negative signs. That's a pattern."

She takes action:

Asks the teacher to reteach distributing negatives

Creates a personal checklist: "Did I distribute the negative?"

Practice 10 extra problems with negatives

November:

No mistakes with negative signs.

The pattern is broken.

The Difference: Pattern Recognition

Same mistakes. Different outcomes.

Student A: Keeps making the same mistake—doesn't see the pattern

Student B: Identifies the pattern → takes targeted action → breaks the pattern

This chapter is about teaching students to recognize error patterns.

What Is Error Pattern Recognition?

Error pattern recognition is the ability to:

Track mistakes over time

Identify recurring errors—patterns

Categorize mistakes by type

Take targeted action to address patterns

Why this matters:

Individual mistakes teach individual lessons.

Patterns reveal systemic issues:

Conceptual gaps—"I don't understand how fractions work."

Procedural weaknesses—"I always skip this step."

Behavioral habits—"I rush through word problems."

Metacognitive patterns—"I don't check my work."

When students see patterns, they can:

Focus their practice—work on what they actually struggle with

Seek targeted help—ask specific questions

Break bad habits—before they become ingrained

Build metacognition—understand how they learn

The Three Levels of Pattern Recognition

Students develop pattern recognition in stages:

Level 1: Single Mistake Analysis

What it looks like:

The student makes a mistake. Uses the Mistake Analysis Protocol. Learns from that one mistake.

Example:

"I got this problem wrong. I forgot to add the exponents when multiplying. I'll remember that next time."

This is good. But it's not pattern recognition yet.

Level 2: Noticing Repetition

What it looks like:

The student makes the same mistake twice. Notices: "I did this before."

Example:

"Wait, I made this same exponent mistake last week. Why do I keep doing this?"

This is the beginning of pattern recognition.

But the student doesn't know what to do with the pattern yet.

Level 3: Systematic Pattern Analysis and Action

What it looks like:

Student:

Tracks mistakes over time

Identifies patterns—themes, categories

Analyzes why the pattern exists

Takes targeted action to break the pattern

Monitors whether the pattern improves

Example:

"I've made 3 mistakes with exponents in the last month. The pattern is: I forget the rules when multiplying versus dividing. I need to create a reference sheet and practice these specific rules."

This is full pattern recognition.

This is the goal.

The Five Types of Error Patterns

Students' mistakes fall into categories.

Teaching students these categories helps them identify patterns.

Pattern Type One: Conceptual Patterns

What it is:

Repeated mistakes caused by misunderstanding a concept.

Examples:

"I keep getting fractions wrong because I don't understand equivalent fractions."

"I keep making thesis statement mistakes because I don't understand what a thesis is."

"I keep confusing photosynthesis and cellular respiration because I don't understand the relationship."

How to identify:

The student makes different mistakes, but they all stem from the same misunderstood concept.

What to do:

Action: Reteach the concept—different explanation, different approach.

Not: More practice. Practice won't help if the concept is misunderstood.

Pattern Type Two: Procedural Patterns

What it is:

Repeated mistakes caused by skipping a step or following incorrect procedures.

Examples:

"I keep forgetting to distribute negative signs."

"I keep forgetting to cite sources."

"I keep forgetting to balance chemical equations."

How to identify:

Student understands the concept but makes execution errors—always the same step.

What to do:

Action: Create a checklist or procedural reminder.

Example:

"Before I finish any equation with a negative, I'll ask: 'Did I distribute the negative?'"

Pattern Type Three: Careless Patterns

What it is:

Repeated mistakes caused by rushing, not checking work, or not reading carefully.

Examples:

"I keep miscalculating simple arithmetic—7 × 8, 6 + 9, etc."

"I keep misreading questions—answering area instead of perimeter."

"I keep making typos in my essays."

How to identify:

Student can do it correctly if they slow down and check.

The pattern is about habits, not understanding.

What to do:

Action: Build checking habits—slow down, use checkpoints, verify work.

Example:

"I'll circle key words in questions before answering."

"I'll use a calculator to verify my arithmetic."

"I'll read my essay out loud to catch typos."

Pattern Type Four: Performance Patterns

What it is:

Mistakes that occur in specific contexts—tests, presentations, and timed work.

Examples:

"I understand the content, but I freeze during tests."

"I know the material, but I rush when there's a timer."

"I do well on homework but poorly on quizzes."

How to identify:

A student performs differently in different contexts.

Practice: Success

Performance: Struggle

What to do:

Action: Address the performance anxiety or context-specific issue.

Example:

Practice under test conditions—simulate the environment.

Learn test-taking strategies—time management, how to approach questions

Address test anxiety—breathing techniques, reframing

Pattern Type Five: Metacognitive Patterns

What it is:

Repeated mistakes caused by not monitoring your own thinking.

Examples:

"I don't realize I'm confused until it's too late."

"I think I understand, but then I can't apply it."

"I don't know when to ask for help."

How to identify:

Student struggles to self-assess or self-monitor.

What to do:

Action: Build metacognitive habits—self-questioning, self-checking.

Example:

"After each problem, I'll ask: 'Does this answer make sense? Can I explain why?"

How to Teach Pattern Recognition

Students don't automatically see patterns.

You need to teach them.

Step 1: Introduce the 5 Pattern Types

Teach students the categories explicitly.

Create a poster or handout:

The 5 Types of Error Patterns

1. **Conceptual:** I don't understand the concept.
2. **Procedural:** I skip a step or use the wrong procedure.
3. **Careless:** I rush or don't check my work.
4. **Performance:** I struggle in specific contexts—tests, presentations.
5. **Metacognitive:** I don't monitor my own thinking.

Walk through examples of each type. Ask students: "Which type do you think you make most often?"

Step 2: Model Pattern Recognition with Your Own Teaching

Share your own teaching mistakes and identify patterns.

Example:

"I've noticed a pattern in my teaching. Three times this semester, I've planned an activity and run out of time before we finish. That's a procedural pattern—I'm not estimating time accurately. Here's what I'm going to do differently: I'm going to add 10 minutes of buffer time to every activity plan. And I'll set a timer halfway through to check if we're on track."

Students see that even the teacher identifies and addresses patterns.

Step 3: Provide a Tracking Tool

Give students a way to log mistakes over time.

Option A: Mistake Tracker—Simple

Date	Assignment	Mistake	Type	Pattern?
9/10	Quiz 2	Forgot to distribute the negative	Procedural	
9/17	Homework 5	Miscalculated 7 × 8	Careless	
9/24	Quiz 3	Forgot to distribute the negative	Procedural	REPEAT

Option B: Mistake Log—Detailed

Date: ___________

Assignment/Test: ______________________________

Mistake: ____

Category—check one:

☐ Conceptual

☐ Procedural

☐ Careless

☐ Performance

☐ Metacognitive

Is this a repeat mistake? ☐ Yes ☐ No

If yes, how many times have I made this mistake? _______

What pattern do I notice? ____________________________________

Students fill this out after using the Mistake Analysis Protocol.

Step 4: Teach Students to Review Their Tracker Regularly

Once a month or at the end of each unit:

Students review their Mistake Tracker and answer:

Pattern Reflection Questions:

1. What mistakes have I made more than once?
2. What type of pattern is this? Conceptual, Procedural, Careless, Performance, Metacognitive
3. Why does this pattern keep happening?
4. What specific action will I take to break this pattern?
5. How will I know if the pattern is improving?

This is the moment when students identify patterns and plan to address them.

Step 5: Provide Time for Targeted Practice

Once students identify a pattern:

Give them time/resources to address it.

Options:

A) Office hours/tutoring:

"I've identified that I have a conceptual gap in fractions. Can we schedule time to reteach this?"

B) Targeted practice:

"I keep making procedural errors with distributing negatives. I'm going to do 10 practice problems focusing on that."

C) Strategy sessions:

"I have a performance pattern—I freeze on tests. Can we talk about test-taking strategies?"

D) Peer support:

"I keep making careless mistakes because I rush. I'm going to ask my lab partner to check my work before I submit."

The key:

Pattern recognition is only useful if it leads to action.

Pattern Recognition at Different Grade Levels

K-2: Simple Tracking

At this age:

Students track mistakes visually, not in writing.

Activity: "Oops Board" with categories

Create columns on a bulletin board:

I need more practice—procedural

I need to slow down—careless

I need help understanding—conceptual

When students make a mistake, they add a sticky note to the appropriate column.

At the end of the week, look at the board together:

"We have a lot of notes in 'I need to slow down.' That's a class pattern. Let's talk about how we can remember to check our work."

3-5: Basic Pattern Recognition

Students keep a simple Mistake Log.

Once a month, they review it and answer:

"What mistake have I made more than once?"

"What will I do to fix it?"

The teacher helps identify patterns:

"I notice you've made 3 mistakes with adding fractions. That's a pattern. Let's reteach adding fractions."

6-8: Systematic Tracking Plus Analysis

Students use the full Mistake Tracker.

They categorize mistakes by type: Conceptual, Procedural, Careless, Performance, and Metacognitive.

They identify patterns independently.

They create action plans to address patterns.

Monthly Pattern Reflection is built into the routine.

9-12: Metacognitive Mastery

Students not only identify patterns but also analyze why patterns exist.

Advanced questions:

"What conditions make this mistake more likely?"—fatigue, time pressure, complex problems

"How does this pattern connect to other areas of my learning?"—transfer

"What does this pattern reveal about how I learn best?"—metacognition

Example—high school student:

"I've noticed a pattern: I make more mistakes on problems that require multiple steps. I think this is because I lose track of where I am in the process. I'm going to start writing out each step explicitly, even if it takes more time. I'll also ask myself after each step: 'What do I need to do next?'"

What to Do with Class-Wide Patterns

Pattern recognition isn't just individual.

You can identify class-wide patterns.

How:

After a test/quiz, tally common mistakes.

Example:

Test on systems of equations.

Common mistakes:

15 students: Made arithmetic errors

12 students: Forgot to check their solution

8 students: Used the wrong method—substitution instead of elimination

What this tells you:

Class-wide pattern: Arithmetic errors and not checking work.

Your action:

Reteach: "A lot of us made arithmetic errors on this test. That's a class pattern. Let's talk about strategies for avoiding arithmetic mistakes."

Strategies you might teach:

Use a calculator for arithmetic—focus on the algebra

Do arithmetic on scratch paper, not in your head

Double-check arithmetic before moving to the next step

Then:

Build in checkpoints:

"Before you finish a problem, verify your arithmetic."

Class-wide patterns inform instruction.

You reteach what students actually struggle with, not what you assumed they would.

Common Student Patterns—By Subject

Here are patterns you're likely to see:

Math Patterns

Common patterns:

Arithmetic errors—Careless: Miscalculating simple operations

Sign errors—Procedural: Forgetting to distribute negatives, mixing up +/-

Order of operations—Procedural: Not following PEMDAS

Misreading problems—Careless: Solving for the wrong variable, answering the wrong question

Conceptual confusion—Conceptual: Mixing up formulas, not understanding when to use which operation

Writing Patterns

Common patterns:

Weak thesis—Conceptual: Thesis is too vague or not arguable

Lack of evidence—Procedural: Forgetting to support claims with evidence

Organization—Procedural: Paragraphs don't flow logically

Grammar/mechanics—Careless: Run-ons, fragments, comma splices

Citation errors—Procedural: Missing citations, incorrect format

Science Patterns

Common patterns:

Confusing similar concepts—Conceptual: Photosynthesis versus cellular respiration, mitosis versus meiosis

Not controlling variables—Procedural: Changing multiple variables in an experiment

Misinterpreting data—Conceptual: Drawing incorrect conclusions from graphs/tables

Skipping steps—Procedural: Not writing hypotheses, not labeling diagrams

Unit errors—Careless: Forgetting to include units, using the wrong units

History/Social Studies Patterns

Common patterns:

Surface-level analysis—Conceptual: Describing events without explaining why they happened

Weak evidence—Procedural: Not citing sources, using unreliable sources

Presentism—Conceptual: Judging historical events with modern values without historical context

Confusing dates/events—Careless: Mixing up chronology

Not answering the prompt—Careless/Metacognitive: Writing about the topic but not addressing the specific question

When you know common patterns, you can:

Anticipate them—teach prevention strategies

Identify them faster—when you see them in student work

Address them systematically—targeted intervention

Real Teacher Story: Ms. Patel's Pattern Breakthrough

Ms. Patel taught 7th-grade science.

For years, she noticed:

Students kept making the same mistakes in labs—not controlling variables and not writing hypotheses.

She would reteach. Students would nod. Then they'd make the same mistakes on the next lab.

Year 4, she introduced the Mistake Tracker.

After each lab, students logged their mistakes.

After 3 labs, she had students review their trackers and answer:

"What mistakes have I made more than once?"

What students discovered:

Top 3 patterns—class-wide:

Not writing a hypothesis—8 students

Not controlling variables—12 students

Not labeling diagrams—10 students

Ms. Patel's response:

She addressed each pattern systematically:

Pattern One: Not writing a hypothesis

Action: Created a hypothesis template:

"If [independent variable], then [dependent variable] because [reasoning]."

Required students to use the template for the next 2 labs.

Pattern Two: Not controlling variables

Action: Created a pre-lab checklist:

"Before you start your experiment, fill out this chart:"

What am I changing?	What am I measuring?	What am I keeping the same?
Independent variable	Dependent variable	Controlled variables

Pattern Three: Not labeling diagrams

Action: Added a checkpoint to the lab procedure:

"Step 5: Label your diagram. Check: Does every part have a label?"

Results:

The patterns broke. Students stopped making these mistakes.

Students became self-aware: "I know I have a pattern of rushing. I need to slow down."

Lab reports improved dramatically.

Ms. Patel reflected:

"Before, I was treating every mistake as a one-off. Now I see patterns. And when you address patterns, you address the root cause. Students don't just fix one mistake—they fix a whole category of mistakes."

The Bottom Line

Individual mistake analysis is good.

Pattern recognition is better.

Why?

Patterns reveal root causes:

Conceptual gaps

Procedural weaknesses

Behavioral habits

Performance issues

Metacognitive blind spots

To teach pattern recognition:

Teach the 5 pattern types—Conceptual, Procedural, Careless, Performance, Metacognitive

Provide a tracking tool—Mistake Tracker or Log

Build in reflection time—monthly Pattern Reflection

Support targeted action—reteaching, practice, strategy sessions

Identify class-wide patterns—inform instruction

When students master pattern recognition:

They don't just fix individual mistakes.

They break entire categories of errors.

They become strategic, self-aware learners.

REFLECTION QUESTIONS

Personal Reflection:

1. Do you track patterns in student mistakes? Or do you treat each mistake as an isolated case?
2. What patterns do you notice in your students' mistakes? List 3-5 common errors
3. Do your students know their own patterns? How do you know?
4. What would change if students could identify and address their own patterns?

Pattern Audit:

Look at recent student work—tests, quizzes, assignments.

Identify:

What's the most common mistake?

Is it Conceptual, Procedural, Careless, Performance, or Metacognitive?

How many students made this mistake?

What would you need to reteach/adjust to address this pattern?

Action Planning:

This week/month:

☐ Teach the 5 pattern types—Conceptual, Procedural, Careless, Performance, Metacognitive

☐ Introduce a Mistake Tracker—simple table or detailed log

☐ Model pattern recognition—share your own teaching patterns

☐ Have students complete a Pattern Reflection—review their tracker, identify patterns

☐ Provide targeted support—reteach based on patterns, offer practice

☐ Identify class-wide patterns—tally common mistakes after a test/quiz

☐ Address one class pattern systematically—reteach, create a checkpoint, provide a tool

Further Exploration

Read:

- *Visible Learning for Teachers* by John Hattie—on using assessment data to inform instruction
- *Embedded Formative Assessment* by Dylan Wiliam—on using student errors to adjust teaching

Students can now identify patterns in their mistakes.

Next: Revision as Learning

How do students use mistake analysis and pattern recognition actually to improve their work?

Ready?

CHAPTER 14

REVISION AS LEARNING—NOT JUST "FIXING"

Teaching Students That Iteration Is the Heart of Learning

Two students got back their essays with feedback.

Student A: Revision as Compliance

Teacher feedback on essay:

"Weak thesis. Add more evidence. Reorganize paragraph 3."

Grade: C

Student's response:

Sighs. Opens document.

Changes:

Makes thesis slightly more specific—bare minimum

Adds one piece of evidence—without analysis

Moves paragraph 3 to a different spot—but doesn't revise it

Submits.

Time spent: 15 minutes.

Thought process: "I just need to do what she said so my grade goes up."

Result:

New grade: C+

What the student learned: How to make surface-level changes to satisfy a teacher.

Did not learn: How to actually write a better essay.

Student B: Revision as Learning

Same feedback:

"Weak thesis. Add more evidence. Reorganize paragraph 3."

Grade: C

Student's response:

Reviews feedback carefully.

Thinks:

"My thesis is weak. Why? What makes a thesis strong?"

Looks at thesis examples from class.

"Oh—strong theses make a specific, arguable claim. Mine just states a fact. Let me rewrite it."

Rewrites thesis 3 different ways. Chooses the strongest.

"I need more evidence. Where? Let me look at my outline. Paragraph 2 has a claim but only one piece of evidence. I need at least two."

Researches. Finds stronger evidence. Adds it. Explains how it supports the claim.

"Paragraph 3 needs reorganization. Why isn't it working? Let me read it out loud."

Reads. Realizes the paragraph jumps between two different ideas.

"I need to split this into two paragraphs. One idea per paragraph."

Revises structure.

Submits.

Time spent: 90 minutes.

Thought process: "I'm figuring out what makes writing strong. This will help me with the next essay, too."

Result:

New grade: A-

What the student learned:

How to write a strong thesis

How to use evidence effectively

How to organize paragraphs logically

Most importantly: How to think like a writer—analyze, revise, improve

The Difference: Revision as Learning

Same feedback. Different approaches. Different outcomes.

Student A:

Revision equals compliance

"Fix what the teacher said so my grade improves."

Focus: Grade

Result: Surface changes. No deep learning.

Student B:

Revision equals learning

"Understand why this didn't work. Figure out how to make it better."

Focus: Understanding

Result: Deep changes. Transferable skills. This chapter is about teaching students that revision is the heart of learning—not an annoying extra step.

Why Students Resist Revision

Most students hate revision.

Why?

Reason One: They Think Revision Equals Punishment

Students have learned:

"If my work needs revision, I did something wrong. Revision is what happens when you fail the first time."

This comes from:

Traditional grading: First draft is graded. Low grade equals you failed. Revision is damage control.

Red pen culture: Feedback looks like criticism. Revision feels like fixing failures.

No time for revision: In many classes, you submit, get graded, and move on. No revision allowed.

What this teaches:

"Good students get it right the first time. If I need to revise, I'm not good enough."

Reason Two: They Don't See the Value

Students think:

"I already wrote it. Why do I have to do it again? This is busywork."

Why?

They don't understand that first drafts are supposed to be rough

They've never experienced revision, making their work significantly better

They don't see how revision develops skills—it just feels like extra work

Reason Three: They Don't Know How to Revise—They Just "Fix"

Students think revision means:

"Fix the errors the teacher marked."

So they:

Change spelling/grammar mistakes

Tweak a few sentences

Make minimal changes to satisfy the teacher

They don't:

Rethink their argument

Reorganize structure

Deepen their analysis

Clarify their thinking

Why?

They've never been taught how to revise deeply.

Reason Four: They Think "Done" Means "Finished"

Students operate with a factory mindset:

"I completed the assignment. I submitted it. It's done. Why are we revisiting it?"

They don't understand:

In a lab, "done" means "ready for the next iteration."

Scientists run experiments → analyze results → revise hypothesis → run again.

Writers write drafts → get feedback → revise → draft again

Designers prototype → test → revise → prototype again

Iteration is the process.

"Done" is temporary.

The Paradigm Shift: Revision as Learning

To build a Mistake Lab, you need to shift how students think about revision.

From:

Revision equals fixing failures

To:

Revision equals how learning happens

From:

"Good students get it right the first time."

To:

"Good students revise strategically."

From:

"I'm revising because I failed."

To:

"I'm revising because that's how you get better."

From:

"Fix the errors the teacher marked."

To:

"Rethink, reorganize, and improve the work."

The Five Principles of Revision as Learning

Here are the core principles you need to teach:

Principle One: First Drafts Are Supposed to Be Rough

Teach students:

"First drafts are not supposed to be perfect. They're supposed to be exploratory."

"A first draft is where you figure out what you want to say. Revision is where you say it well."

Author Anne Lamott:

"All good writers write shitty first drafts. This is how they end up with good second drafts and terrific third drafts."

In your classroom:

Change the language:

Instead of: "First draft due Friday"—sounds final

Say: "Exploratory draft due Friday"—sounds like a starting point

Change the expectations:

Don't grade first drafts on quality.

Grade them on:

Completion—did you try?

Effort—did you engage with the task?

Risk-taking—did you try something challenging?

What this teaches:

"It's safe to submit rough work. That's expected. The learning happens during revision."

Principle Two: Revision Is Where Learning Happens

Teach students:

"You learn more from revising one essay three times than from writing three essays once."

Why?

Repetition without revision equals practicing mistakes.

Revision equals deliberate practice of improvement.

Research:

Spaced repetition plus revision is more effective than mass practice—writing many different things without revising.

In your classroom:

Assign fewer things, revise more.

Instead of: 5 essays per semester—write once, grade, move on

Try: 3 essays per semester—write, revise, revise again based on feedback

What this teaches:

"Depth greater than breadth. Quality greater than quantity. Iteration greater than completion."

Principle Three: Feedback Is Fuel for Revision—Not Judgment

Teach students:

"Feedback isn't telling you what you did wrong. It's telling you what to work on next."

Shift the framing:

Instead of: "Here's what's wrong with your work."

Say: "Here's what to focus on in your next draft."

In your classroom:

Give feedback in stages—not all at once.

Draft 1 feedback: Focus on big things—thesis, argument, structure

Draft 2 feedback: Focus on medium things—evidence, paragraph organization

Draft 3 feedback: Focus on small things—grammar, mechanics

Why this works:

Students aren't overwhelmed.

They focus on one level of revision at a time.

What this teaches:

"Feedback is a roadmap, not a report card."

Principle Four: Revision Is Rethinking—Not Just Editing

Teach students the difference between editing and revising.

Editing:

Fixing spelling

Correcting grammar

Changing word choice

Surface-level changes.

Revising:

Rethinking your argument

Reorganizing structure

Deepening analysis

Clarifying thinking

Deep-level changes.

Both are important. But revising comes first.

If you edit before you revise, you're polishing something that might need to be completely rewritten.

In your classroom:

Teach the hierarchy:

1. Revise first—big picture: ideas, structure, argument
2. Edit second—details: grammar, spelling, mechanics

Give students a Revision versus Editing Checklist:

Revision—Big Picture	**Editing—Details**
Is my thesis clear and arguable?	Did I spell everything correctly?
Does my evidence support my claims?	Did I use correct grammar?
Are my paragraphs organized logically?	Did I vary my sentence structure?
Is my argument persuasive?	Did I use strong word choice?

Students work through revision first. Then editing.

What this teaches:

"Revision is about thinking. Editing is about polishing. Do the hard thinking first."

Principle Five: Revision Never Ends—Iteration Is Ongoing

Teach students:

"There's no such thing as 'perfect.' There's always another iteration."

"Even published authors say: 'I could keep revising this forever.'"

In your classroom:

Set a revision limit—so students don't revise endlessly—but normalize ongoing improvement.

Example:

"For this essay, you'll submit:"

Draft 1—exploratory

Draft 2—after feedback

Final draft—after second round of feedback

"After that, it's 'done for now.' But if you wanted to keep improving it, you could. Writers always see ways to make their work better."

What this teaches:

"Learning is iterative. You never 'finish' growing."

The Revision Cycle—Systematic Process

Give students a clear, repeatable process for revision.

The 4-Stage Revision Cycle:

Stage 1: Receive Feedback

What students do:

Read feedback carefully—don't just look at the grade

Identify patterns—what's the teacher emphasizing? What's mentioned multiple times?

Ask clarifying questions—if feedback is unclear

Stage 2: Analyze the Feedback—Using Mistake Analysis Protocol

What students do:

Use the 4-step protocol from Chapter 12:

1. What happened?—What did the feedback say?
2. Why did it happen?—Why didn't this work in my draft?
3. What did I learn?—What concept/skill do I need to develop?
4. What will I do differently?—What specific changes will I make?

Example—essay feedback: "Weak thesis":

1. What happened?

"The teacher said my thesis is weak."

2. Why did it happen?

"My thesis is: 'School uniforms are good.' That's not specific or arguable. It's just an opinion without explanation."

3. What did I learn?

"A strong thesis needs to be specific and include reasoning. It should answer: 'Why is this true? What's my argument?"

4. What will I do differently?

"I'll rewrite my thesis using this structure: '[Topic] is important because [reason 1] and [reason 2], and therefore [conclusion].'"

"New thesis: 'School uniforms should be required in public schools because they reduce socioeconomic bullying and increase student focus on academics.'"

Stage 3: Revise Strategically

What students do:

Prioritize big revisions first—ideas, structure, argument.

Then, the medium revisions—evidence, paragraph organization.

Then small revisions—grammar, mechanics.

Create a Revision Plan:

What I'm revising—in order:

1. Thesis—rewrite to be more specific
2. Paragraph 2—add evidence
3. Paragraph 3—reorganize; split into two paragraphs
4. Grammar—fix run-on sentences

Students work through the plan systematically.

Stage 4: Reflect on Revision

What students do:

After revising, answer:

What did I change?

Why did I make those changes?

What did I learn from revising this?

How will this help me on future assignments?

This reflection solidifies the learning.

Students aren't just revising this essay. They're developing skills for next time.

Revision Strategies—By Subject

Revision looks different in different subjects.

Writing Revision Strategies

Strategy One: Reverse Outline

What it is:

After you've written a draft, create a backward outline of what you actually wrote, not what you planned to write.

How:

For each paragraph, write one sentence summarizing the main point.

Why it works:

Reveals organizational problems.

Example:

Student reverse outlines and realizes:

Paragraph 3 and Paragraph 5 are making the same point—combine them

Paragraph 4 introduces a new idea that doesn't fit—delete or move

Strategy Two: Read Out Loud

What it is:

Read your essay out loud—or have someone else read it to you.

Why it works:

You catch:

Awkward phrasing

Run-on sentences

Unclear ideas

Missing transitions

When you stumble while reading, that's where revision is needed.

Strategy Three: Thesis-Evidence Check

What it is:

Highlight your thesis. Then highlight every piece of evidence.

Ask: "Does each piece of evidence directly support my thesis?"

If not, either revise the evidence or revise the thesis.

Strategy Four: Paragraph Equals One Idea

What it is:

Each paragraph should have one main idea.

Revision check:

Read each paragraph. Can you summarize it in one sentence?

If not, the paragraph is doing too much. Split it.

Math Revision Strategies

Strategy One: Retrace Your Steps

What it is:

Go through your work line by line.

At each step, ask: "Why did I do this? Is this correct?"

Why it works:

Catches procedural errors—skipped steps, wrong operations.

Strategy Two: Plug Your Answer Back In

What it is:

After solving, substitute your answer back into the original equation.

Does it work? If not, you made a mistake. Find it.

Why it works:

Verifies correctness. Builds checking habits.

Strategy Three: Solve It a Different Way

What it is:

Solve the problem using a different method.

Example—systems of equations:

Solved using substitution? Try elimination.

Did you get the same answer? If yes, you're likely correct. If not, one method has an error.

Why it works:

Deepens understanding. Reveals errors.

Science Revision Strategies

Strategy One: Variable Check

What it is:

Review your experiment.

Ask:

What am I changing?—Independent variable

What am I measuring?—Dependent variable

What am I keeping the same?—Controlled variables

If you changed more than one thing, revise.

Strategy Two: Data → Conclusion Check

What it is:

Look at your data. Then look at your conclusion.

Ask: "Does my conclusion actually follow from my data? Or am I making assumptions?"

If your conclusion goes beyond your data, revise.

Strategy Three: Peer Replication

What it is:

Have a peer follow your experimental procedure, as written.

Can they replicate your experiment?

If not, your procedure isn't clear enough. Revise.

History/Social Studies Revision Strategies

Strategy One: Evidence Check

What it is:

Highlight every claim you make.

Then highlight every piece of evidence.

Ask: "Do I have evidence for each claim?"

If not, add evidence or remove the unsupported claim.

Strategy Two: "So What?" Test

What it is:

After each paragraph, ask: "So what? Why does this matter?"

If you can't answer, the paragraph might be just describing, not analyzing.

Revise to add analysis.

Strategy Three: Bias Check

What it is:

Review your sources.

Ask:

Who wrote this?

What was their perspective? What biases might they have?

Am I presenting multiple perspectives? Revise to include diverse sources/perspectives.

How to Build Revision Into Your Grading System

If you don't change your grading system, students won't revise meaningfully.

Here's how to make revision central:

Option One: Only Grade Final Drafts

How it works:

Draft 1: Feedback only—no grade

Draft 2: Feedback only—no grade

Final draft: Graded

Why this works:

Students focus on learning, not grades, during early drafts.

Grade reflects final quality—after revision—not first attempt.

Option Two: Grading with Revision Built In

How it works:

Draft 1: Graded—low stakes, worth 20%

Draft 2—after revision: Replaces Draft 1 grade

Or: Weight more heavily—Draft 2 equals 80%

Why this works:

Students see their grades improve through revision.

Incentivizes meaningful revision.

Option Three: Revision Equals Participation/Process Grade

How it works:

Essay grade: Based on final draft quality

Revision grade: Separate grade for the revision process

Did you revise meaningfully, not just surface edits?

Did you address feedback?

Did you reflect on what you learned?

Why this works:

Values the process—revision—separately from the product—final essay.

Option Four: Portfolio Grading

How it works:

Students submit a portfolio at the end of the semester containing:

3 essays—each with Draft 1, Draft 2, Final

Reflection on the revision process for each

Grade based on:

Quality of final drafts

Evidence of meaningful revision

Depth of reflection

Why this works:

Emphasizes growth over time.

Students see their own improvement across multiple revisions.

Teaching Students to Give Feedback for Revision—Peer Review

Peer revision is powerful—if students know how to give useful feedback.

What doesn't work:

Vague feedback:

"Good job!"

"I liked it."

"Maybe add more details?"

Unhelpful.

What works: Structured Peer Review

Use the feedback framework from Chapter 9:

Step 1: Notice—What's working

"I notice..."—specific strengths

Step 2: Wonder—What could improve

"I wonder if..."—curious questions, not judgments

Step 3: Suggest—Concrete ideas

"What if you tried..."—specific suggestions

Example—peer feedback on essay:

Notice:

"I notice your introduction grabs my attention. The question you ask makes me want to keep reading."

Wonder:

"I wonder if your thesis could be more specific? Right now, it says 'social media is bad for teens.' Could you say specifically how it's bad?"

Suggest:

"What if you tried: 'Social media increases anxiety and decreases face-to-face communication among teenagers, and should be limited to 1 hour per day'?"

This is actionable.

The writer knows:

What's working—keep the intro

What needs revision—thesis specificity

How to revise it—use the suggested structure

Peer Review Protocol:

1. Read the draft silently—no marking yet
2. Use the Notice/Wonder/Suggest framework—write feedback
3. Discuss with the writer—conversation, not just written comments
4. Writer asks clarifying questions
5. Writer decides what to revise—they're not required to take all feedback, but they should consider it.

Real Teacher Story: Mr. Thompson's Revision Revolution

Mr. Thompson taught 10th-grade English.

For years, his process:

Assign essay

Students submit

He grades

Hand back

Students look at the grade, throw it away

Move on to the next essay

Students didn't revise. They didn't improve.

Year 5, he changed his system:

New process:

Week 1: Students write exploratory draft—feedback only, no grade

Week 2: Mr. Thompson gives feedback—focused on big picture: thesis, argument, structure

Week 3: Students revise—Draft 2

Week 4: Peer review—using Notice/Wonder/Suggest

Week 5: Students revise again—Final draft

Week 6: Mr. Thompson grades the final draft only

He also required:

Revision Reflection—submitted with final draft:

"What did you change from Draft 1 to Final? Why? What did you learn?"

Results:

Quality improved dramatically—final drafts were significantly better than first drafts.

Students learned how to write—not just write 5 separate essays, but deeply practiced revision. Students asked for feedback—"Can you look at my draft and tell me what to work on?" Students saw their own growth—comparing Draft 1 to Final equals visible improvement.

Mr. Thompson reflected:

"I assign fewer essays now—3 instead of 5—but students learn more. Depth beats breadth every time."

The Bottom Line

Revision isn't fixing failures. Revision is how learning happens.

To build a culture of revision:

Teach that first drafts are supposed to be rough—exploration, not perfection

Show that revision is where learning happens—depth greater than breadth

Frame feedback as fuel for revision—not judgment

Teach the difference between revising and editing—big picture first, details second

Normalize iteration—done equals ready for next draft, not finished forever

Give students:

The 4-Stage Revision Cycle—Receive feedback → Analyze → Revise → Reflect

Subject-specific revision strategies—tools for actually improving work

A grading system that supports revision—grade final drafts, not first attempts

Peer review skills—Notice/Wonder/Suggest framework

When students embrace revision, they stop seeing mistakes as failures. They see them as the raw material for growth.

REFLECTION QUESTIONS

Personal Reflection:

1. Do your students revise their work? Or do they submit once and move on?
2. Do you grade first drafts? If yes, what message does that send about revision?
3. What would change if revision were required, not optional?
4. Do you revise your own teaching? How do you model iteration?

Revision Audit:

Look at one major assignment:

How many drafts do students submit?

Do students receive feedback before grading?

Is revision built into the assignment structure?

Do students reflect on what they learned from revising?

What could you change to make revision more central?

Action Planning:

This semester/year:

☐ Teach the 5 Principles of Revision—first drafts are rough, revision is learning, feedback is fuel, revision does not equal editing, iteration is ongoing

☐ Introduce the 4-Stage Revision Cycle—Receive → Analyze → Revise → Reflect

☐ Give feedback on a draft before grading—feedback only, then revision, then grade

☐ Teach one revision strategy—a subject-specific tool students can use

☐ Require revision on one major assignment—Draft 1 → Feedback → Draft 2 → Grade

☐ Teach peer review using Notice/Wonder/Suggest

☐ Have students complete a Revision Reflection—"What did you change? Why? What did you learn?"

Further Exploration

Read:

- *Bird by Bird* by Anne Lamott—on writing, revision, and "shitty first drafts."
- *Revision Decisions* by Jeff Anderson & Deborah Dean—teaching revision in writing
- *The Writing Revolution* by Judith Hochman & Natalie Wexler—structured approach to revision

Watch:

- Ira Glass on storytelling and revision—"The Gap."
- Austin Kleon on creative revision

Students now understand:

Revision isn't punishment. It's the heart of learning.

Next: Student-Led Conferences

How do students articulate and own their learning journey?

Ready?

CHAPTER 15

STUDENT-LED CONFERENCES

Teaching Students to Own and Articulate Their Learning

Two parent-teacher conferences. Same student. Different approaches.

Conference A: Teacher-Led—Traditional

Setting: Classroom. Teacher's desk. The parent sits across from the teacher. The student sits silently to the side.

Teacher: "Thanks for coming. Let me tell you about Marcus's progress."

Opens gradebook.

"Marcus has a B in my class. He's doing well on most assignments. He struggles with fractions. He needs to participate more in class discussions. He's a good kid."

Parent: "What can he do to improve?"

Teacher: "He should study more for tests. And raise his hand more."

Parent: "Okay. We'll work on that."

Looks at Marcus. "You hear that? Study more. Participate more."

Marcus: Nods silently.

End of conference. 10 minutes.

What Marcus experienced:

Two adults talked about him, not with him.

He was a passive observer of his own education.

Message: "Adults decide what I need to improve. I just comply."

Conference B: Student-Led

Setting: Classroom. Table. A student, a parent, and a teacher sit together. The student runs the conference.

Marcus: "Thanks for coming, Mom. I'm going to show you what I've been learning this semester."

Opens portfolio.

"This is my learning portfolio. I'm going to walk you through my progress, my mistakes, and my goals."

Marcus: "First, here's my grade: B. Let me show you why."

Shows standards tracker.

"I've mastered these standards." Points to 4/4 marks. "I'm still working on these." Points to 2/4 and 3/4 marks. "The one I'm working hardest on is fractions."

Marcus: "Let me show you a mistake I made and what I learned from it."

Shows test with error analysis.

"On this test, I got this fraction problem wrong. I used the Mistake Analysis Protocol to figure out why."

Reads his analysis.

"I learned that when adding fractions, I need to find a common denominator first. I wasn't doing that. So I practiced 15 problems focusing on common denominators. Now look at this quiz." Shows the recent quiz. "I got all the fraction problems right."

Marcus: "Here are my goals for next semester:"

"1. Master fractions—get to 4/4 on that standard
2. Participate more in discussions—I'm working on speaking up even when I'm not 100% sure.
3. Ask for help sooner—I used to wait until I was really lost. Now I'm asking when I first get confused."

Marcus: "Do you have any questions?"

Parent: "I'm impressed. You really know where you are and where you're going."

Teacher: "I agree. Marcus, you've shown real growth this semester. I'm excited to see you hit these goals."

End of conference. 20 minutes.

What Marcus experienced:

He owned his learning.

He articulated his progress, mistakes, strategies, and goals.

Message: "I'm in charge of my learning. I know what I need to work on. I have a plan."

The Difference: Agency

Same student. Different conference structures. Different outcomes.

Conference A—Teacher-led:

Teacher talks

The student is passive

Parent receives information

The student has no agency

Conference B—Student-led:

Student talks

The student is active

Parent hears directly from student

The student has full agency

This chapter is about teaching students to lead their own conferences—to articulate their learning, analyze their growth, and set their own goals.

Why Student-Led Conferences Matter

Student-led conferences are the culmination of everything you've built in your Mistake Lab. Why?

Reason One: Agency

When students lead conferences, they take ownership of their learning.

Traditional model:

"The teacher is in charge of my learning. They tell me how I'm doing. They tell me what to improve."

Student-led model:

"I'm in charge of my learning. I can see my own progress. I know what I need to work on. I set my own goals."

Research—Edward Deci & Richard Ryan, Self-Determination Theory:

Autonomy—feeling in control of your own actions—is one of three core psychological needs.

When students have autonomy, they're more:

Motivated

Engaged

Persistent

Successful

Student-led conferences build autonomy.

Reason Two: Metacognition

To lead a conference, students must:

Reflect on their learning

Identify strengths and areas for growth

Analyze their mistakes

Articulate their thinking process

Set goals

All of these are metacognitive skills.

Student-led conferences force metacognition.

Reason Three: Accountability

When students present their learning to their parents:

They're accountable to themselves and their families—not just the teacher.

This is more powerful than:

The teacher tells parents how the student is doing

Grades on a report card

Why?

Students have to explain their performance, not just receive a grade.

Reason Four: Communication Skills

Students practice:

Organizing information

Speaking clearly

Presenting evidence

Answering questions

Defending their thinking

These are life skills.

Reason Five: Parents See the Learning Process—Not Just the Grade

Traditional conferences:

Parents focus on: "What's the grade? How can we get it higher?"

Student-led conferences:

Parents see:

What the student has learned. What mistakes they've made and learned from

What they're working on. What their goals are

Focus shifts from grade to growth.

What a Student-Led Conference Looks Like

Structure:

Duration: 15-20 minutes

Participants: Student, parent(s), teacher

Leader: Student—teacher facilitates but doesn't lead

Format:

Part 1: Welcome—1-2 minutes

Student opens the conference:

"Thank you for coming. I'm going to share my learning with you today. I'll show you what I've been working on, what I've learned, and what my goals are."

Part 2: Overview of Progress—3-5 minutes

Student shares:

Current grade/standing—"I have a B in this class."

What that grade represents—"Here's what I've mastered and what I'm still working on."

Standards tracker—if using standards-based grading—or grade breakdown—if using traditional grading

Tools students use:

Portfolio—collection of work samples

Standards tracker—visual showing mastery levels on each standard

Grade sheet—breakdown of assignments/assessments

Example:

"I have an 85% in this class right now. Let me show you why."

Shows grade breakdown.

"My test average is 80%. My project grades are 90%. I'm strong at long-term projects, but I need to improve my test-taking."

Part 3: Deep Dive—Mistake Analysis—5-7 minutes

Student shares 1-2 significant mistakes and what they learned from them.

Student shows:

The original work—with the mistake

The Mistake Analysis—4-step protocol

The revised work—if applicable

What they learned

Example:

"Let me show you a mistake I made on a math test."

Shows test problem.

"I got this problem wrong. Here's my mistake analysis."

Reads through the 4 steps: What happened? Why? What did I learn? What will I do differently?

"After I analyzed it, I practiced 10 more problems like this. Here's a quiz I took later."

Shows a quiz where they got similar problems correct.

"I mastered it."

Why this is powerful:

Parents see:

The student made a mistake—that's okay

The student analyzed it—metacognition

The student learned from it—growth

The student improved—evidence of learning

This is mistake literacy in action.

Part 4: Pattern Recognition—3-5 minutes

Student shares a pattern they've identified in their mistakes.

Student shows:

Mistake Tracker—log of mistakes over time

Pattern they noticed

The action they took to address it

Evidence of improvement

Example:

"When I looked at my Mistake Tracker, I noticed a pattern. I keep making careless arithmetic errors. That's happened 5 times this semester."

Shows tracker.

"I figured out why: I do arithmetic in my head instead of writing it down. So I'm rushing and making mistakes."

"Here's what I'm doing differently: I'm using a calculator for arithmetic so I can focus on the algebra. And when I don't have a calculator, I write the arithmetic on scratch paper."

"Since I started doing that, I haven't made arithmetic errors."

Shows recent work without arithmetic errors.

Why this is powerful:

Parents see that the student is:

Self-aware—identifying patterns

Strategic—taking targeted action

Growing—breaking patterns

Part 5: Goals—3-5 minutes

Student shares 2-3 specific goals for the next grading period.

Goals should be:

Specific—not vague like "do better."

Actionable—student knows what to do

Measurable—students will know when they've achieved it

Example:

"Here are my goals for next semester:"

"1. Raise my test average from 80% to 85%

How: Study 30 minutes before each test—instead of cramming the night before. Use my Mistake Tracker to review common errors before tests.

2. Participate in class discussions at least twice per week

How: Prepare one question or comment before each class. Raise my hand even when I'm not 100% sure of the answer.

3. Master fractions—currently at 3/4, goal is 4/4

How: Practice 5 fraction problems per week. Ask for help when I'm stuck instead of avoiding it."

Why this is powerful:

Parents see:

The student has direction

The goals are concrete—not vague

The student has a plan—not just wishful thinking

Part 6: Questions—2-3 minutes

Student invites questions:

"Do you have any questions for me?"

Parent asks. Student answers.

Teacher adds context if needed—but student leads.

Part 7: Closing—1 minute

Student closes:

"Thank you for coming. I'm excited to work on these goals. I'll update you on my progress."

Total time: 15-20 minutes

How to Prepare Students for Student-Led Conferences

Students can't just "wing it."

You need to prepare them systematically.

Step 1: Introduce the Concept—4-6 Weeks Before Conferences

Explain:

"In [Month], we're having parent conferences. But these conferences are different. You will lead them." "You'll present your learning to your parents. You'll show them your progress, your mistakes, what you've learned, and your goals." "This is your chance to show them what you've been working on."

Show a model:

Option A: Teacher models—you present your learning as if you're the student

Option B: Show a video of a student-led conference—if available

Option C: Have a former student come in and model

Students understand: "This is what it looks like."

Step 2: Build the Portfolio—Ongoing

Students need a portfolio of evidence.

What goes in the portfolio:

1. Standards Tracker—or grade breakdown

Shows current standing on each standard/assignment.

2. Work samples

2-3 assignments showing growth—first draft → revised

1-2 tests/quizzes with Mistake Analysis

Projects or major assignments

3. Mistake Tracker

Log of mistakes over time—from Chapter 13.

4. Pattern Recognition

1-2 patterns identified and actions taken.

5. Reflection

Written reflection on growth this semester.

6. Goals

2-3 specific goals for the next grading period. Students compile this over the semester, not all at once at the end.

Tip: Dedicate 10 minutes per week for students to update their portfolios.

Step 3: Teach the Presentation Structure—2-3 Weeks Before

Give students a clear outline:

Student-Led Conference Outline

1. Welcome—30 seconds

"Thank you for coming. I'm going to share my learning with you."

2. Overview of Progress—3-5 minutes

"Here's my current grade and what it represents."

Show standards tracker or grade breakdown.

3. Mistake Analysis—5-7 minutes

"Let me show you a mistake I made and what I learned." Present 1-2 examples using the 4-step protocol.

4. Pattern Recognition—3-5 minutes

"Here's a pattern I noticed in my mistakes and what I did about it." Show Mistake Tracker and action taken.

5. Goals—3-5 minutes

"Here are my goals for next semester and how I'll achieve them."

Present 2-3 SMART goals.

6. Questions—2-3 minutes

"Do you have any questions for me?"

7. Closing—30 seconds

"Thank you for coming." Give students this outline. Post it. Reference it.

Step 4: Practice—1-2 Weeks Before

Students need to practice their presentations.

Practice Round 1: Solo practice

Students practice presenting to themselves—or record themselves on a phone.

Practice Round 2: Partner practice

Students practice with a peer. Partner gives feedback using the Notice/Wonder/Suggest framework (Chapter 9).

Practice Round 3: Teacher observation

You circulate while students practice.

Coach: "Speak louder. Make eye contact."

"Slow down when you explain the mistake analysis."

"Add more detail about your goals."

Practice Round 4: Full dress rehearsal

Students present to the whole class—or small groups—as if parents are there.

Feedback: What's working? What needs adjustment? By conference day, students are ready.

Step 5: Conduct Conferences—Conference Day

Logistics:

Schedule: 15-20 minutes per conference

Setup: Student sits at a table with a portfolio. Parent arrives. Teacher observes—doesn't lead. Student presents.

Teacher facilitates only if needed:

"Tell them about the pattern you identified."

"Show them your goals."

Teacher adds context at the end—if necessary:

"I'd like to add: Marcus has shown tremendous growth this semester. His willingness to analyze mistakes and revise is impressive. I'm confident he'll hit these goals." But the student leads.

Step 6: Reflect After Conferences

Students write a reflection:

Prompts:

How did it feel to present your learning to your parent?

What went well?

What was challenging?

What did you learn about yourself?

What will you do differently for the next conference?

This solidifies the learning.

Tools to Support Student-Led Conferences

Tool One: Portfolio Checklist

Give students a checklist to ensure their portfolio is complete:

Portfolio Checklist

☐ Standards Tracker—or grade breakdown—current

☐ 2-3 Work Samples showing growth—first draft → revised

☐ 1-2 Tests/Quizzes with Mistake Analysis completed

☐ Mistake Tracker—updated through this semester

☐ Pattern Recognition—1-2 patterns identified plus action taken

☐ Reflection on growth this semester—written

☐ Goals for next grading period—2-3 SMART goals written

Check off each item as you complete it.

Tool Two: Conference Script Template

For students who need extra support, provide a script template:

Student-Led Conference Script

Welcome:

"Thank you for coming, [parent name]. I'm excited to share my learning with you today."

Overview:

"I currently have a [grade/level] in this class. Let me show you what that means."

Show standards tracker or grade breakdown.

"I've mastered [list standards or skills]. I'm still working on [list standards or skills]."

Mistake Analysis:

"Let me show you a mistake I made and what I learned from it."

Show work with a mistake.

"I used the Mistake Analysis Protocol to figure out what happened."

"What happened: [describe mistake]."

"Why it happened: [explain cause]."

"What I learned: [lesson]."

"What I'll do differently: [strategy]."

If applicable: "Here's evidence that I've improved: [show revised work or later assessment]."

Pattern Recognition:

"When I looked at my Mistake Tracker, I noticed a pattern: [describe pattern]."

"Here's what I did to address it: [action taken]."

"Here's how I know it's working: [evidence]."

Goals:

"Here are my goals for next semester:"

"Goal 1: [specific goal]. How I'll achieve it: [action plan]."

"Goal 2: [specific goal]. How I'll achieve it: [action plan]."

"Goal 3: [specific goal]. How I'll achieve it: [action plan]."

Questions:

"Do you have any questions for me?"

Pause. Answer questions.

Closing:

"Thank you for coming. I'm looking forward to working on these goals."

Students can customize this, but it gives them structure.

Tool Three: Parent Reflection Form

Give parents a form to fill out after the conference:

Parent Reflection: Student-Led Conference

Student name: ___________________________

Date: ________________

1. What impressed you most about your student's presentation?

2. What did you learn about your student's learning that you didn't know before?

3. What questions do you still have?

4. How can you support your student in achieving their goals?

5. Additional comments:

This gives you feedback on how conferences went.

It also helps parents reflect on how to support their student.

Variations for Different Contexts

Variation One: Virtual Student-Led Conferences

How it works:

Student leads conference via Zoom video call.

Setup:

Student shares screen—shows portfolio documents

Presents the same structure—welcome, overview, mistake analysis, goals, etc. Parent can be on video from home. The teacher observes via video

Works well for:

Remote learning

Parents who can't come in person

Hybrid models

Variation Two: Student-Led Conferences with Multiple Families at Once

How it works:

Instead of one-on-one conferences, students present to their parents in a classroom with multiple families present simultaneously.

Setup:

4-6 students presenting at the same time—at different tables

Each student presents to their own family

Teacher circulates

Why this works:

Efficient—you can do many conferences at once

Students see peers presenting—modeling

Less pressure—not everyone is watching you

Works well for:

Elementary—shorter attention spans, shorter conferences

Time constraints—many families to meet

Variation Three: Portfolio Showcase—Instead of Conference

How it works:

Students create a portfolio—digital or physical.

Parents view the portfolio at home. Students record a video presentation that walks through their portfolios.

Setup:

Student creates portfolio

Students record a 10-minute video presenting their learning. Parent watches the video and fills out the reflection form.

Optional: Follow-up video call for questions

Works well for:

Asynchronous schedules—parents can't come during conference times

Students who are anxious about presenting live

Digital portfolios

Variation Four: Three-Way Conferences—Hybrid

How it works:

Student presents—10 minutes.

The teacher adds 5 minutes of information. Then all three discuss together for 5 minutes. This is less student-led than full student-led conferences but more student-centered than teacher-led conferences.

Works well for:

Transition year—moving from teacher-led to student-led

Younger students—who need more support

High-stakes situations—college prep, IEP meetings

Student-Led Conferences at Different Grade Levels

K-2: Simplified Version

Structure:

The student shows parents 3 things:

Something I'm proud of—work sample

Something I'm working on—work sample showing growth

My goal—simple, 1 goal

Duration: 5-10 minutes

Support needed: High—teacher helps students prepare, prompts during conference

Example:

"This is my writing from September." Shows. "This is my writing from now on." Shows. "I got better at using periods!" "I'm still working on capital letters. See? I forgot some here." "My goal is to remember capital letters at the start of sentences."

3-5: Basic Structure

Structure:

Welcome

Show 2 work samples—before/after showing growth

Explain 1 mistake and what I learned

Share 2 goals

Duration: 10-15 minutes

Support needed: Medium—teacher provides templates, students practice

6-8: Full Structure

Structure:

Full structure as outlined above—welcome, overview, mistake analysis, pattern recognition, goals, questions, closing.

Duration: 15-20 minutes

Support needed: Medium—students can do most of it independently with practice

9-12: Advanced Structure

Structure:

Full structure plus:

Deeper analysis—metacognitive reflection on the learning process

Connection to future—how does this learning prepare me for college/career?

Self-assessment against standards—detailed rubric analysis

Duration: 20-25 minutes

Support needed: Low—students should be largely independent

Example additions for high school:

"This semester, I've noticed that I learn best when I can make connections to real-world applications. For example, when we studied [topic], I connected it to [real-world example], which helped me understand it more deeply. I'm going to keep using this strategy."

"My goal of improving my analytical writing will help me in college, where I'll need to write research papers. I'm building this skill now."

Real Teacher Story: Ms. Rodriguez's Student-Led Conference Transformation

Ms. Rodriguez taught 7th-grade science.

For 10 years, she did traditional parent-teacher conferences:

She talked for 10 minutes

Parents asked a few questions

The student sat silently

Everyone left

She always felt: "I'm doing all the work. The student isn't engaged."

In Year 11, she switched to student-led conferences.

Preparation—over 6 weeks:

Introduced the concept in September

Students built portfolios throughout the semester

Dedicated 10 minutes/week to portfolio updates

Practiced presentations for 2 weeks before conferences

Conference day:

First conference: Anxious. The student stumbled. But got through it.

By the 5th conference, Students were confident. Parents were impressed.

What parents said:

"I've never seen my child talk about their learning like this."

"I learned more in 15 minutes than I usually do in these conferences."

"I'm so proud of how they analyzed their mistakes. That's mature."

What students said:

"I was nervous, but I liked showing my parents what I learned."

"It made me realize how much I've grown."

"I feel like I'm in control of my learning now."

Results:

Student engagement—students took ownership

Parent buy-in—parents saw the process, not just the grade

Metacognition—students reflected deeply to prepare

Accountability—students were accountable to themselves and their families

Ms. Rodriguez reflected:

"I'll never go back to teacher-led conferences. Student-led conferences require more upfront work—preparing students—but they're so much more powerful. Students own their learning in a way they never did before."

The Bottom Line

Student-led conferences are the culmination of your Mistake Lab.

They require students to:

Reflect on their learning

Analyze their mistakes

Identify patterns

Articulate their growth

Set goals

All of this equals agency.

To implement student-led conferences:

Introduce the concept early—4-6 weeks before

Build portfolios throughout the semester—10 minutes/week

Teach the presentation structure—give a clear outline

Practice extensively—solo, partner, teacher observation, dress rehearsal

Conduct conferences—student leads, teacher facilitates

Reflect afterward—students plus parents

When students lead conferences:

They're not passive recipients of their education.

They're active agents in their own learning. That's the goal of the Mistake Lab.

REFLECTION QUESTIONS

Personal Reflection:

1. Have you ever done student-led conferences? Why or why not?
2. What would it take to shift from teacher-led to student-led conferences in your context?
3. What resistance might you face—from admin, parents, students? How would you address it?
4. How would student-led conferences change the way students think about their learning?

Conference Audit:

Think about your last parent-teacher conference:

Who talked the most? You? Student? Parent?

Was the student an active participant or passive observer?

Did the student articulate their own learning? Or did you do it for them?

What could you change to give students more agency?

Action Planning:

This semester/year:

☐ Introduce student-led conferences to students—explain what they are and why

☐ Have students start building portfolios—standards tracker, work samples, mistake analysis, goals

☐ Teach the presentation structure—give an outline, model it

☐ Schedule practice time—solo, partner, dress rehearsal

☐ Conduct student-led conferences—student leads, you facilitate

☐ Collect feedback—from students and parents

☐ Reflect and adjust—what worked? What needs improvement for next time?

Further Exploration

Read:

- *Student-Led Conferences* by Rick Stiggins—a comprehensive guide
- *The Power of Student Agency* by Michael McDowell & Ethan Braden—on student ownership

Watch:

- Videos of student-led conferences—search YouTube for examples at different grade levels.

Students can now lead conferences and articulate their own learning.

Next—final chapter of Part 3: Student Voice and Choice

How do students design their own learning experiences in the lab?

Ready?

CHAPTER 16

STUDENT VOICE AND CHOICE—AGENCY IN THE LAB

Designing Learning Experiences Students Actually Own

Two classrooms. Same unit on ecosystems.

Classroom A: Teacher-Designed—No Choice

Teacher assigns:

"Everyone will create a poster about food chains. It must include producers, consumers, and decomposers. Use the template I provided. Due Friday."

What happens:

25 students create identical posters

Students follow the template—no creativity

Some students are bored—they already understand food chains

Some students are lost—the poster format doesn't help them learn

Everyone turns in a poster on Friday. Teacher grades 25 nearly-identical posters.

Student reaction:

"This is boring. I'm just doing what she told me to do. I'm not learning anything new."

Engagement: Low

Learning: Surface-level—compliance, not understanding

Classroom B: Student Choice

Teacher frames the challenge:

"Your goal: Demonstrate your understanding of how energy flows through an ecosystem. You choose how to demonstrate it."

"Options:"

Create a poster

Build a 3D model

Write and perform a skit

Create a video

Design a board game

Write a children's book

Code an interactive simulation

Or: Propose your own idea—get it approved first

"Requirements—must include:"

Producers, consumers, decomposers

Energy transfer between organisms

At least one specific ecosystem example

"Due Friday."

What happens:

Student A: Creates a video showing energy flow in a coral reef—uses animation software they already know

Student B: Builds a 3D model of a forest ecosystem with labeled organisms—hands-on learner

Student C: Writes a children's book about "The Journey of Energy" from sun to decomposer—loves writing and illustration

Student D: Designs a board game where players are organisms competing for energy—game designer at heart

Student E: Creates a poster—prefers traditional format, and that's okay

Student reaction:

"I got to show what I know in a way that makes sense to me. I actually enjoyed this."

Engagement: High

Learning: Deep—students thought creatively about content, made it their own

The Difference: Student Voice and Choice

Same content. Different approaches. Different outcomes.

Classroom A:

Teacher decides everything—format, process, product

Students comply—follow directions

One-size-fits-all—everyone does the same thing

Low agency

Classroom B:

The teacher sets learning goals—what students must demonstrate

Students choose how to demonstrate it—format, process, product

Multiple pathways—students use their strengths

High agency

This chapter is about the final piece of your Mistake Lab: giving students voice and choice in their learning.

What Are Student Voice and Choice?

Student Voice:

Students have input into their learning.

They can:

Express preferences

Share ideas

Give feedback on what's working/not working

Co-design learning experiences

Student Choice:

Students make decisions about their learning.

They choose:

How to learn—methods, strategies

How to demonstrate learning—product type

What to learn—topics within a unit

Who to work with—partners, groups

Where to work—seating, location

When to work—pacing, deadlines within limits

Why this matters in a Mistake Lab:

Agency is the endpoint.

You've taught students:

Mistakes equal data—Chapter 6

How to analyze mistakes—Chapter 12

How to identify patterns—Chapter 13

How to revise—Chapter 14

How to lead conferences—Chapter 15

Now the final step:

Students use all these tools to design and drive their own learning.

They become independent learners.

Why Student Voice and Choice Matter

Reason One: Intrinsic Motivation

Research—Deci & Ryan, Self-Determination Theory:

Humans have three core psychological needs:

1. Autonomy—feeling in control
2. Competence—feeling capable
3. Relatedness—feeling connected

When all three are met → intrinsic motivation.

When autonomy is missing, there is either compliance or resistance.

Choice builds autonomy:

"I chose this. I'm not just doing what I was told. I'm invested."

Traditional classroom:

Teacher controls everything → students feel controlled → extrinsic motivation—grades, compliance

Classroom with choice:

Students have autonomy → intrinsic motivation—curiosity, interest, ownership

Reason Two: Engagement

When students choose:

They pick what interests them

They use their strengths

They feel ownership

They engage more deeply

Research—John Hattie, Visible Learning:

Student agency has an effect size of 0.70—a strong impact on achievement.

When students have control over their learning, achievement improves.

Reason Three: Differentiation—Without the Teacher Doing All the Work

Traditional differentiation:

The teacher creates a different version of each assignment to meet different student needs.

Exhausting.

Choice-based differentiation:

The teacher creates the framework—learning goals, success criteria.

Students choose the pathway that works for them.

Sustainable.

Students differentiate for themselves:

Advanced students choose challenging formats

Students who need support choose formats that scaffold

Students use their strengths—visual, kinesthetic, verbal, etc.

Reason Four: Real-World Preparation

In the real world:

You choose:

What career to pursue

What projects to work on

How to solve problems

Who to collaborate with

No one gives you a template and says, "Do this exactly."

Classrooms with choice prepare students for:

Decision-making

Problem-solving

Self-direction

Ownership

Skills they'll need forever.

Reason Five: Equity

One-size-fits-all assignments disadvantage students who:

Learn differently—neurodivergent students

Have different strengths—not everyone is a strong writer

Have different access to resources—not everyone can do a project requiring expensive materials

Choice-based assignments:

Students can choose formats that:

Match their learning style

Use their strengths

Work with their resources

More equitable.

The Spectrum of Student Choice

Choice isn't all-or-nothing.

There's a spectrum:

Level 1: No Choice—Full Teacher Control

Teacher decides:

What students learn

How do they learn it

How they demonstrate it

When it's due

Student role: Comply

Example:

"Everyone will write a 5-paragraph essay on Romeo and Juliet. Use MLA format. Due Friday."

Level 2: Limited Choice—Product Options

Teacher decides:

Learning goals—what students must demonstrate

Process—how they learn it

Students choose:

How they demonstrate learning—from teacher-provided options

Example:

Demonstrate your understanding of Romeo and Juliet. Choose one:

Write an essay

Create a visual storyboard

Perform a scene with analysis

Level 3: Moderate Choice—Process Plus Product Options

Teacher decides:

Learning goals

Students choose:

How they learn—readings, videos, research

How they demonstrate learning—from options or propose their own

Example:

"Goal: Understand the theme of fate versus free will in Romeo and Juliet."

"How you learn it: Read the play, watch film adaptations, research critical essays—your choice."

"How you demonstrate it: Choose a format—essay, video essay, podcast, creative project—or propose your own."

Level 4: High Choice—Student-Designed

Teacher provides:

Broad essential question or theme

Students design:

What they'll learn—within the theme

How will they learn it

How they'll demonstrate it

Who they'll work with

Timeline—within boundaries

Example:

"Essential question: What makes a tragedy tragic?" "Choose a tragedy—Shakespeare, Greek, modern. Design a project that explores this question. Propose your plan to me by Friday."

Level 5: Full Autonomy—Genius Hour/Passion Projects

Students choose:

What they want to learn—within broad boundaries

How will they learn it

How they'll demonstrate it

Everything

Teacher role: Coach, facilitator, resource

Example:

"Genius Hour: Spend 1 hour per week learning something you're passionate about. Document your learning. Share it at the end of the semester."

Where should you be on the spectrum?

It depends: Grade level—younger students need more structure. Student readiness—have they learned decision-making skills? Learning goals—some objectives require specific methods. Your comfort level—start small, build up.

Recommendation: Start at Level 2-3. Build toward Level 4-5 over time.

The Six Dimensions of Choice

Students can have a choice in different dimensions of learning.

You don't have to give a choice in all dimensions.

Pick the ones that make sense for your context.

Dimension One: Content—What to Learn

What it looks like:

Students choose:

Which topic to explore—within a unit

Which texts to read

Which aspect of a concept to study deeply

Examples:

Elementary—social studies:

"We're studying community helpers. Choose one to research: firefighter, teacher, doctor, farmer, or engineer."

Middle school—science:

"We're studying ecosystems. Choose one ecosystem to become an expert on: rainforest, desert, ocean, tundra, or wetland."

High school—literature: "We're studying the Harlem Renaissance. Choose 3 authors/poets from this list to study deeply."

Why this works:

Students explore what interests them within their learning goals.

Dimension Two: Process—How to Learn

What it looks like:

Students choose:

How they access information—read, watch videos, listen to podcasts, interview experts

What strategies do they use to learn

In what order do they tackle concepts

Examples:

Elementary—reading:

"Today's goal: Practice fluency. Choose how:"

Read with a partner—choral reading

Listen to an audiobook while following along

Record yourself reading and listen back

Middle school—math:

"Goal: Learn how to multiply fractions. Choose your pathway:."

Watch Khan Academy videos plus practice problems

Work through examples in the textbook

Use manipulatives—fraction tiles

Ask me to teach a small group

High school—history:

"Goal: Understand causes of WWI. Choose your sources:"

Textbook chapters

Documentary films

Primary source documents

Podcast series on WWI

Why this works:

Students learn in ways that match their strengths.

Dimension Three: Product—How to Demonstrate Learning

What it looks like:

Students choose how they'll show what they know.

Examples:

Elementary—science:

"Show me what you learned about the water cycle. Choose:"

Draw and label a diagram

Build a 3D model

Write a story from a water droplet's perspective

Create a song or rap

Middle school—English:

"Analyze the theme in this novel. Choose your format:."

Traditional essay

Video essay

Podcast episode

Creative project—with written analysis

High school—any subject:

Demonstrate mastery of [concept]. Choose:

Written test

Oral presentation

Project

Portfolio of evidence and propose your own idea

Why this works:

Students use their strengths—writing, speaking, visual, and kinesthetic.

Dimension Four: Pace—When to Work

What it looks like:

Students have flexibility in:

When to complete work—within a window

What order to tackle assignments

When to take assessments

Examples:

Elementary:

Here are this week's 5 activities. Complete them by Friday. You choose the order.

Middle school:

"Unit test window: April 15-22. Schedule your test anytime during that week."

High school:

"This semester, you have 3 essays due. Deadlines: October 15, November 15, December 15. If you want to turn one in early and get feedback before the deadline, you can."

Why this works:

Students manage their own time—a real-world skill.

Reduces stress—not everyone has to perform on the same day.

Dimension Five: Place—Where to Work

What it looks like:

Students choose:

Where to sit

Whether to work alone or with others

Indoor or outdoor—if available

Examples:

Elementary:

"During independent reading, you can sit at your desk, on the rug, at a table, or in the reading corner. Your choice."

Middle school:

"During work time, you can work anywhere in the classroom. Choose what helps you focus."

High school:

"You can work in the classroom, library, study hall, or—with permission—outside. Show me you can use this freedom responsibly."

Why this works:

Some students focus better:

Alone in a quiet corner

At a table with peers

Standing at a desk

Moving around

Let them choose what works.

Dimension Six: Partnership—Who to Work With

What it looks like:

Students choose:

Whether to work alone or with others

Who to work with

Group size

Examples:

Elementary:

"You can work on this project alone, with a partner, or in a group of 3. Your choice."

Middle school:

"Choose a lab partner for this experiment. Or work alone if you prefer."

High school:

"Form groups of 2-4. Or work solo. You decide."

Why this works:

Some students:

Work better alone

Thrive in partnerships

Need group energy

Let them choose.

Important note:

Even with choice, you still set boundaries:

"You can choose your partner, but everyone must participate equally. If I see one person doing all the work, I'll reassign groups."

How to Implement Choice—Step-by-Step

Start small. Build gradually.

Step 1: Start with Low-Stakes Choice

Don't start by giving students full control over a major project.

Start with small, low-stakes choices:

Examples:

"Choose which problem set to work on first—A or B."

"Choose where to sit during independent work."

"Choose whether to work alone or with a partner."

Why start small:

Students learn to make decisions

You learn to facilitate choice

Low risk if it doesn't go perfectly

Step 2: Teach Decision-Making Skills

Students need to learn how to choose wisely.

Teach them:

Decision-making framework:

1. What's the goal?—What am I trying to learn/demonstrate?
2. What are my options?—List them
3. What are my strengths?—What am I good at? What do I enjoy?
4. What are the requirements?—What must I include?
5. What will I choose?—Make a decision
6. Why?—Justify your choice

Example—student choosing project format:

Goal: Demonstrate understanding of photosynthesis

Options: Poster, model, video, written explanation

Strengths: I'm good at drawing and visualizing processes

Requirements: Must show inputs—CO_2, water, sunlight—process—chloroplasts—outputs—glucose, O_2

Choice: I'll create a poster

Why: I can draw the process step-by-step, which will help me understand it and show what I know. Practice this framework together before giving high-stakes choices.

Step 3: Provide Structure—Choice Within Boundaries

Choice does not equal chaos. Students need structure.

Provide:

Clear learning goals—what they must demonstrate

Success criteria—what quality looks like

Options—not unlimited choice; 3-5 options

Requirements—what must be included

Deadlines—timeframe

Resources—where to find help

Example:

"Goal: Demonstrate understanding of the American Revolution."

"Success criteria: Explain causes, key events, and outcomes. Use at least 3 specific examples."

"Options: Essay, timeline with annotations, video documentary, podcast episode, historical fiction story."

Requirements: 3 sources cited. Due March 15.

"Resources: Library databases, textbook, me—office hours."

Choice within structure.

Step 4: Model Examples

Show students what strong work looks like in each format.

Don't assume they know what a "good podcast" or "good video essay" looks like.

Provide models:

Show exemplars from previous students—with permission

Show professional examples—real podcasts, documentaries, etc.

Create a rubric that defines quality.

Example—for video essay option:

"Here's an example of a strong video essay. Notice:"

A clear thesis is stated in the first 30 seconds

Visual evidence—images, clips—supports narration

Organized into clear sections

3-5 minutes long

"Here's the rubric I'll use to assess video essays."

Now students know what quality looks like.

Step 5: Require a Proposal—For Complex Projects

For high-choice projects, require students to submit a proposal before they start.

Proposal template:

Name: ____________________

Project topic: ______________________________________

Format I'm choosing: ______________________________________

Why I chose this format: ______________________________________

What I'll include—to meet requirements: ______________________________________

Timeline:

Week 1: ______________________________________

Week 2: ______________________________________

Week 3: ______________________________________

Resources I'll need: ______________________________

Questions I have: ______________________________

You review proposals and give feedback:

"Approved! This plan will work."

Or:

"This plan needs adjustment. You need to include [X]. Revise and resubmit."

Why this works:

Ensures students have a viable plan

Catches problems early

Teaches planning skills

Step 6: Check In During the Process

Don't just assign choice projects and walk away.

Build in checkpoints:

Example—3-week project:

Week 1 checkpoint: Proposal approved

Week 2 checkpoint: Draft/prototype—show progress

Week 3 checkpoint: Peer review

Week 4: Final submission

At each checkpoint:

Students show what they've done

You give feedback

Students adjust before final submission

Why this works:

Students don't procrastinate until the last minute

You catch issues early

Students revise as they go—iteration

Step 7: Reflect on the Choice

After students complete choice-based work:

Have them reflect:

Reflection prompts:

What format did you choose? Why? Was this format a good fit for you? Why or why not? What did you learn about yourself as a learner?

If you did this again, what would you choose differently?

How did having a choice affect your engagement/learning?

This builds metacognition:

Students become aware of what works for them.

Common Challenges—And Solutions

Challenge One: "Students Choose the Easiest Option"

What it looks like:

All students choose the same "easy" format—poster—rather than trying something more challenging.

Why does this happen:

Students are risk-averse—they choose what's familiar. The "easy" option isn't scaffolded differently—same rigor expected. Students don't see the value of challenging themselves

Solutions:

A) Make all options equally rigorous

Don't let "poster" equal "easy"; "video" equal "hard". All formats must meet the same success criteria. "Whether you create a poster or a video, you must include 3 causes, 5 key events, and 2 outcomes. Same rigor, different format."

B) Require students to try different formats over time

"This semester, you'll do 3 choice projects. You must try 3 different formats. No repeats." Forces variety.

C) Frame challenge as growth

"I want you to choose a format that will stretch you. If you always choose posters, try something new this time. Growth happens outside your comfort zone."

Challenge Two: "I Don't Know How to Grade Different Formats Fairly"

What it looks like: Student A submits an essay. Student B submits a video. How do you grade them fairly?

Solution: Use a single rubric that assesses content—not format.

Example rubric—works for any format:

Criteria	Proficient	Developing	Beginning
Understanding	Demonstrates deep understanding of [concept]	Shows partial understanding	Shows minimal understanding
Evidence	Uses 3+ specific, relevant examples	Uses 1-2 examples	Uses vague or no examples
Organization	Ideas are clearly organized and easy to follow	Some organizations, occasionally unclear	Disorganized; hard to follow
Accuracy	Information is accurate	Mostly accurate; minor errors	Significant inaccuracies

This rubric works for:

Essay

Video

Podcast

Model

Poster

Anything

You're assessing learning, not format.

Challenge Three: "Students Don't Know How to Choose"

What it looks like:

Student stares at options. "I don't know which one to pick."

Why does this happen?

Decision fatigue—too many options

Fear of choosing wrong

Never been taught to make decisions

Solutions:

A) Limit options

Instead of unlimited choice: "Choose 1 of these 4 formats."

B) Use the decision-making framework—from Step 2

Walk students through:

What's your goal?

What are your strengths?

What will you choose? Why?

C) Allow "choice counseling."

"If you're stuck, come talk to me. I'll help you think through it."

Challenge Four: "Some Students Need More Structure"

What it looks like:

Students choose to "design their own project." Has no plan. Produces low-quality work.

Solution:

Differentiate the amount of choice based on student readiness:

High-readiness students: Full choice—design your own

Medium-readiness students: Choose from 4-5 options

Low-readiness students: Choose from 2-3 highly-scaffolded options—with templates/supports

This is choice-based differentiation.

Challenge Five: "Choice Takes Too Much Time"

What it looks like:

Students spend 3 days deciding on a format. Only 2 days are actually working.

Solution:

Set a decision deadline:

"You have 1 class period to choose your format and submit your proposal. After that, you start working."

Prevents endless deliberation.

Examples of Choice-Based Assignments—By Subject

Math: Choice in Demonstration

Learning goal: Solve systems of equations

Assignment:

Demonstrate that you can solve systems of equations. Choose how:

Option A: Problem Set

Solve 10 problems—varying difficulty. Show your work.

Option B: Create a Tutorial

Create a video or written tutorial teaching someone else how to solve systems. Include 3 example problems.

Option C: Real-World Application

Find a real-world scenario that uses systems of equations—business, engineering, etc. Solve it. Explain your process.

Option D: Design Your Own

Propose your own way to demonstrate mastery. Get approval first.

Science: Choice in Topic Plus Format

Essential question: How do human activities impact ecosystems?

Assignment:

"Choose one human activity—deforestation, pollution, overfishing, climate change, etc.—and one ecosystem—coral reef, rainforest, wetland, etc."

"Demonstrate how this activity impacts this ecosystem."

"Choose your format:."

Research paper

Documentary-style video

Infographic with detailed annotations

Podcast interview—you interview an "expert"; can be scripted

3D model with explanation

English: Choice in Text Plus Product

Essential question: How do authors use symbolism to convey a theme?

Assignment: "Choose a novel, play, or film from this list." Provide 8-10 options. "Analyze how the author uses symbolism to convey the theme."

"Choose your format:."

Literary analysis essay

Video essay

Podcast episode analyzing symbolism

Creative project—symbol map, visual analysis—plus written explanation

Annotated screenplay/chapter

History: Choice in Research Question Plus Format

Unit: Civil Rights Movement

Assignment: "Choose one of these research questions—or propose your own:"

How did music influence the Civil Rights Movement?

What role did young people play?

How did media coverage shape public opinion?

How did the movement vary in different regions?

"Research your question. Present your findings."

"Choose your format:."

Research paper, documentary, museum exhibit—digital or physical

Podcast series—3 episodes

Historical fiction story with research notes

Elementary: Choice Board

Unit: Community helpers

Assignment: "Complete 3 activities from this choice board—choose 1 from each row."

Row 1: Research	Row 2: Create	Row 3: Reflect
Read a book about a community helper	Draw a poster showing what they do	Write: Why is this job important?
Interview someone with this job	Build a model of where they work	Write: Would you want this job? Why?
Watch a video about their work	Create a costume for this job	Write: How does this job help our community?

Genius Hour/Passion Projects—Maximum Choice

What it is:

Students pursue self-directed learning on a topic of their choice.

Structure:

1. Choose a topic

"What do you want to learn? It can be anything—within school-appropriate boundaries."

2. Set a learning goal

"What specifically do you want to learn about this topic?"

3. Plan your learning

"How will you learn it? Books, videos, experts, practice, experiments, etc."

4. Document your process

"Keep a learning journal. What are you learning? What's challenging? What's exciting?"

5. Share what you learned

"At the end of the semester, present your learning to the class—format of your choice."

Teacher role:

Coach: Check in weekly. "How's it going? What do you need?"

Resource connector: "You want to learn coding? Here's a free resource."

Accountability partner: "Show me your progress."

Why this works:

100% student-driven.

Students learn:

How to pursue their interests

How to set goals

How to learn independently

How to overcome obstacles

Skills for life.

Real Teacher Story: Mr. Jackson's Choice Transformation

Mr. Jackson taught high school English.

For 15 years, everyone wrote essays. Same prompt. Same format.

In Year 16, he introduced choice.

New assignment—novel unit:

"Analyze the theme in this novel. Choose your format:."

Traditional essay

Video essay

Podcast

Creative project plus written analysis

Propose your own

First attempt: Messy.

Half the class chose video—overwhelmed him with tech support questions

Quality varied wildly—he hadn't shown models

Some students chose "creative project" with no plan, and produced low-quality work

He adjusted:

Attempt Two—next semester:

Required proposal with a detailed plan

Showed models of each format—what quality looks like

Capped how many students could choose each format—max 5 videos, so he wasn't overwhelmed

Required checkpoints—draft/prototype due Week 2

Results:

Engagement skyrocketed—students excited to create in formats they enjoyed

Quality improved—students put in more effort when they had ownership

Differentiation happened naturally—advanced students chose complex formats; struggling students chose formats that scaffolded them

Students learned about themselves—"I learned I'm better at explaining things out loud than in writing."

Mr. Jackson reflected:

"I was scared to give up control. But choice gave students ownership in a way I never could by assigning everything. Now I'll never go back."

The Bottom Line

Student voice and choice are the final piece of your Mistake Lab.

You've taught students:

Mistakes equal data—Chapter 6

How to analyze mistakes—Chapter 12

How to identify patterns—Chapter 13

How to revise—Chapter 14

How to lead conferences—Chapter 15

Now: Students use all these tools to design their own learning.

To implement choice:

Start small—low-stakes choices first. Teach decision-making—a framework for choosing wisely. Provide structure—choice within boundaries. Model examples—show what quality looks like. Require proposals for complex projects. Check in during the process—at checkpoints and for feedback. Reflect on choices—metacognition.

Six dimensions of choice:

1. Content—what to learn
2. Process—how to learn
3. Product—how to demonstrate
4. Pace—when to work
5. Place—where to work
6. Partnership—who to work with

Pick 1-3 dimensions to start. Build over time.

When students have voice and choice:

They're not just learning content. They're learning how to learn.

They're becoming independent, self-directed, agentive learners. That's the goal of the Mistake Lab.

REFLECTION QUESTIONS

Personal Reflection:

1. On a scale of 1-5, how much choice do students have in your classroom?

1 = No choice—I decide everything

5 = High choice—students make most decisions

Your rating: _____

2. Which dimension of choice feels most comfortable to you? Content, process, product, pace, place, partnership
3. Which dimension feels most uncomfortable? Why?
4. How did you feel when you had a choice as a student? How does that shape your teaching now?

Choice Audit:

Look at one recent assignment:

What did you decide? Topic, format, deadline, etc.

What could students have decided?

How could you redesign this assignment to include choice?

Action Planning:

This semester/year:

☐ Start with one low-stakes choice—seating, partner, order of work

☐ Teach decision-making framework—goal, options, strengths, requirements, choice, justification

☐ Redesign one assignment to include choice—product options

☐ Provide structure—learning goals, success criteria, options, deadlines

☐ Show models—exemplars of each format

☐ Require proposals for complex projects

☐ Build in checkpoints—monitor progress

☐ Have students reflect on their choices—what worked? What didn't? What did you learn?

Further Exploration

Read:

- *The Power of Student Agency* by McDowell & Braden
- *Learner-Centered Innovation* by Katie Martin
- *Drive* by Daniel Pink—on autonomy, mastery, purpose
- *Choice Words* by Peter Johnston—language that builds agency

Watch:

- Genius Hour videos—examples from classrooms
- AJ Juliani talks about student choice

PART 3 RECAP

You've completed Part 3. Here's what you've built:

Chapter 12: The Mistake Analysis Protocol

4-step process: What happened? Why? What did I learn? What will I do differently?

Students analyze their own mistakes systematically. Transforms mistakes from failures into learning opportunities. Makes metacognition visible and actionable

Chapter 13: Error Pattern Recognition

5 types of patterns: Conceptual, Procedural, Careless, Performance, Metacognitive

Students track mistakes over time—Mistake Tracker

Monthly Pattern Reflection—identify trends, take targeted action

Breaking patterns equals addressing root causes, not just symptoms

Chapter 14: Revision as Learning

5 principles: First drafts are rough, revision is where learning happens, feedback is fuel, revision does not equal editing, iteration is ongoing

4-Stage Revision Cycle: Receive feedback → Analyze → Revise → Reflect

Subject-specific revision strategies

Grading systems that support revision—grade final drafts, not first attempts

Chapter 15: Student-Led Conferences

Students present their own learning to parents

7-part structure: Welcome, overview, mistake analysis, pattern recognition, goals, questions, closing

Builds agency, metacognition, accountability, and communication skills

Parents see the learning process, not just grades

Chapter 16: Student Voice and Choice

Choice builds intrinsic motivation, engagement, differentiation, and equity

Spectrum of choice: No choice → Limited → Moderate → High → Full autonomy

6 dimensions: Content, process, product, pace, place, partnership

Start small, provide structure, teach decision-making, model examples

Students now have the full toolkit:

Part 1: Foundation—science, vulnerability, safety, language, core concept

Part 2: Culture—first week, teacher as co-researcher, peer norms, grading revolution, equity

Part 3: Protocols—mistake analysis, pattern recognition, revision, conferences, voice/choice

What's next: Part 4

Working Within the System

How do you sustain a Mistake Lab when:

Standardized tests exist

Admin expects traditional grading

Parents push back

The system resists

Ready to continue?

PART 4

WORKING WITHIN THE SYSTEM

Sustaining Your Mistake Lab in a Traditional Education System

You've built your Mistake Lab.

You've:

Laid the foundation—Part 1

Established the culture—Part 2

Equipped students with protocols—Part 3

But here's the reality:

Your Mistake Lab doesn't exist in a vacuum.

It exists within:

A school with policies. A district with mandates

A state with standardized tests. A society with expectations

Parents with concerns. Administrators with priorities

Part 4 addresses the hard questions:

How do you prepare students for standardized tests while maintaining a mistake-literate culture?

How do you navigate grading policies when your district requires traditional grades?

How do you respond when parents push back?

How do you sustain this work when the system resists change?

In Part 4, you'll learn:

Chapter 17: Standardized Tests and Mistake Literacy—They're Not Incompatible

Chapter 18: Navigating School and District Policies—Working Within and Changing the System

Chapter 19: When Parents Push Back—Communication and Advocacy

Chapter 20: Sustaining the Work—Avoiding Burnout, Building Community

This is the reality check.

The idealism of Parts 1-3 meets the pragmatism of the education system.

Let's navigate it together.

CHAPTER 17

STANDARDIZED TESTS AND MISTAKE LITERACY

They're Not Incompatible—Here's How

The concern teachers raise most often:

"This all sounds great. But my students have to take standardized tests. I'm evaluated on their test scores. I don't have time for mistake literacy. I need to teach to the test."

The assumption behind this concern:

Mistake literacy and test prep are mutually exclusive.

You have to choose one or the other.

This chapter argues:

That's a false choice. Mistake literacy doesn't compete with test performance.

It improves test performance. And you can prepare for tests without abandoning mistake literacy.

Why Teachers Think They Have to Choose

The traditional test-prep mindset:

Assumption One: "Test Prep Equals Drills and Practice Tests"

The logic:

"Standardized tests require specific knowledge and skills. The way to prepare is to repeatedly practice test-like questions. Drills equal higher scores."

What this leads to:

Weeks of practice tests

Worksheets mimicking test format

Memorization of test-taking strategies

Elimination of "non-tested" content—art, music, inquiry, creativity

No time for mistake analysis, revision, or deep learning

The problem:

This approach:

May raise scores short-term—students learn test-taking tricks

Doesn't build deep understanding—students forget after the test

Kills engagement—drills are boring

Increases anxiety—high-stakes practice creates pressure

Disadvantages of students who don't test well—one-size-fits-all approach

Assumption Two: "Mistakes Waste Time"

The logic:

"If students make mistakes, I have to reteach. That takes time. I can't afford to let them fail. I need to prevent mistakes by explaining everything clearly up front."

What this leads to:

The teacher does most of the cognitive work—lectures, explains

Students passively receive information—take notes

Little time for practice—can't risk mistakes

No time for mistake analysis—we're moving fast to cover everything

The problem:

Students:

Don't develop a deep understanding—because they didn't struggle with it

Don't retain information—passive learning doesn't stick

Can't apply knowledge in new contexts—they memorized, didn't understand

Result on tests:

May do okay on straightforward questions—memorization

Struggle on application/analysis questions—require deep understanding

Assumption Three: "Standardized Tests Measure Performance, Not Learning"

The logic:

"Tests measure one-shot performance on a specific day. Mistake literacy is about iterative learning over time. Those are different things."

What this leads to:

"I'll teach mistake literacy during the year. But when test season comes, we abandon it and drill."

The problem:

This sends a mixed message:

"Learning from mistakes matters... except when it counts. When it really matters—tests, grades—you need to be perfect."

Students internalize: "Mistake literacy is nice, but it's not what actually matters."

The Truth: Mistake Literacy Improves Test Performance

Here's what research actually shows:

Finding One: Deep Learning Greater Than Shallow Coverage

Research—John Hattie, Dylan Wiliam, Robert Marzano:

Shallow coverage—racing through content to "cover" everything on the test: Students don't retain information

Can't apply knowledge to new contexts

Forget everything after the test

Deep learning—teaching less content, but ensuring students understand it: Students retain information longer

Can apply knowledge in new situations

Perform better on complex test questions

Translation:

Test questions aren't just recall.

Standardized tests increasingly include:

Application—use this concept in a new context

Analysis—break down complex information

Synthesis—combine multiple concepts

These require deep understanding.

Mistake literacy builds deep understanding—because students analyze why things work, not just memorize procedures.

Finding Two: Metacognition Improves Performance

Research—Dunlosky, Bjork, Brown/Roediger/McDaniel, "Make It Stick":

Students who are metacognitively aware of their own thinking:

Self-monitor during tests—"Does this answer make sense? Let me check."

Use strategies effectively—"This is a two-step problem. What's step 1?"

Manage their time—"I'm spending too long on this. Move on and come back."

Students who aren't metacognitive:

Rush through without checking

Don't notice errors

Don't use strategies

Mistake literacy develops metacognition.

When students analyze mistakes, they:

Think about their thinking. Identify patterns in their errors

Develop strategies to avoid mistakes. This directly improves test performance.

Finding Three: Growth Mindset Reduces Test Anxiety

Research—Carol Dweck, Angela Duckworth:

Students with a fixed mindset:

See tests as measuring their intelligence

High test anxiety—"If I fail, I'm not smart."

Give up when tests are hard—"I can't do this."

Students with a growth mindset:

See tests as measuring current understanding

Lower test anxiety—"This shows what I still need to learn."

Persist when tests are hard—"I can figure this out."

Mistake literacy builds a growth mindset.

Students learn: "Mistakes don't mean I'm not smart. They mean I'm learning."

Result: Lower anxiety, better performance.

Finding Four: Feedback Plus Revision Greater Than One-Shot Practice

Research—Ruth Butler, Dylan Wiliam, Paul Black:

One-shot practice tests:

Students take a test

Get score

Don't learn from mistakes—just move to the next practice test

Practice with feedback plus revision:

Students take a practice test

Analyze mistakes

Revise understanding

Demonstrate improvement

Which approach leads to better test scores?

Feedback plus revision.

Why?

Students actually learn from practice—not just perform.

Translation:

Mistake literacy practices—analyzing errors, revising, and improving—lead to better test performance than drill-and-kill.

How to Prepare for Tests Without Abandoning Mistake Literacy

Here's the approach:

Strategy One: Embed Test Skills Throughout the Year—Don't Save Them for Test Season

Traditional approach:

September-March: Teach content

April-May: Test prep—practice tests, drills

Mistake Lab approach:

All year: Teach content plus test-taking skills integrated

What this looks like:

Throughout the year, teach:

How to read test questions carefully—underline key words, identify what's being asked

How to eliminate wrong answers—process of elimination

How to check your work—does this answer make sense? Plug it back in

How to manage time—don't get stuck on one question

How to approach different question types—multiple choice, open response, and data analysis

Build these skills into regular instruction:

Example—math:

After teaching a concept, give students a few multiple-choice questions in test format.

Have students:

Solve the problem

Choose the correct answer

Then: Explain why the wrong answers are wrong—error analysis

This teaches:

Content—solving the problem

Test-taking—eliminating wrong answers

Mistake literacy—analyzing why wrong answers are tempting

No need for a separate "test prep" unit.

Test skills are woven throughout.

Strategy Two: Use Practice Tests as Learning Tools—Not Just Performance Assessments

Traditional approach:

Give practice test → grade it → move on

Mistake Lab approach:

Give practice test → analyze mistakes → reteach based on patterns → retake if needed

What this looks like:

Week 1: Practice test

Students take a practice test—timed, test conditions.

Week 2: Mistake analysis

Students don't just get a score.

They:

Identify which questions they got wrong

Categorize mistakes:

Conceptual error—didn't understand the concept

Procedural error—knew the concept, made a calculation/process error

Careless error—misread question, arithmetic mistake

Test-taking error—ran out of time, didn't eliminate wrong answers

Complete Mistake Analysis Protocol for 2-3 significant errors

Week 3: Targeted reteaching

You, the teacher, look at class-wide patterns.

If 15 students missed questions on fractions: Reteach fractions—different approach.

If 10 students made careless errors: Reteach checking strategies.

If 8 students ran out of time, teach time management.

Targeted intervention based on data.

Week 4: Retake—optional

Students who want to improve can retake—after reteaching plus practice.

Why this works:

Practice tests become learning opportunities, not just measurements.

Students improve because they analyze mistakes.

Strategy Three: Teach Students to Analyze Released Test Items

Most states release some test items each year.

Use them.

Activity: Error Analysis with Released Items

Step 1: Give students a released multiple-choice question—with the correct answer revealed.

Step 2: Students analyze the wrong answers.

"Why might someone choose A? What misconception would lead to that answer?"

"Why might someone choose C? What mistake would produce that answer?"

Step 3: Students reverse-engineer the test question.

"What concept is this question testing? What do you need to know to answer it correctly?"

Example—math:

Question: Which of the following is equivalent to 3(x + 2)?

A) 3x + 2

B) 3x + 6

C) x + 6

D) 3x + 5

Correct answer: B

Error analysis:

"Why might someone choose A?" "They distributed the 3 to the x but forgot to distribute it to the 2."

"Why might someone choose C?" "They added the 3 and the x instead of distributing."

"Why might someone choose D?"

"Arithmetic error. They distributed but calculated 3 × 2 = 5 instead of 6."

What students learn:

Common mistakes to avoid

How test-makers design wrong answers—to catch specific errors

How to approach these questions strategically. This is mistake literacy applied to test prep.

Strategy Four: Build Stamina Gradually—Don't Cram

Traditional approach:

Students take full-length practice tests weekly in April-May to "build stamina".

Result: Burnout, anxiety, diminishing returns.

Mistake Lab approach:

Build stamina gradually throughout the year.

September-October:

Short practice—10-15 questions, 20 minutes

November-December:

Medium practice—20-25 questions, 30 minutes

January-February:

Longer practice—full section, 45 minutes

March-April:

Full-length practice—entire test, with breaks

Why this works:

Students build stamina without burning out.

By test day, they're ready.

Strategy Five: Address Test Anxiety with Mistake Literacy

Test anxiety is real.

Students who fear mistakes experience higher anxiety.

How mistake literacy reduces test anxiety:

When students believe:

"Mistakes on practice tests equal learning opportunities"—not failures

→ Lower anxiety during practice

"I know how to analyze and fix my mistakes"—agency

→ Greater confidence

"Test scores don't determine my worth"—identity versus data → Less pressure.

Explicit teaching:

Before practice tests:

"This practice test is a learning tool. The mistakes you make will help you improve. This isn't measuring your intelligence. It's showing you what to study."

After practice tests:

"Now we analyze mistakes. This is where the learning happens."

On actual test day:

"You've practiced. You've learned from mistakes. You're ready. Do your best. One test doesn't define you."

Strategy Six: Don't Abandon Rich Learning for Test Prep

Traditional approach—March-May:

Stop all projects, discussions, labs, and creativity.

Focus 100% on test prep—drills, practice tests.

Mistake Lab approach:

Continue rich learning plus integrate test prep.

Example schedule—April-May: Monday-Wednesday: Continue regular curriculum—projects, discussions, deep learning

Thursday: Test-taking skills plus practice—short practice, analyze mistakes

Friday: Reflection plus targeted review—based on Thursday's patterns

Why this works: Students stay engaged—rich learning maintains interest

Deep learning continues—supports long-term retention

Test prep is targeted—not overwhelming

Students see test prep as part of learning—not a separate "drill and kill" mode.

What to Say to Admin/Parents Who Worry About Test Scores

When they say: "We need higher test scores. Focus on test prep."

You say:

"I'm absolutely committed to strong test performance. Here's my approach:

"**1. I'm teaching for deep understanding, not shallow coverage.**

Research shows deep understanding leads to better test performance, especially on complex questions.

2. I'm teaching metacognition through mistake analysis.

Students who can analyze their own thinking perform better on tests. They self-monitor, catch errors, and use strategies effectively.

3. I'm using practice tests as learning tools.

Students don't just take practice tests—they analyze mistakes, identify patterns, and revise understanding. This leads to greater improvement than drill-and-kill.

4. I'm building test skills throughout the year.

Test-taking strategies are integrated into regular instruction, not crammed in at the end.

5. I'm addressing test anxiety.

Students with lower anxiety perform better. Mistake literacy reduces anxiety by reframing tests as learning opportunities."

Then show data: "Here's what I'm tracking: practice test scores over time, error patterns, student self-assessments. I'll share this data with you monthly so you can see growth."

The key: You're not saying: "Test scores don't matter."

You're saying: "I'm preparing students effectively—in a way that builds lasting skills, not just short-term tricks."

Real Teacher Story: Ms. Chen's Test Prep Transformation

Ms. Chen taught 8th-grade math.

Her state had high-stakes testing in May.

For years, her test-prep approach:

January-May: Weekly practice tests

Drill procedures and formulas

Minimal time for mistake analysis—too busy covering content

Results: Decent scores. But students forgot everything after the test.

In Year 6, she changed her approach.

New system:

September-April: Teach content deeply—fewer topics, but true understanding

Build test-taking skills into regular lessons

After every quiz/test, students complete the Mistake Analysis Protocol

Monthly—September-April: One short practice test—30 minutes, 15 questions

Students analyze mistakes—categorize by type, complete protocol

Ms. Chen identifies class-wide patterns, reteaches based on data

May—test month: Two full-length practice tests—with mistake analysis after each

Targeted review based on patterns

Test-taking strategies review

Confidence-building—not panic-inducing

Results—Year 6: Test scores improved—higher than previous years, with a drill-heavy approach

Students were less anxious—they felt prepared, not panicked

Students retained knowledge—asked about concepts in high school; still remembered

Ms. Chen reflected: "I used to think test prep meant abandoning deep learning. Now I know: deep learning is the best test prep. When students understand why, they can handle any question the test throws at them."

The Bottom Line

Mistake literacy and standardized tests are not incompatible.

In fact, mistake literacy improves test performance because:

Deep learning—from analyzing mistakes—greater than shallow coverage

Metacognition—from error analysis—leads to better test-taking

Growth mindset—from mistake literacy—leads to lower anxiety

Feedback plus revision—from Mistake Lab—greater than drill-and-kill

To prepare for tests without abandoning mistake literacy:

Embed test skills throughout the year—don't save them for test season

Use practice tests as learning tools—analyze mistakes, reteach, retake

Teach error analysis with released items—understand common misconceptions

Build stamina gradually—don't cram

Address test anxiety—mistake literacy reduces pressure

Don't abandon rich learning—continue projects, deep learning, plus integrate test prep

When admin or parents worry:

Show them the research. Show them your data. Show them that mistake literacy is the best test prep.

REFLECTION QUESTIONS

Personal Reflection:

1. How do you currently prepare students for standardized tests?
2. Do you feel pressure to choose between deep learning and test prep? Where does that pressure come from?
3. How do your students feel about standardized tests? Anxious? Confident? Indifferent?
4. Have you ever used practice tests as learning tools—with mistake analysis? If not, what would that look like?

Test Prep Audit:

Look at your test prep approach:

How much time do you spend on test prep? Hours per week in March-May?

What does test prep look like? Practice tests? Drills? Content review? Mistake analysis?

Do students analyze their mistakes on practice tests? Or just get a score?

How could you integrate mistake literacy into test prep?

Action Planning:

This semester/year:

☐ Embed test skills throughout the year—don't save for test season

☐ After the next practice test, have students complete the Mistake Analysis Protocol

☐ Identify class-wide error patterns and reteach based on data

☐ Use released test items for error analysis—analyze wrong answers, reverse-engineer questions

☐ Build stamina gradually—short practice → medium → full-length over time

☐ Address test anxiety explicitly—teach that practice tests equal learning tools

☐ Continue rich learning during test season—don't abandon projects/discussions

Further Exploration

Read:

- *Embedded Formative Assessment* by Dylan Wiliam—using assessment to improve learning
- *Make It Stick* by Brown, Roediger, McDaniel—effective learning strategies
- *Visible Learning for Teachers* by John Hattie—what actually improves achievement

Mistake literacy and standardized tests can coexist.

In fact, mistake literacy is the best test prep.

Next: Navigating School and District Policies

What do you do when your grading system, your curriculum, or your admin's expectations conflict with mistake literacy?

Ready?

CHAPTER 18

NAVIGATING SCHOOL AND DISTRICT POLICIES

Working Within—and Changing—the System

The email lands in your inbox:

From: Principal

Subject: Grading Policy Reminder

"Dear Staff,

As a reminder, all grades must be entered in the gradebook by Friday. Per district policy:

All assignments must be graded for accuracy—not completion

Late work receives a 10% deduction per day

Final grades must be calculated as the average of all assignments

No retakes without documented accommodations

Thank you for your compliance."

You stare at the email.

You've spent months building a Mistake Lab:

Students analyze mistakes

Grades reflect current mastery—not averages

Revision is expected

Late work is accepted—within reason

And now this email says: "Follow district policy. Comply."

You think:

"Everything I've built contradicts this policy. Do I abandon my Mistake Lab? Do I quietly rebel? Do I try to change the policy? What do I do?"

This chapter is about navigating the tension between:

What you know is best for students—mistake literacy, learning-focused practices

And

What the system requires—policies, mandates, compliance

The Reality: Schools Are Systems

Schools don't operate in isolation.

They're nested systems:

You—the teacher

↓

Your classroom—your practices, your culture

↓

Your school principal, colleagues, and school policies

↓

Your district—superintendent, school board, district policies

↓

Your state department of education, state standards, and state tests

↓

Federal government—federal mandates, funding

Each level has:

Policies

Expectations

Mandates

Priorities

Sometimes these align with mistake literacy.

Sometimes they conflict.

Your challenge:

Navigate the system strategically.

Work within constraints when necessary.

Advocate for change when possible.

This chapter shows you how.

The Five Most Common Policy Conflicts

Let's address the policies that most often conflict with mistake literacy:

Conflict One: Grading Policies

Common district policies: "All assignments must be graded for accuracy."

"Grades must be averaged."

"Late work equals automatic deduction."

"No retakes without IEP/504 accommodation"

Why does this conflict with mistake literacy:

Grading for accuracy during practice equals high-stakes mistakes—students are afraid to fail

Averaging grades equals early mistakes haunt students forever—not current mastery

Late penalties equal grading compliance, not learning

No retakes equals one-shot performance—no iteration

What to do:

Option A: Work Within the Policy—Find Loopholes

If the policy says: "All assignments must be graded for accuracy."

You can still:

Grade practice assignments on a different scale

"Practice assignments are graded on a 0-4 effort/completion scale. Performance assessments are graded on a 0-100 accuracy scale."

Technically, everything is graded. But practice is low-stakes.

Weight categories differently

"Practice equals 10% of the final grade. Assessments equal 90%."

Practice is graded—policy satisfied—but it barely affects the final grade—students can fail practice safely.

If the policy says: "Grades must be averaged."

You can still:

Drop the lowest scores

"I dropped your two lowest quiz grades."

The average includes this accommodation. But early failures don't haunt students.

Weight recent assessments more heavily

"Quizzes 1-3 are worth 10 points each. Quizzes 4-6 are worth 20 points each."

Later quizzes—after learning has occurred—count more. Technically, it's an average. But it prioritizes current mastery.

If the policy says: "Late work equals 10% deduction per day."

You can still:

Extend deadlines for everyone

"This assignment is due Friday. But you can turn it in through Monday without penalty—I'm giving everyone a 3-day grace period."

No late penalty if they turn it in by Monday.

Accept "revisions" instead of "late work."

"If you turn in a draft by the deadline, you can revise it later without penalty."

Frame late submissions as "revisions"—allowed—rather than "late work"—penalized.

If the policy says: "No retakes."

You can still:

Offer "revisions"—not retakes

"You can't retake the test. But you can revise your test corrections and earn back partial credit."

Not technically a retake. But students can improve their grades through revision.

Give "alternate assessments."

"You can demonstrate mastery through an alternate assessment—project, oral exam, etc.—if your test score doesn't reflect your understanding."

Not a retake. A different assessment format.

These are workarounds. You're technically complying with the policy while preserving the principles of mistake literacy.

Option B: Advocate for Policy Change

If you want the policy itself to change:

Here's how to advocate strategically:

Step 1: Build evidence

Collect data showing:

Student growth with your approach—test scores, work samples, student reflections

Student engagement—attendance, participation, survey data

Parent/student feedback—testimonials, survey results

Example:

"Since implementing learning-focused grading practices, my students' test scores have improved by 15%. Here's the data. Here's what students and parents are saying."

Step 2: Find allies

Identify:

Other teachers interested in grading reform

Admins who are open to innovation. Parents who support your approach

District leaders who prioritize equity/learning. You're stronger as a coalition than alone.

Step 3: Propose a pilot

Don't ask to change the policy district-wide immediately. Ask to pilot an alternative approach in your classroom/school.

Proposal:

"I'd like to pilot standards-based grading in my classroom this semester. I'll collect data on student outcomes and share results. If it's successful, we can consider expanding."

Pilots are less threatening than wholesale policy changes.

Step 4: Frame it around district priorities

Don't say: "I want to change grading because I believe in mistake literacy."—They don't care about your beliefs.

Say: "I want to pilot an approach that aligns with our district's equity goals. Research shows that traditional grading disadvantages marginalized students. Here's an alternative that closes achievement gaps."

Connect your proposal to their priorities—equity, achievement, college readiness, etc.

Step 5: Be patient

Policy change is slow.

You might: Pilot for 1-2 years

Present data multiple times

Face resistance

Make compromises

Keep advocating. Incremental change is still change.

Option C: Quietly Push Boundaries—Strategic Non-Compliance

Some teachers choose strategic non-compliance:

They implement practices that technically violate policy, but:

Don't advertise it

Produce strong results—hard to argue with success

Build relationships with admin—so admin looks the other way

Example:

Policy says: "No retakes."

You: Allow retakes quietly. Don't announce it. Don't publicize it. Just do it.

When the admin asks: "My students are learning. Look at their growth."

If results are strong, the admin may not push back.

Caution:

This is risky.

You could:

Get reprimanded

Be told to stop

Face consequences if results don't justify the risk

Only pursue this if: You have strong relationships with the admin

You're producing undeniable results

You're prepared to defend your practices

Conflict Two: Pacing Guides/Curriculum Mandates

Common district mandates:

"All teachers must follow the pacing guide—teach Unit 1 in September, Unit 2 in October, etc."

"Use the district-adopted curriculum—specific textbook/program."

"All teachers teaching the same course must give common assessments on the same day."

Why does this conflict with mistake literacy:

Pacing guides prioritize coverage over mastery—move on even if students haven't learned

Rigid timelines don't allow for revision—no time to reteach/retake if you're racing to stay on pace

Common assessments on the same day equal one-shot performance—no flexibility for students who need more time

What to do:

Option A: Follow the Pacing Guide—But Adapt How You Teach

You can follow the pacing guide and still practice mistake literacy.

Here's how:

Teach fewer topics deeper—within each unit

Instead of: Covering every standard in the unit superficially

Try: Prioritizing the most important standards, teaching them deeply, letting students master them

You're still teaching the unit. But you're making choices about what to emphasize.

Use formative assessment to inform instruction—within the timeline.

Example:

Unit 3—October: Fractions

Week 1: Teach adding fractions. Formative quiz—Friday.

Weekend: Analyze quiz. 60% of students are struggling with finding common denominators.

Week 2: Reteach common denominators—different approach. Practice. Reassess.

You're still "on pace" for Unit 3. But you're responsive to student needs within the timeline.

Spiral back to previous units during warm-ups/homework.

If you had to move on from Unit 2 before students mastered it:

Continue practicing Unit 2 concepts in:

Warm-ups—5-10 minutes daily

Homework—mix in old concepts with new

Review days

You moved on—pacing guide satisfied—but you're still supporting mastery.

Option B: Advocate for Flexible Pacing

Propose to admin:

"Can we shift from a rigid pacing guide to a 'pacing range'?"

Instead of: "Teach Unit 3 in October"

Try: "Teach Unit 3 sometime between mid-October and mid-November—4-week window"

This allows teachers to adjust based on student needs while still ensuring all teachers cover the same content.

Or propose:

"Can we identify 'power standards'—the most essential concepts—and give teachers flexibility on the rest?"

Teachers must teach power standards—depth required.

Other standards can be covered more flexibly.

Option C: Use Common Assessments as Formative—Not Summative

If common assessments are required:

Reframe them:

Instead of: Common assessment equals final grade—summative

Propose: Common assessment equals diagnostic—formative

Students take the common assessment. But:

Results inform instruction—what needs reteaching?

Students can revise/retake after intervention.

You're still giving the common assessment—policy satisfied.

But you're using it to support learning—not just measure it.

Conflict Three: Homework Policies

Common district policies:

"Students must receive homework nightly."

"Homework must be graded."

Why does this conflict with mistake literacy:

Homework is practice.

Practice should be low-stakes—safe to make mistakes.

If homework is graded for accuracy, students:

Copy answers—to avoid mistakes

Don't take risks—only do what they're confident about

Feel punished for struggling

What to do:

Option A: Grade Homework on Completion/Effort—Not Accuracy

You're grading homework—policy satisfied.

But you're grading:

Did you attempt it? ✓

Did you show effort? ✓

Not:

Did you get it right? ✗

Students can make mistakes on homework without penalty.

Option B: Use Homework as Formative Assessment

You review homework to see:

Who's struggling?—offer intervention

What misconceptions exist?—reteach

What patterns emerge?—adjust instruction

But you don't put homework scores in the gradebook.

You track completion for accountability, but it doesn't affect grades.

Option C: Make Homework Optional But Valuable

If policy allows:

Homework is optional.

But you design it so students want to do it:

Scaffolded practice—helps prepare for assessments

Low-stakes feedback—students get feedback but no grade

Connected to interests—choice in homework tasks

Students do homework because it helps them learn, not because they're forced.

Conflict Four: Required Programs/Curricula

Common district mandates:

"All teachers must use [specific program/textbook/curriculum]."

"Fidelity to the program is required."

Why does this conflict with mistake literacy:

Scripted curricula often:

Don't allow time for mistake analysis—racing through lessons

Emphasize one-shot performance—tests at the end of each unit, no retakes

Prioritize compliance over student agency—teacher follows script, students follow directions

What to do:

Option A: Use the Required Curriculum as a Foundation—But Supplement

You teach the required curriculum.

But you add:

Mistake Analysis Protocol—after assessments

Revision opportunities—after students demonstrate learning needs

Student choice—how they practice, how they demonstrate learning

You're using the required materials. But you're layering mistake literacy on top.

Option B: Advocate for "Flexibility Within Fidelity"

Fidelity doesn't mean robotically following a script.

Propose:

"I'll teach the required curriculum with fidelity to the standards/objectives, but I'll adapt the methods based on student needs."

Core content: Required curriculum

Instructional methods: Your choice—including mistake literacy practices

Option C: Pilot Alternative Approaches

If you have strong relationships with admin:

Propose:

"I'd like to pilot a different approach to teaching [unit/concept]. I'll still cover the same standards, but I'll use a different method. I'll compare results to classes using the required curriculum."

If your results are better, you have evidence to support flexibility.

Conflict Five: Teacher Evaluation Systems

Common evaluation criteria:

"Teacher delivers clear, direct instruction."

"Students are on-task and compliant."

"Lesson follows prescribed format—I Do, We Do, You Do."

Why does this conflict with mistake literacy:

Mistake Labs are messy:

Students work independently—not all eyes on the teacher

Students make mistakes—not always "on-task" in a traditional sense

Teacher facilitates, not lectures—not "delivering instruction."

Evaluators might see:

"Students are off-task"—actually: experimenting and problem-solving

"Teacher isn't teaching"—actually: facilitating student-led learning

"Lesson lacks structure"—actually: student choice means varied pathways

What to do:

Option A: Educate Your Evaluator—Before the Observation

Before an observation, send an email: "I'm excited for you to observe my class on [date]. Here's what you'll see:."

"Students will be working in groups, analyzing mistakes from yesterday's quiz. You'll see students using the Mistake Analysis Protocol. Some groups may be at different stages. This is intentional—students are working at their own pace."

"I'll be circulating, asking probing questions, and facilitating discussions. I won't be at the front of the room lecturing, because students are doing the cognitive work."

"This aligns with [evaluation rubric item]: 'Teacher facilitates student-centered learning.'" Now the evaluator knows what to look for.

They won't misinterpret your methods.

Option B: Connect Your Practices to the Evaluation Rubric

Most evaluation rubrics include:

Student engagement

Critical thinking

Differentiation

Formative assessment

Student-centered learning

Your Mistake Lab hits all of these.

Make the connections explicit in your post-observation reflection:

"Student engagement: Students were actively analyzing their own mistakes—not passively receiving information."

"Critical thinking: Students identified error patterns and proposed strategies to address them."

"Differentiation: Students worked at their own pace on their own identified areas of need."

"Formative assessment: Students used quizzes as formative data to guide their learning."

Option C: Invite Your Evaluator Into the Process

Instead of being evaluated on your Mistake Lab:

Invite the evaluator to be a partner in building it.

Ask:

"I'm implementing mistake literacy practices. Would you be willing to observe multiple times this semester and give me feedback on what's working? I'd love your input."

Now they're invested in your success—not just evaluating you.

How to Build Allies for Systemic Change

Individual workarounds are useful. But systemic change requires collective action. Here's how to build a coalition:

Step 1: Find Other Teachers Who Share Your Values

Look for teachers who:

Question traditional grading

Prioritize learning over compliance

Are frustrated with current policies

Are willing to try new approaches

Have informal conversations:

"Have you ever thought about how grading for averages doesn't reflect learning?"

"I've been experimenting with allowing retakes. Want to collaborate?"

Step 2: Start a Study Group/Professional Learning Community (PLC)

Propose:

"Would anyone be interested in a monthly PLC on grading practices? We could read research, share strategies, and support each other."

Or:

"I'm reading 'Grading for Equity.' Anyone want to read it together and discuss?"

Study groups built:

Shared knowledge

Collective commitment and mutual support

Step 3: Pilot Collaboratively

Instead of one teacher piloting alone:

3-5 teachers pilot together.

Propose:

"We'd like to pilot standards-based grading in our classrooms this semester. We'll meet monthly to share data and troubleshoot. At the end of the semester, we'll present findings to the admin." Strength in numbers.

Step 4: Share Results Publicly

When you have data:

Student growth

Improved engagement

Positive feedback from students/parents

Share it:

Faculty meetings

PLC presentations

School board meetings—if appropriate

District professional development

Articles in district newsletters

Make your work visible.

Step 5: Engage Parents as Advocates

Parents are powerful advocates.

If parents support your approach:

They can advocate at school board meetings

They can email the admin/district leaders

They can share testimonials

How to engage parents:

After implementing mistake literacy practices, send a survey:

"How has [student-led conferences/revision opportunities/mistake analysis] impacted your students' learning?"

Collect testimonials. Share them with the admin.

Example:

"My daughter used to hate math. Now she analyzes her mistakes and sees growth. This approach has transformed her confidence." —Parent.

These testimonials carry weight.

Step 6: Connect to Broader Movements

Grading reform is happening nationally.

Organizations working on this:

Teachers Going Gradeless—a network of teachers rethinking grading

Equitable Grading Project—Joe Feldman's work

Standards-Based Learning initiatives—many districts are piloting

Connect your local work to these broader movements.

Share resources. Learn from others. Build momentum.

Real Teacher Story: Mr. Thompson's Policy Navigation

Mr. Thompson taught high school history.

His district had rigid policies:

All assignments are graded for accuracy

Grades averaged

No retakes

Strict pacing guide

He wanted to implement mistake literacy.

But he felt stuck.

Year 1: He worked within the system

He:

Graded assignments for accuracy—policy requirement

But weighted formative assignments at 20%, summative at 80%—so practice mistakes didn't tank grades.

Averaged grades—policy requirement

But dropped the two lowest quiz scores, so one bad day didn't ruin the students.

Didn't offer retakes officially—policy prohibition

But offered "alternate assessments" for students who wanted to demonstrate mastery differently

Followed the pacing guide—policy requirement

But spiraled back to the previous content in warm-ups and homework

Result: He implemented mistake literacy principles within policy constraints.

Student outcomes improved.

Year 2-3: He built a coalition

He:

Started a PLC with 4 other teachers interested in grading reform

They read *Grading for Equity* together

They shared strategies

They collected data on student growth

After 2 years, they had compelling evidence:

Test scores improved in all 5 teachers' classes

Student engagement increased

Parents reported positive changes

Year 4: They proposed a pilot

The PLC proposed to the admin:

"We'd like to pilot standards-based grading in our 5 classrooms next year. We'll track student outcomes and report back. If results are positive, consider expanding."

Admin approved the pilot—low risk for admin; only 5 teachers, not district-wide.

Year 5: The pilot succeeded

Data showed:

Higher test scores

Increased student engagement

Reduced achievement gaps

Positive parent feedback. The PLC presented results to the school board. The board approved expanding standards-based grading to the entire school.

Mr. Thompson reflected:

"Year 1, I felt powerless. But I worked within the system and proved it could work. Then I built a coalition. We advocated together. Change was slow—5 years—but we changed the system, not just our individual classrooms. That's lasting impact."

The Bottom Line

School and district policies will sometimes conflict with mistake literacy.

You have options:

Option A: Work Within the System

Find loopholes

Adapt policies creatively

Technically comply while preserving principles

Option B: Advocate for Change

Build evidence

Find allies

Propose pilots

Frame around district priorities

Be patient—change is slow

Option C: Strategic Non-Compliance

Push boundaries quietly

Produce strong results

Build relationships with the admin

Risky—only if you're prepared to defend

The most effective approach: Combine Option A plus Option B. Work within the system—short-term—while advocating for change—long-term.

Systemic change requires: Collective action—coalitions, not individuals

Data—evidence of impact

Strategic framing—align with district priorities

Patience—incremental change over the years

Persistence—keep advocating even when it's slow

You can navigate policies. And you can change them. But it takes strategy, evidence, allies, and time.

REFLECTION QUESTIONS

Personal Reflection:

1. Which district/school policies conflict most with your mistake literacy practices?
2. Have you tried to work within those policies? What creative workarounds have you found?
3. Have you advocated for policy change? What happened?
4. Who are potential allies in your school/district? Other teachers, admin, parents?

Policy Audit:

List 3 policies that conflict with mistake literacy:

1. ______________________________
2. ______________________________
3. ______________________________

For each policy, ask:

Can I work creatively within this policy?

Can I advocate for a change in this policy?

What data/evidence would I need to support change?

Who would I need as allies?

Action Planning:

This semester/year:

☐ Identify one policy you can work within creatively—find a loophole/workaround

☐ Collect data on student outcomes—to support future advocacy

☐ Find 2-3 allies—other teachers interested in similar changes

☐ Start a study group/PLC—read and discuss grading/mistake literacy

☐ Propose a pilot—small-scale change in your classroom or with a few teachers

☐ Engage parents—survey them on your practices, collect testimonials

☐ Present findings—share data with admin/colleagues

Further Exploration

Read:

- *Grading for Equity* by Joe Feldman—a comprehensive guide to grading reform, plus how to navigate policies
- *Hacking Assessment* by Starr Sackstein—workarounds for traditional grading systems
- *Leading Impact Teams* by Paul Bloomberg & Barb Pitchford—building teacher coalitions for change

Connect:

- Teachers Going Gradeless—online community: teachersgoinggradeless.com
- Equitable Grading Project—resources: gradingforequity.org

You can navigate policies. You can advocate for change. You don't have to choose between compliance and your values.

Work within the system. And work to change it.

Next: When Parents Push Back

How do you respond when parents don't understand—or don't support—mistake literacy?

Ready?

CHAPTER 19

WHEN PARENTS PUSH BACK

Communication and Advocacy

The email arrives Monday morning:

From: Parent—Sarah's mom

Subject: Concerns about grading

"Dear Ms. Rodriguez,

I'm concerned about Sarah's grade in your class. She worked very hard on her first essay and received a C. Now you're saying she can revise it and improve her grade?

This doesn't seem fair. In the real world, you don't get second chances. You need to get it right the first time. I'm worried you're not preparing her for college.

Also, I noticed you haven't graded homework. Sarah says you only give 'feedback.' How am I supposed to know if she's doing her work correctly?

I'd like to schedule a meeting to discuss this.

Sincerely,

Mrs. Patterson"

You read the email.

Your first reaction: Defensive. "She doesn't understand what I'm doing. Revision is how learning happens. This is research-based!"

Your second reaction: Doubt. "Am I doing the right thing? What if she's right?"

Your third reaction: Anxiety. "What if she complains to the admin? What if other parents feel this way?"

This chapter is about:

How to respond when parents push back on mistake literacy practices.

Why Parents Push Back

Parents aren't pushing back to make your life difficult.

They're pushing back because:

Reason One: Your Approach Is Different from What They Experienced

Most parents went to school in the 1980s-2000s.

Their experience:

One-shot assignments—no revision

Graded everything—homework, classwork, tests

Averages—early failures haunted them

No retakes—test scores were final

Mistakes equal bad—red X's, point deductions, shame

Your approach is unfamiliar.

What's unfamiliar equals threatening.

They think: "This isn't how school worked for me. How do I know it will work for my child?"

Reason Two: They Equate Rigor with Traditional Grading

Parents often believe:

"Strict grading equals high standards."

"Allowing revisions equals lowering the bar."

"If you let students retake tests, they'll slack off."

They conflate:

Rigor—high expectations plus support to meet them

With

Harshness—punishment for mistakes, no second chances

They don't understand:

You can have high expectations and support revision.

In fact, revision raises the bar—students must demonstrate mastery, not just turn in something mediocre.

Reason Three: They're Worried About Their Child's Future

Parents think:

"College won't allow retakes."

"Jobs won't give second chances."

"The real world is harsh. I need to prepare my child for that."

They see revision/retakes as:

Coddling. Protecting kids from reality.

They don't see:

Revision is what the real world requires—drafts, prototypes, iterations.

Reason Four: They Don't Understand the Research

You know the research:

Feedback without grades → better learning—Ruth Butler

Grades reflect current mastery, not averages → more accurate—Dylan Wiliam

Revision → deeper learning—John Hattie

Growth mindset → higher achievement—Carol Dweck

Parents don't know this research.

They're operating on the belief that "This is how I learned, so it must be right."

Reason Five: They're Confused About What Grades Mean

Traditional grading is familiar:

"My child has a 92%. I know exactly what that means. They're doing well."

Your grading might be different:

"My child is 'proficient' on 3 standards, 'developing' on 2."

Parent thinks: "What does that mean? Is that good? How does this translate to college?"

Confusion breeds anxiety.

Anxiety breeds pushback.

Reason Six: Their Child Is Struggling—and They're Scared

Sometimes, pushback isn't really about your grading system.

It's about:

"My child is failing. I'm scared. I don't know how to help. I'm looking for someone to blame." Your grading system equals a convenient target.

Underneath the complaint:

Fear. Worry. Helplessness. Not anger at you personally.

The Five Principles of Responding to Parent Concerns

When parents push back, follow these principles:

Principle One: Listen First—Don't Defend

Your instinct: Jump in and defend your practices.

"Actually, research shows..."

Resist this urge.

Instead:

Listen fully.

Ask questions:

"Tell me more about your concerns."

"What specifically worries you?"

"What would you like to see happen?"

Why this works:

Parents feel heard—they're not just being lectured to

You understand the real concern—often it's not what they said initially

You build rapport—listening equals respect

Example:

Parent says: "I don't think you should allow retakes. It's not fair."

Don't immediately say: "Actually, research shows retakes improve learning..."

Instead, ask: "Tell me more. What about retakes feels unfair to you?"

The parent might say: "Well, my older child's teacher didn't allow retakes. He had to study hard the first time. I'm worried my younger child won't develop good study habits if she can just retake."

Now you understand: The real concern is about study habits, not retakes per se.

You can address that concern.

Principle Two: Validate Their Concern—Even If You Disagree

After listening:

Validate their feelings.

This doesn't mean agreeing with them. It means acknowledging their concern is real.

Examples:

"I hear that you're worried about preparing your child for the real world. That's a legitimate concern."

"I understand that this approach is different from how you learned. Change can feel uncertain."

"It sounds like you're concerned about whether your child is developing good work habits. That's an important question."

Why this works:

People are more receptive to new information after they feel heard.

If you jump straight to "here's why you're wrong," they shut down.

If you validate first, they're open to listening.

Principle Three: Educate—With Empathy, Not Condescension

After validating:

Explain your approach.

But frame it as:

"Let me share why I do this, and you can tell me what you think."

Not:

"Let me tell you why you're wrong."

Use:

Research—but translate it to plain language

Examples—specific stories from your classroom

Analogies—connect to things they know

Example—addressing revision concerns:

"I understand your concern about retakes. Let me share why I use them."

"When engineers design a product, they build prototypes, test them, identify what doesn't work, and redesign. They don't get it perfect the first time. Revision is built into the process."

"I want students to learn the same way. The first draft of an essay is like a prototype. They get feedback, revise, and improve. The goal is mastery, not one-shot performance."

"Research shows students who revise learn more deeply and retain information longer than students who only do one draft. And here's what I see in my classroom: [specific example of student growth through revision]."

"What do you think?"

Why this works:

Real-world analogy—engineers revise; relatable

Research—but simplified, not jargon-heavy

Classroom example—concrete, not abstract

Invites dialogue—not lecturing

Principle Four: Connect to Their Values

Find common ground.

What do you both care about?

Their child's success

Preparation for the future

Deep learning—not just memorization

Confidence and growth

Frame your practices as supporting their values.

Example:

Parent says: "I'm worried this won't prepare my child for college."

You say:

"I share that concern. I want every student to be ready for college. Let me tell you how this approach actually prepares them better."

"In college, professors expect students to:"

Revise drafts—writing courses require multiple drafts

Seek feedback—office hours, writing centers

Self-assess—reflect on their learning

Take ownership—professors won't chase you; you have to advocate for yourself.

"That's exactly what I'm teaching. Students analyze their own mistakes, seek feedback, revise their work, and take ownership of their learning. These are the skills colleges expect."

You've reframed:

Your practices support college readiness—not undermine it.

Principle Five: Invite Partnership—Not Confrontation

Frame the conversation as:

"We're on the same team. Let's work together to support your child."

Not:

"You're wrong. I'm the expert."

Examples:

"I'd love to partner with you to support Sarah's learning. Here's what I'm doing in class. What are you noticing at home? How can we work together?"

"I'm always learning and improving my teaching. If you have concerns, I want to hear them. Let's figure this out together."

How to Respond to Specific Parent Concerns

Here are the most common concerns and how to address them:

Concern One: "Allowing Retakes Isn't Fair. Students Should Get It Right the First Time."

Listen:

"Tell me more about what feels unfair to you."

Validate:

"I hear that you're concerned about fairness and accountability. Those are important values."

Educate:

"Let me share how retakes work in my class and why I use them."

"First, retakes aren't 'free.' Students have to:."

Complete error analysis—identify what went wrong

Attend a reteaching session—office hours or tutoring

Show evidence of additional study/practice

"So students are working harder, not less hard, when they retake."

"Second, the goal is mastery. If a student didn't understand fractions on October 15 but does understand them by October 30, their grade should reflect current understanding, not their confusion two weeks ago."

"Research shows that when students can revise and demonstrate growth, they learn more deeply and retain information longer."

Connect to values:

"I know you want your child to be prepared for the real world. In most careers—medicine, engineering, business—people get feedback and revise constantly. One-shot performance is actually the exception, not the rule."

Invite partnership:

"I'd love to hear if you see your child developing better study habits through this process. Let's check in again in a few weeks."

Concern Two: "You're Not Grading Homework. How Do I Know If My Child Is Learning?"

Listen:

"What worries you about homework not being graded?"

Validate:

"I understand. You want to know how your child is doing. That's completely reasonable."

Educate:

"Let me explain how I use homework."

"Homework is practice. It's where students try new skills and make mistakes. If I grade practice for accuracy, students are afraid to fail, so they copy answers or only do what they're sure about."

"Instead, I give feedback on homework. I look at it, identify mistakes, and write comments like: 'You're doing well with X. You're still working on Y. Here's what to focus on.'"

"Students get more information from feedback than from a grade. A grade tells you, 'you got 75%.' Feedback tells you 'here's specifically what you need to improve.'"

"Research shows that when students get grades plus feedback, they ignore the feedback and focus on the grade. When they get feedback only, they actually use it to improve."

Connect to values:

"I know you want to know how your child is doing. Here's how you can tell:"

Look at the feedback I wrote on the homework

Check the gradebook for test scores—those are graded for accuracy

Ask your child: 'What are you working on? What's challenging? What have you learned?'

Invite partnership:

"I send home progress reports every 3 weeks showing exactly what your child has mastered and what they're still working on. Does that give you the information you need?"

Concern Three: "My Child Says They Can Turn in Work Late. That's Not Teaching Responsibility."

Listen:

"Tell me more about your concern."

Validate:

"I hear that you're worried about responsibility and meeting deadlines. Those are important life skills."

Educate:

"Let me clarify my late work policy."

"I do have deadlines. Assignments are due on [date]. But I also understand that life happens—illness, family emergencies, struggling with the material."

"So I accept late work within a reasonable timeframe—usually 1 week. But there's a catch: if work is consistently late, I conference with the student to figure out what's getting in the way and how to help them stay on track."

"My goal isn't to punish lateness. It's to teach time management and problem-solving."

"Research shows that when we grade timeliness instead of learning, we conflate the two. A student could understand the content perfectly but get a lower grade because they turned it in late. That grade doesn't accurately reflect learning."

Connect to values:

"I want students to learn responsibility. But I also want them to learn that when you're overwhelmed, the responsible thing is to communicate and problem-solve, not give up."

"In the real world, if you're going to miss a deadline, you communicate with your boss and negotiate an extension. That's what I'm teaching."

Invite partnership:

"If you're noticing your child turning things in late regularly, let's talk. We can work together to help them develop better time management."

Concern Four: "This Feels Like You're Lowering Standards. My Child Needs to Be Challenged."

Listen:

"What makes you feel like standards are being lowered?"

Validate:

"I hear that you want high expectations for your child. So do I."

Educate:

"Let me clarify what I mean by 'mistakes as learning opportunities.'"

"I have very high standards. I expect students to demonstrate mastery of complex concepts."

"But I also know that learning is messy. Students don't master things on the first try. They need practice, feedback, and revision."

"Allowing revision doesn't lower the bar. In fact, it raises it. Because students can't turn in mediocre work and be done with it, they have to keep revising until it meets the standard."

"So instead of accepting a C as 'good enough,' I'm saying: 'This doesn't meet the standard yet. Here's what needs to improve. Revise it.'"

Connect to values:

"I think we both want the same thing: for your child to deeply understand the material, not just memorize and forget it."

"That's what revision achieves. Students who revise learn more deeply."

Invite partnership:

"I'd love to show you examples of student work—first drafts versus final drafts. You'll see the growth. Does that sound helpful?"

Concern Five: "My Child Is Used to Getting Straight A's. Now They Have a B. What's Going On?"

Listen:

"Tell me about what you're noticing."

Validate:

"I understand this is frustrating. Your child has worked hard and is used to high grades."

Educate:

"Let me explain how my grading works."

"In my class, grades reflect mastery of standards, not completion of assignments or effort."

"A B means: 'You're proficient. You understand most of the material. There are a few areas where you're still developing."

"This might be different from previous classes where grades were based on completing assignments or averaging all attempts."

"Here's what I see with your child: [specific standards mastered, specific standards still developing]."

"The good news: Your child can improve their grade by demonstrating mastery of the standards they're still developing. Here's how: [specific actions]."

Connect to values:

"I know you want your child to succeed. I do too. My grading system is designed to give accurate information about what your child knows so we can target support where it's needed."

Invite partnership:

"Let's work together to help your child master the remaining standards. What support can we provide at school and at home?"

Concern Six: "This Is Too Different. I Don't Understand It."

Listen:

"What's most confusing?"

Validate:

"I completely understand. This is different from how most of us learned, and that can feel disorienting."

Educate:

"Let me walk you through how it works, step by step." Use visuals, examples, and simple language. "Would it help if I sent you a one-page overview you can reference?"

Connect to values:

"The reason I'm doing this is that research shows it leads to deeper learning. But I know it's a shift. I'm here to answer any questions."

Invite partnership:

"What would help you understand this better? A meeting? A written guide? A chance to see your child's work portfolio?"

Proactive Communication—Prevent Pushback Before It Starts

The best way to handle parent concerns:

Prevent them.

How?

Communicate proactively.

Strategy One: Explain Your Approach at the Beginning of the Year

Back-to-School Night/Welcome Letter:

Don't wait for parents to be confused.

Explain upfront:

How grading works

Why do you use mistake literacy practices

What research supports this

How parents can support at home

Sample welcome letter excerpt:

"Welcome to 7th-grade science! I'm excited to work with your child this year."

"I want to share how learning works in my classroom. My goal is for every student to deeply understand scientific concepts, not just memorize facts for tests."

"Here's how I approach learning:"

1. Mistakes are learning opportunities

"When students make mistakes, we analyze them. Students use a 4-step protocol to figure out what went wrong, why it went wrong, and what to do differently. This builds metacognition and problem-solving skills."

2. Grades reflect current mastery

"Grades show what your child knows now, not an average of all attempts. Students can revise work and retake assessments after demonstrating additional learning."

3. Practice is separate from performance

"Homework and classwork are practice—graded on completion/effort. Tests and projects are performance—graded on mastery."

"This approach is based on research showing that students learn more deeply when they can learn from mistakes without penalty."

"I know this may be different from how you learned. I'm happy to answer any questions. You can reach me at [email]." This sets expectations early. Parents aren't surprised later.

Strategy Two: Send Regular Updates

Don't wait for parent-teacher conferences.

Communicate regularly:

Weekly/biweekly email updates—what we're learning, upcoming assessments, how parents can support

Monthly progress reports—what students have mastered, what they're working on, and specific growth

Student-created updates—students email parents explaining their learning; builds ownership

Example monthly email:

"Dear families,

Here's what we've been working on in October:"

Students analyzed ecosystems and identified energy flow

We practiced error analysis after the Unit 2 test—students identified patterns in their mistakes

Students revised their lab reports based on feedback

"Next month, we'll study chemical reactions. Here's how you can support at home: [specific suggestions]."

"Questions? Reach out anytime."

Strategy Three: Invite Parents Into the Process

Make parents partners, not observers.

Invite them to:

Student-led conferences—students present their learning; parents see mistake analysis in action

Portfolio nights—students showcase work, including mistake analysis and revisions

Classroom observations—open invitation: "Come see us in action anytime."

When parents see the work:

They understand it better than when you just tell them.

Strategy Four: Share Student Success Stories

Regularly share examples of student growth.

In newsletters, emails, or parent nights:

"I want to share a success story. A student struggled with fractions all semester. They made the same mistake repeatedly. But they used the Mistake Analysis Protocol to identify the pattern, practiced intentionally, and now they've mastered it. This is what learning looks like in our classroom."

Stories make the abstract concrete.

When to Involve Administration

Most parent concerns can be resolved through communication.

But sometimes you need admin support.

Involve administration when:

1. The parent is hostile/aggressive

If a parent is threatening, verbally abusive, or making unreasonable demands, loop in the admin.

Say:

"I want to resolve this, but I think it would be helpful to have [principal] join our conversation."

2. The concern is about school/district policy—not just your classroom

If a parent is questioning policies beyond your control—such as the district-mandated grading system, curriculum requirements, etc.—the admin needs to be part of the conversation.

3. The parent demands you change your practices in ways that harm learning

If a parent insists you stop allowing retakes, stop giving feedback, grade homework for accuracy—and you've explained why you do what you do—the admin can support you.

Say:

"I've explained my approach and the research behind it. This is what's best for students. I'd like [principal] to join this conversation."

4. You've tried to resolve it, and the parent is unsatisfied

If you've had multiple conversations, explained your approach, offered compromises, and the parent is still escalating, it's time to escalate to admin.

How to involve admin:

Don't surprise them.

Loop them in early:

"I wanted to let you know I'm meeting with a parent who has concerns about my grading practices. I'm confident I can address their concerns, but I wanted you to be aware in case they reach out to you."

Keep them updated:

"I met with the parent. Here's what we discussed. Here's the plan moving forward."

This way, if the parent escalates, the admin already knows the context.

Real Teacher Story: Mr. Davis's Parent Turnaround

Mr. Davis taught 9th-grade English.

He implemented mistake literacy: revision was expected, grades reflected current mastery, and student-led conferences were held.

Month 2: He got an angry email from a parent.

Parents' concern: "My son turned in an essay and got a C. Now you're letting him revise it? He should have done it right the first time. This isn't preparing him for college. I want a meeting."

Mr. Davis's initial reaction: Defensive. "She doesn't understand. This is how college works."

But he took a breath. Followed the principles.

The meeting:

Step 1: Listen

Mr. Davis: "Thank you for meeting. Tell me about your concerns."

Parent: "I just don't think you should let him revise. He needs to learn to do it right the first time. College won't give him second chances."

Step 2: Validate

Mr. Davis: "I hear that you're worried about preparing him for college. That's a completely legitimate concern. I share it."

Step 3: Ask questions—to understand the real concern

Mr. Davis: "Can I ask—what worries you most about revision?"

Parent: "I'm worried he'll procrastinate. He'll think, 'Oh, I can just revise later,' and not try his best the first time."

Ah. The real concern: Effort, not revision itself.

Step 4: Educate

Mr. Davis: "That's a great question. Let me show you how revision works in my class."

Shows the rubric, the student's first draft with feedback, and the revision process.

"He can't just change a few sentences and resubmit. He has to:."

Analyze what didn't work—using the Mistake Analysis Protocol

Meet with me to discuss revisions

Substantially revise the essay—not just surface edits

"So revision requires more work, not less."

"And here's why I think this prepares him for college: In college writing courses, professors require multiple drafts. That's the standard. No one writes a perfect essay on the first try."

Step 5: Show evidence

Mr. Davis: "Let me show you your son's first draft versus his revised draft."

Shows both. "Look at the improvement. He learned so much through revision. That's deep learning."

Step 6: Invite a partnership

Mr. Davis: "I'd love to partner with you to make sure he's developing strong work habits. Here's what I'm seeing in class. What are you seeing at home?"

Result:

The parent left the meeting satisfied. A month later, she emailed: "Thank you for explaining your approach. I see my son engaging more with his writing than he ever has. He's proud of his work. I'm on board."

Mr. Davis reflected:

"I almost went into that meeting defensive. But when I listened first, I realized her concern wasn't really about revision. It was about effort. Once I addressed that, she understood."

The Bottom Line

Parents push back because:

Your approach is unfamiliar

They equate rigor with traditional grading

They're worried about their child's future

They don't understand the research

They're confused about what grades mean

They're scared—their child is struggling

When parents push back:

Listen first—don't defend. Validate their concern—even if you disagree. Educate—with empathy, not condescension. Connect to their values—find common ground. Invite partnership—we're on the same team.

Prevent pushback through proactive communication:

Explain your approach at the start of the year. Send regular updates.

Invite parents into the process—student-led conferences, portfolio nights

Share success stories

Most parent concerns can be resolved through communication.

When they can't, involve the admin for support.

Parents are your allies—even when they push back.

They want what's best for their child.

So do you. Find that common ground. Work together.

REFLECTION QUESTIONS

Personal Reflection:

1. Have you experienced pushback from parents on your teaching practices? What happened?
2. When parents question your methods, what's your first reaction? Defensive? Anxious? Confident?
3. How do you currently communicate with parents about your grading/teaching approach?
4. What's one thing you could do to communicate more proactively?

Scenario Practice:

Imagine a parent says:

"I don't think you should allow retakes. My child needs to learn to get it right the first time."

Write your response using the 5 principles:

1. Listen:
2. Validate:
3. Educate:
4. Connect to values:
5. Invite partnership:

Action Planning:

This semester/year:

☐ Create a welcome letter explaining your approach—send at the start of the year or semester

☐ Send a monthly update email—what we're learning, how parents can support

☐ Hold student-led conferences—invite parents to see mistake literacy in action

☐ Prepare responses to common concerns—practice the 5 principles

☐ Loop in admin proactively—let them know your approach, share research

☐ Collect parent testimonials—from parents who support your approach; use these to educate others

Further Exploration

Read:

- *Grading for Equity* by Joe Feldman—Chapter on communicating with parents
- *The Parents We Mean to Be* by Richard Weissbourd—Understanding Parent Anxieties

You can navigate parent pushback.

Listen. Validate. Educate. Partner.

Most parents will come around when they understand.

Next—final chapter of Part 4: Sustaining the Work

How do you avoid burnout? How do you keep this going year after year?

Ready?

CHAPTER 20

SUSTAINING THE WORK

Avoiding Burnout, Building Community

Year 1 of your Mistake Lab:

You're energized. Excited. Every day feels purposeful.

You're:

Teaching mistake analysis

Giving feedback instead of just grades

Having students lead conferences

Building a culture where failure is safe

It's working. Students are engaged. They're learning.

You think: "I'll never go back to the old way."

Year 2:

Still going strong.

You've refined your systems. You know what works.

But you're also:

Spending 15 hours a week giving feedback—you don't just grade; you write meaningful comments

Staying after school for retake sessions

Answering parent emails at 10 PM

Revising your grading system—again—because district policies changed

You think: "This is a lot of work. But it's worth it."

Year 3:

You're tired.

You notice:

You're skipping feedback on some assignments—you just don't have the energy

You're allowing fewer retakes—the logistics are overwhelming

You're cutting corners on mistake analysis—students do it, but you don't check as carefully

You're resentful when parents push back—you think: "I'm working so hard and they're complaining?"

You think: "Maybe the old way was easier."

Year 4:

You're burned out.

You've quietly abandoned some practices:

Students don't lead conferences anymore—too much prep

You grade homework for completion—not feedback; faster

Retakes are rare—you can't keep up

You think: "I tried. But I can't sustain this."

This is the trajectory of burnout.

It happens to passionate teachers who don't build sustainable systems.

This chapter is about:

How to sustain mistake literacy work for the long term—without burning out.

Why Teachers Burn Out on Reform Work

Burnout doesn't happen because the work isn't worth it.

Burnout happens when:

Reason One: You're Trying to Do Everything Alone

You think:

"I'm the only one doing this. My colleagues don't get it. I'm on my own."

Result:

No one to share the workload

No one to troubleshoot with

No one to celebrate successes with

Isolation

Isolation equals burnout.

Reason Two: You're Doing Too Much at Once

You think:

"I need to implement all the practices from this book: mistake analysis, pattern recognition, revision, student-led conferences, choice, grading reform, etc."

Result:

Overwhelming workload

Can't do any of it well—spread too thin

Constant stress

Overcommitment equals burnout.

Reason Three: You're Not Setting Boundaries

You think:

"Good teachers work nights and weekends. If I'm not giving feedback at 11 PM, I'm not doing enough."

Result: No work-life balance

Physical exhaustion

Resentment

No boundaries equals burnout.

Reason Four: You're Swimming Upstream—System Resistance

You think:

"I'm fighting district policies, admin expectations, parent pushback, and standardized tests. It's exhausting."

Result: Constant battles

Feeling like Sisyphus—pushing a boulder uphill

Demoralization

System resistance without support equals burnout.

Reason Five: You're Not Seeing Results—or Not Noticing Them

You think: "I'm working so hard. But students still make the same mistakes. Parents still complain. Nothing's changing."

Result: Loss of motivation

Questioning if it's worth it

Giving up. Lack of visible progress equals burnout.

Reason Six: You've Lost Connection to Your "Why"

Year 1, you were clear:

"I'm doing this because students deserve better than shame-based grading. I want them to see mistakes as learning opportunities."

Year 4, you've forgotten:

"Why am I doing this again? I'm exhausted."

Result:

Work feels like an obligation—not a purpose

No emotional fuel

Burnout

Loss of purpose equals burnout.

The Seven Strategies for Sustaining the Work

Here's how to sustain mistake literacy without burning out:

Strategy One: Build Community—Don't Do It Alone

The antidote to isolation: Community.

Find your people:

Option A: Build a Local Community—Your School/District

Start or join a PLC—Professional Learning Community—focused on:

Grading reform

Formative assessment

Mistake literacy

Student agency

What this looks like:

3-5 teachers meet monthly or biweekly.

Agenda:

Share what's working

Troubleshoot challenges

Read the research together

Support each other

Why this works:

- You're not alone—others are doing this too
- Shared problem-solving—collective wisdom greater than individual struggle
- Accountability—you're more likely to sustain practices when others are counting on you
- Celebration—someone celebrates your wins with you

How to start:

Step 1: Identify 2-3 teachers interested in this work.

Step 2: Propose a monthly meeting—"Want to meet once a month to discuss grading practices? We could read articles, share strategies, and support each other."

Step 3: Set a regular time—same day/time each month; easier to commit

Step 4: Keep it informal—coffee, someone's classroom, virtual if needed

Step 5: Rotate facilitation—don't put all the work on one person

Option B: Join a National/Online Community

If you can't find local allies:

Join online communities:

Teachers Going Gradeless (teachersgoinggradeless.com)

Online community of teachers rethinking grading

Forums, webinars, resources

Twitter: #TeachersGoingGradeless

Mastery Collaborative/Competency-Based Learning Network

Teachers implementing standards-based/mastery-based grading

Share resources, troubleshoot together

Facebook Groups:

"Grading for Equity Teachers"

"Ungrading Educators"

"Standards-Based Grading Teachers"

Why this works:

- Access to hundreds/thousands of teachers doing this work
- Ask questions, get answers quickly
- See what's possible—schools/districts that have fully implemented these practices
- Less isolation

Option C: Find a Thought Partner—One Person

Even if you can't build a full PLC:

Find one person who gets it.

Could be:

A colleague at your school

A teacher at another school—meet virtually

A former colleague or grad school friend

What you do:

Check in monthly—or weekly.

15-30 minutes.

Share:

What worked this week?

What flopped?

What do I need help with?

What am I celebrating? This is your thought partner. You're not alone.

Strategy Two: Start Small and Build Gradually—Don't Do Everything at Once

You don't have to implement everything from this book in Year 1.

In fact, you shouldn't.

Sustainable implementation equals gradual layering.

Year 1: Pick 2-3 core practices.

Examples:

- Core Practice 1: Mistake Analysis Protocol—students analyze errors on all assessments
- Core Practice 2: Feedback before grades—on major assignments
- Core Practice 3: One revision opportunity per semester—students revise one major assignment

That's it. Master those three things.

Year 2: Add 2-3 more practices.

Examples:

- Add: Pattern recognition—students track mistakes over time
- Add: Student-led conferences—once per semester
- Add: Grading reform—weight formative lightly, summative heavily

Now you have 6 practices. Still manageable.

Year 3: Add more—if you're ready.

Examples:

- Add: Student choice—on one unit per semester
- Add: Full standards-based grading—if you're ready for the shift

By Year 3-5, you've built a comprehensive Mistake Lab.

But you did it gradually.

You didn't try to do it all at once.

The key:

Depth greater than breadth.

Do a few things well rather than many things poorly.

Strategy Three: Systemize and Streamline—Reduce Workload

Some mistake literacy practices are time-intensive.

Feedback takes longer than grading.

Retakes require logistics.

But you can make it more sustainable through systems.

Systemize Feedback

Don't reinvent feedback every time.

Create reusable systems:

Feedback banks:

Keep a document of common feedback comments you give.

Example—writing:

"Your thesis is too broad. Try making it more specific by adding: [specific claim] because [reasoning]."

"Your evidence is strong, but you need to explain how it supports your claim. Add analysis after the quote."

"Your paragraphs jump between ideas. Reorganize so each paragraph has one main point."

Copy-paste these into student work.

Saves time. Still meaningful.

Voice feedback:

Instead of writing comments, record yourself giving feedback—use a tool like Mote, Kami, or just voice memos.

Talk for 2 minutes about their work.

Faster than typing. Often more personal.

Peer feedback first:

Before you give feedback, students give feedback to each other—using a structured protocol from Chapter 9.

You only give feedback after peer feedback.

This catches surface-level issues—so you can focus on deeper feedback.

Systemize Retakes

Don't manage retakes individually—chaos.

Create a system:

Retake window:

"Retakes are available during the last week of each unit. Sign up by Wednesday. Retakes happen Thursday/Friday."

All retakes happen at once—not scattered throughout the semester.

Retake requirements—checklist:

Before retaking, students must:

☐ Complete test corrections—error analysis

☐ Attend reteaching session—office hours or after-school tutoring

☐ Complete practice problems

Submit the checklist. Then retake.

This ensures students don't just retake without learning.

Alternate retake formats:

Not every retake equals taking another test.

Alternatives:

Oral exam—you ask questions, student explains

Project—demonstrate mastery through application

Written explanation—student explains the concept in their own words

Less time grading tests. Still assesses mastery.

Systemize Student-Led Conferences

Don't prepare every student individually—it's time-consuming.

Build preparation into class time:

Weekly portfolio updates—10 minutes:

Every Friday, students spend 10 minutes updating their portfolio:

Add recent work

Update standards tracker

Write a reflection

By conference time, the portfolio is ready—no last-minute scramble.

Practice in class:

Students practice presentations with peers (Chapter 15).

You're not prepping 25 students individually.

They're prepping each other.

Strategy Four: Set Boundaries—Protect Your Time and Energy

Sustainable teaching requires boundaries.

Boundaries to set:

Time Boundaries

Work hours:

"I work until 5 PM on weekdays. After 5 PM, I'm off."

Exceptions: Rare—conferences, events. Stick to it.

Email boundaries:

"I respond to emails during school hours—8 AM to 5 PM. If you email me at 9 PM, I'll respond the next day."

Set an auto-responder if needed:

"Thank you for your email. I respond to messages during school hours and will get back to you within 24 hours."

Weekend boundaries:

"I don't work on Sundays."

Protect one day completely.

Workload Boundaries

Feedback boundaries:

"I give detailed feedback on major assignments—essays, projects. On smaller assignments—homework, quizzes—I give brief comments or use feedback codes."

You can't give extensive feedback on everything.

Prioritize.

Retake boundaries:

"Students can retake each unit test once. After that, their grade stands."

You can't offer unlimited retakes.

Set a limit.

Revision boundaries:

"Students can revise major assignments—essays, projects—once. Drafts must be submitted by [deadline]. After that, no revisions."

Clear boundaries prevent endless revision cycles.

Emotional Boundaries

You can't save every student.

You can't fix every problem.

You can't carry every burden.

Permit yourself:

"I will do my best. I will support students. But I can't fix everything. And that's okay."

Therapy/counseling support:

If you're carrying emotional weight from students' struggles:

Connect students to counselors, social workers, and outside resources.

You're a teacher, not a therapist.

You can care without carrying.

Strategy Five: Track Wins—Notice Progress

When you're exhausted, it's easy to focus on what's not working.

You think: "Students still make the same mistakes. This isn't working."

But you're not noticing the wins.

Combat this by tracking progress intentionally:

Keep a "Wins" Journal

Every week, write down:

One student success—"Marcus analyzed his own mistake without prompting!"

One teaching success—"The revision protocol worked really well today."

One moment of joy—"A student said: 'I used to hate failing. Now I see it as data.'"

When you're discouraged, read this journal.

You'll see it's working.

Collect Student Reflections

At the end of each semester, ask students:

"How has this class changed how you think about mistakes?"

"What did you learn about yourself as a learner?"

Read these reflections.

They remind you why you're doing this.

Example student reflection:

"I used to think mistakes meant I was dumb. Now I know mistakes mean I'm learning. This changed everything for me."

That's impact.

That's why you do this.

Track Data

Collect data on:

Test score improvement—after mistake analysis plus revision

Student engagement—surveys, attendance

Revision rates—how many students revise? How much do grades improve?

Data shows progress even when you can't feel it.

Strategy Six: Reconnect to Your "Why"—Revisit Your Purpose

When burnout creeps in, you've lost touch with your "why."

Reconnect:

Write Your "Why" Statement

Why do you teach this way?

What do you believe about students, learning, and mistakes?

Example: "I teach this way because I believe every student deserves to learn without shame. Mistakes are not moral failures—they're data. I want students to leave my class knowing they're capable of growth, not limited by a single bad test or a single rough draft. This is my 'why.'"

Write this. Post it somewhere visible.

Read it when you're discouraged.

Revisit a Transformational Moment

Think of a moment when you saw the impact of mistake literacy:

A student who used to shut down now analyzes their errors

A student who said, "I used to think I was bad at math. Now I know I'm just still learning."

A parent who said, "This approach changed my child's confidence."

Revisit that moment when you need fuel.

Talk to Former Students

If possible, reach out to former students:

"How did what you learned in my class affect you?"

Their answers remind you of long-term impact.

Strategy Seven: Give Yourself Permission to Adjust—Perfection Isn't the Goal

You will not implement mistake literacy perfectly.

Some weeks, you'll:

Skip feedback—because you don't have time

Not analyze mistakes deeply—because you're overwhelmed

Cut corners—because you're human

That's okay.

Perfectionism is the enemy of sustainability.

Aim for consistency, not perfection.

Mantras:

"Done is better than perfect."

"I'm doing the best I can with the time and energy I have."

"Progress, not perfection."

Some years will be better than others.

Some semesters will be smoother.

That's normal. Keep going.

When to Take a Break—and How to Come Back

Sometimes, despite your best efforts, you need a break.

Signs you need a break:

You dread going to work

You're irritable with students when you're usually patient

You're not sleeping well—work stress keeps you up

You're getting sick frequently—stress impacts the immune system

You're fantasizing about quitting

If 3 or more of these are true, you need a break.

Option 1: Micro-Breaks—During the Year

You can't take a semester off.

But you can take micro-breaks:

One week "light" schedule:

"This week, I'm not giving extensive feedback. I'm grading for completion only. I'm taking care of myself."

One week won't destroy your Mistake Lab.

It will prevent burnout.

One unit "traditional":

"This unit, I'm not doing student-led conferences. I'm not offering revisions. I'm simplifying."

Then, in the next unit, you return to the topic of literacy practices.

Mental health day:

Use a sick day for mental health.

Take a Friday. Rest. Come back Monday refreshed.

Option 2: Summer Reset

Summer is your reset.

Use it to:

Rest—don't work the first 2 weeks; truly rest

Reflect—what worked last year? What didn't?

Revise systems—streamline what felt overwhelming. Reconnect to your "why." Prepare for next year—but not obsessively; balance rest plus prep

Option 3: Sabbatical/Leave—If Possible

If your district offers sabbaticals or leaves:

Consider taking one.

Use the time to:

Rest deeply

Pursue additional learning—grad school, professional development.

Write, research, or create resources

Come back refreshed. Teaching is a marathon. You need rest stops.

Building a Mistake-Literate School—Beyond Your Classroom

The most sustainable Mistake Labs exist at the school level—not just individual classrooms.

When the whole school adopts mistake literacy:

You're not alone

Practices are reinforced across grades/classes

Admin supports it

Parents understand it—because it's consistent

How to build toward a school-wide Mistake Lab:

Step 1: Start with Your Classroom—Prove It Works

You can't convince others without evidence.

Implement in your classroom.

Collect data:

Student outcomes—test scores, growth

Student engagement—surveys, reflections. Parent feedback

Step 2: Share Your Work—Make It Visible

Present at: Faculty meetings

PLC meetings

District professional development

Conferences—local, state, national

Share: What you're doing

Why you're doing it—research

What results you're seeing—data

How others can start—practical steps

Step 3: Build a Coalition—Recruit Allies

Identify teachers who:

Are interested in this work

Are frustrated with traditional practices

Are you willing to try something new

Form a pilot group.

Implement together.

Step 4: Propose a School-Wide Pilot

After 1-2 years of evidence:

Propose:

"We'd like to pilot mistake literacy practices school-wide next year. Here's the research. Here's our data from individual classrooms. Here's the plan."

Pilots are less threatening than wholesale change.

Step 5: Provide Support for Teachers

If the admin approves a pilot:

Don't just tell teachers to "do it."

Provide:

Professional development—workshops on mistake analysis, grading reform, etc.

Coaching—peer coaching, admin coaching

Resources—templates, protocols, examples

Time—PLC time to collaborate

Step 6: Iterate and Expand

After the pilot:

Evaluate:

What worked?

What didn't?

What needs adjustment?

Then expand:

"The pilot was successful. Let's expand to all grade levels/all departments."

Building a school-wide Mistake Lab takes years.

But it's the most sustainable model.

Because you're not doing it alone.

Real Teacher Story: Ms. Lee's Sustainability Journey

Ms. Lee taught 4th grade.

Year 1: Energized

She implemented mistake analysis, revision, and student-led conferences.

Students thrived.

She worked 60-hour weeks.

"It's worth it," she thought.

Year 2: Overwhelmed

She added more practices—pattern recognition, grading reform.

She was exhausted.

Giving feedback took 20 hours/week.

She started skipping weekends with family. "I can't keep this up," she thought.

Year 3: Burned out

She was resentful.

She quietly stopped giving extensive feedback.

She stopped offering revisions.

She thought about quitting teaching.

Summer after Year 3: Reset

She took the first 3 weeks of summer off—no schoolwork.

She reflected.

She realized: "I tried to do too much alone. I need community. I need boundaries."

Year 4: Sustainable systems

She:

- Found a thought partner—another 4th-grade teacher; they met biweekly
- Streamlined feedback—created feedback bank, used voice comments
- Set boundaries—no work after 5 PM, no work on Sundays
- Scaled back—kept 3 core practices, let go of others
- Tracked wins—kept a journal of student successes

Year 5-10: Thriving

She sustained the work. It was manageable. She recruited 2 other teachers and formed a PLC. By Year 8, her whole grade-level team was implementing mistake literacy. By Year 10, the school adopted it school-wide.

Ms. Lee reflected:

"Year 3, I almost quit. But I learned: Sustainability requires community, boundaries, and self-compassion. Now I can do this work for the long haul."

The Bottom Line

Sustaining mistake literacy requires:

Strategy 1: Build community—don't do it alone; find your people

Strategy 2: Start small and build gradually—don't try to do everything at once

Strategy 3: Systemize and streamline—reduce workload through smart systems

Strategy 4: Set boundaries—protect your time and energy

Strategy 5: Track wins—notice progress; keep a wins journal

Strategy 6: Reconnect to your "why"—revisit your purpose when discouraged

Strategy 7: Give yourself permission to adjust—progress, not perfection

When you need a break:

- Take micro-breaks—one week light, one unit simplified
- Use summer to reset—rest, reflect, revise
- Consider sabbatical/leave—if burnout is severe

Long-term sustainability:

- Build toward a school-wide Mistake Lab—you can't do it alone forever

This work is a marathon, not a sprint.

Pace yourself.

Build community.

Set boundaries.

Celebrate wins.

You can sustain this. But only if you take care of yourself.

REFLECTION QUESTIONS

Personal Reflection:

1. On a scale of 1-10, how sustainable does your current workload feel?

1 = Completely unsustainable—heading toward burnout

10 = Very sustainable—could do this for years

Your rating: _____

2. Which of the 6 burnout reasons resonates most with you?

☐ Doing it alone—isolation

☐ Doing too much at once—overcommitment

☐ No boundaries—working constantly

☐ System resistance—fighting policies

☐ Not seeing results—demoralization

☐ Lost connection to "why"—loss of purpose

3. What boundaries do you need to set? Time? Workload? Emotional?
4. Who could be your thought partner or community? Name 1-3 people

Sustainability Audit:

Current practices: List all the mistakes in literacy practices you're currently implementing:

1. ______________________________
2. ______________________________
3. ______________________________
4. ______________________________
5. ______________________________

For each practice, ask: Is this sustainable? Can I do this for years?

If not, how could I streamline it? Could I do this less often but still have an impact?

Action Planning:

This semester/year:

☐ Find 1-2 people to form a thought partnership or PLC

☐ Choose 2-3 core practices to focus on—let go of the rest for now

☐ Streamline one practice—create a system to reduce workload

☐ Set one boundary—time, email, workload, or emotional

☐ Start a wins journal—write down one win per week

☐ Write your "why" statement—post it somewhere visible

☐ Schedule a micro-break—one week this semester, where you simplify

Further Exploration

Read:

- *Onward* by Elena Aguilar—sustaining resilience as an educator
- *The Courage to Teach* by Parker Palmer—reconnecting to purpose
- *Teach Like Finland* by Timothy Walker—sustainable teaching practices

Listen:

- "Cult of Pedagogy" podcast episodes on teacher burnout and self-care
- "Angela Watson's Truth for Teachers" podcast

PART 4 RECAP

You've completed Part 4. Here's what you've learned:

Chapter 17: Standardized Tests and Mistake Literacy

They're not incompatible—mistake literacy improves test performance

Deep learning, with greater coverage than shallow learning, leads to better scores on complex questions. Metacognition—from error analysis—leads to better test-taking

Use practice tests as learning tools—analyze mistakes, reteach, retake

Don't abandon rich learning for drill-and-kill

Chapter 18: Navigating School and District Policies

Work within policies—find loopholes, creative workarounds

Advocate for policy change—build evidence, find allies, propose pilots

Strategic non-compliance—risky but sometimes necessary

Build coalitions for systemic change—strength in numbers

Change is slow—be patient and persistent

Chapter 19: When Parents Push Back

Parents push back because: unfamiliar approach, worry about rigor, fear for child's future, don't know the research. Respond with: Listen, Validate, Educate, Connect to values, Invite partnership. Communicate proactively—welcome letters, regular updates, student-led conferences. Most concerns can be resolved through communication. Loop in the admin when needed

Chapter 20: Sustaining the Work

Build community—don't do it alone; find thought partners, PLCs, online communities. Start small and build gradually—don't try everything at once

Systemize and streamline—reduce workload through smart systems

Set boundaries—protect time, energy, emotional health

Track wins—notice progress, keep wins journal. Reconnect to "why"—revisit purpose when discouraged. Give yourself permission to adjust—progress, not perfection.

You now have the complete Mistake Lab framework: **Part 1:** Foundation—science, vulnerability, safety, language, core concept. **Part 2:** Culture—first week, co-researcher, peer norms, grading, equity. **Part 3:** Protocols—mistake analysis, patterns, revision, conferences, choice. **Part 4:** Systems—tests, policies, parents, sustainability.

What's left: **Part 5:** Sustaining the Lab—Final Thoughts

This is the conclusion—tying it all together. Ready for the final part?

PART 5

SUSTAINING THE LAB

Final Thoughts and Next Steps

You've reached the end of the book.

You've learned:

Part 1: The Foundation—science, vulnerability, psychological safety, language, core concept

Part 2: The Lab Culture—first week, co-researcher, peer norms, grading revolution, equity

Part 3: Lab Protocols—mistake analysis, pattern recognition, revision, student-led conferences, voice and choice

Part 4: Working Within the System—standardized tests, policies, parents, sustainability

Now what?

How do you take all of this and actually do it?

How do you move from reading to implementation?

How do you sustain it?

CONCLUSION

YOUR NEXT EXPERIMENT

Remember Mr. Harrison and Ms. Rodriguez from the Introduction?

Mr. Harrison's classroom:

Theater—students perform, hide mistakes, one shot to get it right

Maya gets a math problem wrong, feels shame, and stops participating

Students learn: "Don't be wrong in public. Mistakes equal failure."

Ms. Rodriguez's classroom:

Lab—students experiment, analyze mistakes, iterate

James gets a math problem wrong, analyzes it with curiosity, and corrects it

Students learn: "Mistakes are data. That's how scientists work."

When I introduced you to these classrooms, I asked:

Which classroom do you want to build?

You've now learned how to build Ms. Rodriguez's classroom.

The question is:

Will you?

The Choice Ahead

You have a choice.

Choice One: Do Nothing

Put this book down.

Go back to teaching the way you've always taught.

Keep:

Grading everything for accuracy

Averaging grades

Not allowing revisions

Treating mistakes as failures

It's familiar. It's what the system expects. It's easier.

But here's what you know now:

This approach:

Harms students—perfectionism, fixed mindset, fear of failure

Doesn't reflect learning—grades measure compliance, not understanding

Perpetuates inequity—disadvantages marginalized students

Kills curiosity—students play it safe, don't take risks

You can't unknow this.

Choice Two: Try Everything at Once

Implement every practice from this book tomorrow.

Mistake analysis, pattern recognition, revision, student-led conferences, grading reform, student choice—all of it.

Go big. Transform everything.

But here's what will happen:

You'll burn out in 6 months.

It's too much, too fast.

You'll abandon it all.

And you'll think: "I tried. It didn't work."

Choice Three: Start Small, Build Sustainable Systems, Grow Over Time

Pick 1-3 practices.

Implement them deeply.

Build sustainable systems.

Reflect. Adjust. Add more when ready.

Over 3-5 years, build a comprehensive Mistake Lab.

This is the choice I'm inviting you to make.

Not "all or nothing."

But: "Start small. Build steadily. Sustain it."

Your Next Experiment

Think of this as your next experiment.

You're the scientist now.

Your hypothesis:

"If I implement mistake literacy practices, students will develop growth mindsets, learn more deeply, and take ownership of their learning."

Your experiment:

Pick 1-3 practices to pilot this semester/year.

Collect data:

Student outcomes—test scores, work quality, growth

Student engagement—reflections, surveys, participation

Your observations—what's working? What's challenging?

Analyze the data. Adjust your approach. Iterate.

This is what scientists do.

You're modeling it.

Where to Start: The Three Entry Points

Depending on your context, start with one of these:

Entry Point One: Start with Mistake Analysis—Chapter 12

Best for: Teachers who want to start small, build a foundational practice, and see immediate impact.

What you do:

Teach the 4-step Mistake Analysis Protocol—Chapter 12

After every quiz/test, students analyze 2-3 mistakes

Students keep a Mistake Log—track mistakes over time

Monthly: Students identify patterns—Chapter 13

Why start here:

Immediate impact—students start thinking metacognitively right away

Low barrier to entry—doesn't require grading reform or policy changes

Builds the foundation—once students can analyze mistakes, everything else flows

Timeline:

Week 1: Introduce the protocol, model it

Weeks 2-8: Students use it after every assessment

Month 2: Students identify patterns

Semester 2: Add revision opportunities—Entry Point Two

Entry Point Two: Start with Grading Reform—Chapter 10

Best for: Teachers who are frustrated with traditional grading, ready to make a bigger shift.

What you do:

Separate practice from performance—practice equals feedback only or completion, performance equals graded. Allow one revision opportunity per semester—for major assignments, students revise after feedback. Weight recent assessments more heavily—or drop the lowest scores.

Why start here:

Changes the incentive structure—mistakes during practice are safe

Students see grades improve through revision—motivating

Aligns with mistake literacy—grades reflect current mastery, not averages

Timeline:

Week 1: Explain your grading system to students and parents

Weeks 2-10: Implement—feedback on practice, grades on performance

Mid-semester: Offer first revision opportunity

End of semester: Reflect and adjust for next semester

Entry Point Three: Start with Student-Led Conferences—Chapter 15

Best for: Teachers who want students to develop agency and metacognition, and schools that already hold conferences.

What you do:

Students build portfolios throughout the semester—10 minutes/week

Students prepare presentations—practice in class

Students lead parent conferences—presenting their learning, mistakes, and goals

Why start here:

High visibility—parents see mistake literacy in action

Builds agency—students take ownership

Culminating experience—brings everything together

Timeline:

Week 1: Introduce student-led conferences

Weeks 2-15: Students build portfolios—10 minutes/week

Weeks 13-14: Students practice presentations

Week 16: Student-led conferences

Pick Your Entry Point

Which one resonates with you?

Entry Point One—Mistake Analysis:

Best if you want to start small and build foundational skills.

Entry Point Two—Grading Reform:

Best if you're ready to change the system, frustrated with traditional grading.

Entry Point Three—Student-Led Conferences:

Best if you want high-impact, visible practice that builds agency.

You don't have to pick just one.

But start with one.

Master it. Then add more.

The 30-Day Challenge

If you want a concrete starting point:

Try this 30-day challenge.

Week 1: Teach the Concept

Day 1-2: Teach students: Mistakes equal Data, Not Identity—Chapter 6 lesson, age-appropriate

Day 3: Model vulnerability—share your own mistake, analyze it

Day 4: Co-create lab norms—how we respond to mistakes

Day 5: First low-stakes experiment—students try something, make mistakes, analyze them

Week 2: Introduce the Protocol

Day 1: Teach the 4-step Mistake Analysis Protocol—Chapter 12

Day 2: Model the protocol—with your own mistake or a sample student mistake

Day 3: Students practice—guided, whole-class

Day 4: Students practice—individual, with a real mistake from recent work

Day 5: Reflection—what did you learn from analyzing your mistake?

Week 3: Build the Routine

Give a quiz/formative assessment.

Students analyze mistakes using the protocol.

You give feedback on their analysis:

"You described what happened. Now dig deeper—why did it happen?"

"Good analysis. What's your specific plan for next time?"

Make this routine.

Every assessment → mistake analysis.

Week 4: Introduce Pattern Recognition

Students review their Mistake Log—3-4 weeks of mistakes.

Prompt:

"What mistakes have you made more than once?"

"What pattern do you notice?"

"What will you do to address this pattern?"

Students identify one pattern and create an action plan.

End of 30 Days:

You've built the foundation:

Students understand mistakes equal data

Students can analyze mistakes systematically

Students are identifying patterns

The culture is shifting

Now continue:

Month 2: Keep the routine going. Add targeted reteaching based on patterns.

Month 3: Introduce revision opportunities—on one major assignment.

Semester 2: Add student-led conferences or student choice—depending on readiness.

By the end of the year:

You've built a functioning Mistake Lab.

Not everything from the book. But the core.

And it's sustainable.

What If It Doesn't Work?

You might be thinking:

"What if I try this and it doesn't work?"

"What if students don't engage?"

"What if parents push back?"

"What if the admin shuts it down?"

Here's what I want you to know:

It will be messy.

Students won't immediately embrace mistake analysis.

Some will resist.

Some parents will question you.

Some practices won't work perfectly the first time.

But here's the thing:

That's okay.

This is an experiment.

Experiments sometimes fail.

When things don't work:

You analyze what happened.

You adjust.

You try again.

You're modeling the exact process you're teaching students.

Mistakes → analysis → adjustment → improvement.

So if it doesn't work perfectly:

That's not failure.

That's data.

Final Thoughts

I want to end where we started.

Two classrooms.

Mr. Harrison's theater. Ms. Rodriguez's lab.

In Mr. Harrison's classroom:

Students hide mistakes. They perform. They fear failure.

Result: Some students "succeed"—those who can perform perfectly. Many students disengage.

In Ms. Rodriguez's classroom:

Students make mistakes publicly. They analyze them. They learn from them.

Result: All students grow. They develop resilience, metacognition, and agency.

The difference isn't the students.

The difference is the culture.

The structures. The language. The practices.

You can build Ms. Rodriguez's classroom.

You now know how.

But more importantly:

You can build something even better than Ms. Rodriguez's classroom.

Because you're not just copying someone else's lab.

You're designing your lab.

For your students.

In your context.

This book gave you the principles, the research, and the practices.

But you will adapt them.

You will make them your own.

You will iterate and improve.

That's what scientists do.

Your Next Experiment

So here's my invitation:

Try one thing. Just one. For 30 days.

Teach students the Mistake Analysis Protocol.

Or

Allow one revision opportunity.

Or

Have students lead one conference. Pick one. Try it. See what happens.

Collect data:

What did students learn?

How did they respond?

What surprised you?

What would you adjust?

Then decide:

"Do I want to continue this experiment?"

If yes:

Keep going. Add another practice when you're ready.

Build your lab steadily.

If no:

That's okay too.

You tried.

You learned.

Maybe you'll try again later.

Or maybe this isn't the right fit for you.

But I'm betting:

Once you see students analyzing their own mistakes...

Once you see a student say, "I used to think I was bad at this. Now I know I'm still learning..."

Once you see the transformation that happens when mistakes become data...

You won't go back.

The Mistake Lab Manifesto

Let me leave you with this:

We believe:

Every student can learn—intelligence is not fixed

Mistakes are essential to learning—not obstacles to avoid

Grades should reflect learning—not compliance or averages

Students deserve agency—ownership over their learning

Classrooms should be labs—places to experiment, fail, and grow

Teachers should be co-researchers—not infallible experts

Learning is iterative—revision, not one-shot performance

All students deserve access—mistaken literacy is an equity issue

We reject:

Perfectionism culture—mistakes equal shame

Fixed mindset—"I'm just not good at this"

Grading as punishment—mistakes lower grades permanently

One-size-fits-all—every student does the same thing the same way

Theater classrooms—perform perfectly or fail

Teacher as sage—the teacher knows everything, students receive

We commit to:

Building psychological safety—students feel safe to fail

Teaching metacognition—students analyze their own thinking

Modeling vulnerability—we make mistakes too

Using learning-focused language—not yet, still learning, mistakes equal data

Revising our practices—we're experimenting too

Sustaining the work—this is a marathon, not a sprint

This is the Mistake Lab.

Will you build it?

Go Build Your Lab

You have everything you need.
The science. The practices. The tools.
Now go.
Start small.
Build steadily.
Sustain it.
Your students are waiting.
They're waiting for a classroom where:
Mistakes are safe
Learning is messy
Growth is possible
They can be themselves
Go build that classroom.
Go build your Mistake Lab.
Your next experiment starts now.

ABOUT THE AUTHOR

Jeffrey O. Porter is an educational consultant, leadership coach, and founder of The JP Moment Educational Consultants, LLC. With more than 25 years of experience in education, he has served in multiple roles across the educational system, giving him firsthand insight into the challenges schools face and the conditions needed for students and educators to thrive.

Jeffrey's work centers on helping schools build stronger instructional practices, healthier learning cultures, and systems that increase student ownership and engagement. Through coaching, professional development, and leadership support, he works with teachers, school leaders, and districts to create environments where growth, reflection, and learning are part of the culture—not just the expectation.

His work is grounded in a simple belief: students learn best in environments where mistakes are treated as part of the process, not proof of failure.

That belief became the foundation for *The Mistake Lab*, a framework designed to help educators create classrooms where students feel safe thinking, struggling, revising, and growing.

Known for his practical approach, direct communication style, and ability to connect with educators, Jeffrey focuses on strategies that can be implemented immediately and sustained over time.

Through The JP Moment Educational Consultants, LLC, he continues to support schools and organizations in building systems that strengthen instruction, leadership, and student learning.

For speaking engagements, professional development, or consulting inquiries, visit:

www.themistakelab.com
www.thejpmoment.com

REFERENCES

Dweck, C. S. (2006). *Mindset: The New Psychology of Success*. Random House.
Explains how beliefs about intelligence shape effort, persistence, and response to mistakes.

Hattie, J. (2009). *Visible Learning: A Synthesis of Over 800 Meta-Analyses Relating to Achievement*. Routledge.
Identifies the instructional practices that have the greatest impact on student learning.

Hattie, J., & Clarke, S. (2018). *Visible Learning: Feedback*. Routledge.
Clarifies how feedback can move learning forward when it is specific, timely, and actionable.

Black, P., & Wiliam, D. (1998). *Inside the Black Box: Raising Standards Through Classroom Assessment*. Phi Delta Kappan.
Shows how formative assessment strengthens learning by making thinking visible and adjustable.

Brookhart, S. M. (2017). *How to Give Effective Feedback to Your Students* (2nd ed.). ASCD.
Provides practical ways to give feedback that supports growth instead of judgment.

Duckworth, A. (2016). *Grit: The Power of Passion and Perseverance*. Scribner.
Highlights the role of persistence and sustained effort in long-term success.

Sousa, D. A. (2017). *How the Brain Learns* (5th ed.). Corwin.
Connects brain research to classroom practice, including how students process errors.

Medina, J. (2014). *Brain Rules* (Updated ed.). Pear Press.
Presents key principles about how the brain learns, retains, and responds to challenge.

Fisher, D., Frey, N., & Hattie, J. (2016). *Visible Learning for Literacy, Grades K–12*. Corwin.
Applies high-impact strategies to literacy instruction, including feedback and clarity.

Marzano, R. J. (2007). *The Art and Science of Teaching*. ASCD.
Outlines a framework of instructional strategies that support effective teaching and learning.

FURTHER READING FOR EDUCATORS

Wiliam, D. (2011). *Embedded Formative Assessment*. Solution Tree.
Offers clear strategies for using assessment during instruction to guide next steps.

Knight, J. (2007). *Instructional Coaching: A Partnership Approach to Improving Instruction*. Corwin.
Focuses on reflective practice and coaching conversations that improve teaching.

Hammond, Z. (2015). *Culturally Responsive Teaching and the Brain*. Corwin.
Connects culture, cognition, and instruction to support deeper student engagement.

Lemov, D. (2015). *Teach Like a Champion 2.0*. Jossey-Bass.
Provides concrete classroom techniques that can be adapted to support strong instruction.

Sizer, T. R. (1992). *Horace's School: Redesigning the American High School*. Houghton Mifflin.
Advocates for depth of understanding over surface-level coverage.

Costa, A. L., & Kallick, B. (2008). *Learning and Leading with Habits of Mind*. ASCD.
Promotes thinking habits that support reflection, persistence, and problem-solving.

Ritchhart, R., Church, M., & Morrison, K. (2011). *Making Thinking Visible*. Jossey-Bass.
Provides strategies for helping students articulate and reflect on their thinking.

Fullan, M. (2016). *The New Meaning of Educational Change* (5th ed.). Teachers College Press.
Focuses on leading and sustaining meaningful change in schools.

www.ingramcontent.com/pod-product-compliance
Lightning Source LLC
LaVergne TN
LVHW020652110826
845149LV00012B/1969

* 9 7 9 8 9 9 5 6 7 1 2 0 6 *